Advance Praise for The Next Revolution in Our Credit-Driven Economy: The Advent of Financial Technology

This book is a timely and comprehensive description of the rapidly changing financial world. It covers not only the changing role of financial institutions but is also one of the first to analyze the profound impact of technology and big data on financial institutions and transactions. There is no question that the tens of billions of dollars in fines levied on the banks will change their ways of doing business. But, when a world top bank announces that it is hoping major institutional depositors will withdraw at least a hundred billion dollars in deposits, something serious must have happened. The book covers, in everyday language, the lead-up to and the current status of this transformation. Best of all, the author draws on his extensive BRIC experience to differentiate an increasingly regional market despite much hyped "globalisation." It is also a must read for the practitioner, as the author goes beyond descriptions to investment strategies.

—Charles Liu, founder and former chairman of Hao Capital, and financial technology pioneer in China

Throughout history, dictators have abused their control of finance to subjugate people and destroy economic vitality. Paul Schulte's exceptional understanding and international experience permit him to show simple metrics by which all can measure when and how finance is abused to the detriment of investors. He shows, moreover, that advancements in technology now offer both the means and a process by which the world can end this sad saga, for everyone's benefit.

—Frederick L. Feldkamp, attorney; co-author of *Financial Stability: Fraud, Confidence, and the Wealth of Nations* (Wiley, 2014)

Paul Schulte's book is brilliant, witty and has penetrating simplicity. He moves beyond connecting the dots for a sneak peek on how online-to-offline credit is the Jedi lightsaber which is behind the rise, fall, and renaissance of livelihood, lifestyle and power hubs globally. His book prisms the perfect storms and vast opportunities as Wall Street, Corporates, Government and Digital Continents align and disrupt. Spotlighting the urkraft of bank credit, Schulte presciently lays out how mobile, wireless and cloud data analytics are turbocharging the jump over the garden wall for vast pools of money—the lifeblood of business, nonprofit funding and government. The canvas Schulte unrolls reads like a thriller in fiction—entertaining and more jolting because it is nonfiction.

—Camille Tang, president and co-founder,
ConvenientPower Group

After the global financial crisis of 2008, the Queen of England wondered why all the country's economists had failed to sound warnings. Financial instabilities are inherently unpredictable; all you can do is clean up afterwards, quoth Greenspan. But in this important book Paul Schulte explains how crises can indeed be foreseen. For our lifetimes, economic "growth" has been driven by the expansion of credit. Failure to account adequately for the overwhelming importance of credit has led governments and central banks to miss obvious warning signs. Warning signs of another type are being missed today by many of the world's major banks. The second half of this book analyses how their revenue streams are under attack, while their costs are driven ever higher by regulators and governments. This will inevitably lead to the ultimate irony: "too big to fail" will be rephrased as "so big, it must fail." Customers may be winners; shareholders assuredly will not. At least Queen Elizabeth and Jamie Dimon should read this book. You should, too.

—Nick Sallnow-Smith, former UK Treasury civil servant;
former company treasurer and ex-banker

This book ties together the unethical practices of banks with the growing financial and wealth-gap crisis destabilizing our world.

—Max Keiser, editor and host, *The Kaiser Report*

Credit allows us to spend money we don't have, to buy goods we don't want, to show off to people we don't like. More prosaically, excessive credit creation over the past half century has fuelled a series of rolling asset price booms and busts to which the solution has always been to create even more credit. Schulte, unlike most policymakers, understands the relationship between credit and real life. This timely work explains these inter-linkages and how the technology and big data revolution is spawning new models of financial intermediation that threaten the very existence of traditional banks.

—Simon Ogus, CEO, DSG Asia Limited

Paul is one of the most astute commentators in his understanding of the financial architecture globally. This book gives the reader a ringside seat into the fast evolving creative destruction that is engulfing the financial services industry in the aftermath of the global financial crisis which has altered the regulatory landscape permanently. This interplays with the lightning-speed evolution of Internet-led fulfilment of underserved areas in this space. A tectonic shift is in the making. This book is a must-read for anyone following financial markets.

—Amit Rajpal, global banks portfolio manager,
Marshall Wace

This book will bolster Paul's already substantial reputation as a stimulating, original thinker and skilled polemicist. Written in clear, declarative sentences (as he says, "anyone" can understand the arguments), the first section of The Next Revolution in Our Credit-Driven Economy *argues for the central role of credit and the credit cycle in economic analysis and financial valuation. He offers insightful recommendations on investment in multiple assets classes through the credit cycle. The book's second section is a wakeup call to bankers on the disruptions to commercial banking's "business as usual" attitude posed by new financial technologies. His observations are telling; his conclusions persuasive.*

—Eugene K. Galbraith, deputy president director,
PT Bank Central Asia Tbk

Mr. Schulte brings a definitive element of "been there, done that" to his insightful text about how the financial world truthfully operates. As he states from the beginning, he wants to explain it like he was talking to his grandmother, and he delivers. That which appears to be beyond the grasp of the loudest spokesmen of today's Economic Ivory Towers, Paul lays out with the clearest of common sense and the most obvious of logic—CREDIT MATTERS! This text should be highly recommended to any student of Finance and Economics. It should be made compulsory for any practicing central banker.

—David Dredge, co-chief investment officer,
Convex Strategies Group, Fortress Investment Group

Paul Schulte elucidates the impact of the credit cycle on our economies, our politics, and our lives. In the process he provides tools for us to profit from the cycle and to avoid catastrophe when it turns down. The book should be read by financial professionals, regulators, political leaders, and anyone trying to manage a portfolio, even a personal portfolio, of investments.

—**William Overholt, president, Fung Global Institute**

Paul Schulte's book outlines in depth the growth of credit in our economy and the importance of the credit cycle as a key driver in both economic growth and investment returns. His illustration of the pendulum swing of the credit cycle and identification of the consistent mistakes made during boom/bust cycles will surely be helpful to those who make business and investment decisions across the global markets. Schulte then helps guide us to the beginning of the cross-section of technology and finance, a merger of two worlds that will likely dominate the global economic discussion for the next decade.

—Minh Duc Do, senior vice-president,
Gerson Lehrman Group

Facebook, Alibaba, Big Data, geopolitics, crowdsourcing, the Great Recession and 13,000 pages of the Dodd-Frank Act. What do all have to do with an industrial revolution in banking and financial services? To quote William Gibson, the revolution is already here; it is just unevenly distributed. Bankers and the regulators who are meant to provide the guardrails for the bankers may not quite know that the revolution is underway; the visionaries, the paranoiacs and the insurgents know it already. Once this lucidly written and brilliant account by Paul Schulte is evenly distributed, everyone will know about the revolution, what the revolution is being driven by and who might be expected to survive it. With compelling explanations of the impact of credit on economic fundamentals, the changing global financial architecture and chapters on the anatomy of a credit crisis, readers get a "front row seat in this technological slugfest." Those who do not pick up a copy of this book do so at their peril.

—Bhaskar Chakravorti, senior associate dean of **International Business and Finance, the Fletcher School at Tufts University; founding executive director, Institute for Business in the Global Context**

Schulte has a rare gift for explaining in simple terms the extraordinary importance of banks, credit, and regulators in modern economies—how their irresponsible behavior has devastated lives, toppled governments, and collapsed economies the world over. He adds to this some provocative thoughts on the future of banks and credit in a bit-driven world, posing the question of whether banks as we know them will survive the challenges of the digital revolution. Schulte depicts banking and its uncertain future with rare clarity.

—James Stent, external supervisor, **China Everbright Banking Corporation**

The Next Revolution in Our Credit-Driven Economy

The Next Revolution in Our Credit-Driven Economy

The Advent of Financial Technology

PAUL SCHULTE

WILEY

Other Wiley Editorial Offices

John Wiley & Sons, 111 River Street, Hoboken, NJ 07030, USA

John Wiley & Sons, The Atrium, Southern Gate, Chichester, West Sussex, P019 8SQ, United Kingdom

John Wiley & Sons (Canada) Ltd., 5353 Dundas Street West, Suite 400, Toronto, Ontario, M9B 6HB, Canada

John Wiley & Sons Australia Ltd., 42 McDougall Street, Milton, Queensland 4064, Australia

Wiley-VCH, Boschstrasse 12, D-69469 Weinheim, Germany

Library of Congress Cataloging-in-Publication Data

Schulte, Paul, 1963-
 The next revolution in our credit-driven economy : the advent of financial technology / Paul Schulte.
    pages cm
 Includes index.
  ISBN 978-1-118-98960-9 (hardback), 978-1-118-98962-3 (ePDF), and 978-1-118-98961-6 (e-pub)

1. Banks and banking. 2. Bank loans. 3. Credit. 4. Financial services industry–Information technology.
  I. Title.
 HG1601.S38 2015
 332–dc23
                              2015008523

Cover image: revolutionary fist © Christos Georghiou / Shutterstock
Cover design: Wiley

Typeset in 10/12pt Sabon by SPi Global, Chennai, India

Printed in Singapore by C.O.S. Printers Pte Ltd

10 9 8 7 6 5 4 3 2 1

To Rob Citrone, Eric Bushell, Adam Levinson, and David Halpert—four pairs of sturdy shoulders on which to stand.

Whoever controls the volume of credit in any country is absolute master of all industry and commerce.

—James A. Garfield, 20th President of the United States

O Fortune
Like the moon you are changeable,
Ever waxing and waning.
Hateful Life first destroys wealth and then gives abundance
As Fantasy takes over.
Poverty and power are, in turn, melted like ice.

—Carl Orff, "O Fortuna," *Carmina Burana*

Contents

Acknowledgments

This book has been ripening in my head for several years during the literally thousands of meetings I've had with hedge fund managers, mutual fund managers, and policy makers in central banks, as well as ministers and senior bureaucrats in national development entities on five continents. In addition, when I worked for the Minister of Finance of Indonesia and spent two years working at the White House in Ronald Reagan's second administration, I received a "behind the scenes" look at the way in which this thing called monetary policy is made. It is always a mix of politics, accommodation to bankers, a desire to keep ahead of the guy across the pond, spurious national security considerations, and mostly back-of-the-envelope calculations.

That said, over the years a few very smart people in the money management business have challenged me to leave my comfort zone and push forward into the unknown to answer some thorny questions. And sometimes they have inspired me to write the unpleasant truth about financial markets, which, while working in the crocodilian world of investment banking, had put my career as an analyst at risk from time to time.

So I would like to mention a few of these people who have coerced me to lay it all on the line. Dave Dredge, in particular, has been a great mentor over the past 25 years. Jeremy Kranz has been a wonderful interlocutor. Amit Rajpal has been a great sounding board and I consider him the best bank analyst around. Other intellectual leaders who have helped me are Gao Xiqing, Byron Gill, David Courtney, Chris Mikosh, Jack Malvey, Alex Muncerow, Frank Wang, Tomonori Tani, Simon Ogus, and Todd Tibbetts, a great friend for the past 25 years. A very special thanks goes to Fred Feldkamp, who was gracious enough to go through every line of the book and bring out some vitally important conclusions that were lying just beyond the horizon but were not visible to me from the map room. In addition, I am very grateful to Jim Stent, one of the smartest commercial bankers I have met in my 25 years in Asia. Without fear or favor, he went through the book line by line and made valuable changes.

Thanks to Gavin Liu and Christian Ng for editing and fact checking.

About the Author

Paul Schulte has his own consulting firm called Schulte Research. He is a 25-year veteran of equity and fixed income research in Wall Street firms. He is a Senior Fellow at the Council on Emerging Market Enterprises at the Fletcher School at Tufts University. He has been a Visiting Scholar at Hong Kong University of Science & Technology for eight years. He is also a Visiting Scholar at the University of Hong Kong. He has taught in MBA programs in China, the United States, the United Kingdom, and Brazil, and lives in Hong Kong. He previously worked at the National Security Council in Washington, D.C. His other books are *Cravings for Deliverance* and *Healing Weary Hearts*.

About the Website

Please visit this book's companion website at www.wiley.com/go/Schulte to access learning tools that provide additional coverage of the material presented in each of their respective chapters.

The password for downloading the files is: fintech15

List of slides available on the website:

- 01_Credit_Master.pdf
- 02_Banks_Master.pdf
- 03_Trading_The_LDR_Cycle.pdf
- 04_Plus_Ca_Change.pdf
- 05_Credit_Bubbles_And_Catastrophe.pdf
- 06_The_End_Of_Mercantilism.pdf
- 07_ROC_For_Banks.pdf
- 08_Leadership_in_a_World_of_Folly.pdf
- 09_Why_Now_and_Why_So_Fast.pdf
- 10_Non-Bank_Finance.pdf
- 11_Financial_Technology.pdf
- 12_Alibaba_and_the_Paypal_Gang.pdf

Introduction: A Few Numbers Can Crack the Code

The genesis of this book lies in a simple question that I put to more than a thousand of the M.B.A. students I taught over the past 16 years across five continents, many of whom had degrees in economics from New York University, the University of Chicago, Harvard, Columbia, Berkeley, or the London School of Economics. They would *always* get it wrong.

I would draw a simple supply-and-demand curve on the chalk board and ask students a simple question: What causes a change in demand for goods and services? They would say it was changes in tastes, technology, demographics, income, substituted goods, and so on. These are the usual suspects peppered throughout economics books. They offer a partial explanation, but something far more fundamental is missing.

Yet when I would ask them how they buy just about anything (how they increase demand in their own lives), almost all of them would say they use credit—credit cards, layaway plans, mortgages, student loans, small business loans, vendor financing, loan sharks, and so on. How on earth can we all look at a supply-and-demand curve and leave out the one thing that seems to be the underlying determinant of demand—the availability of credit? The answer is deceptively simple.

It seems that credit is the lifeblood of the economic body, yet we all just assume it is there and will always be there. Why? Because until a few years ago, it *was* always there. And it has been there for the past 70 years. Credit is the oxygen of the economy, yet the study of economics has repeatedly left it out of the equation. Look at the first five chapters of any economics book and you might find a few scattered paragraphs on credit, but typically that is it. Incredible!

Think about it. From cradle to grave, our decisions are based on how much credit we can manage to scrounge up. The kind of christening or bar mitzvah we can have depends on it. When we can own our first home depends on it. The scale and timing of our wedding depends on it. It is vital to the kind of education we can receive. How we retire and how we are buried depends on it. The quality of our health care depends on it. All of our major decisions about life revolve around the availability of credit. And yet none of these very bright students—many of them the cream of the crop, and some of them currently serving as money managers and policymakers—recognized that credit is a critical determinant of demand.

I will concede that this is a reasonable mistake. Since the end of World War II in 1945, the Western world has had positive credit growth in just about every year in and out for 70 years—three generations! These students would need to go back in time to the era of their *great*-grandparents to find a time when credit shrank for a significant period of time. This was during the Great Depression. The reason these students did not realize that credit is a vital determinant of demand is because it has just been there all their lives, like oxygen. Their parents and grandparents depended on it.

Not anymore. In the past few years, we have seen a compression in credit (let's call it a depression in credit) for the first time since the 1930s. What was assumed to be there as a given by a generation of the elite future leaders of our time is simply gone, vanished. As we will see, the warning signs were right there in front of us, just as they were in front of us during the Asian crisis in 1997. Indeed, in the twilight of 2014, we see credit growth for the entire Euro-zone dip into negative territory for the second time in four years.

U.S. credit growth is scrimping along in the single digits after going negative for several quarters from 2009 through 2013. It has only started to take off a little bit since mid-2014. The buoyancy of these numbers is belied by the large amount of credit being thrown at the student loan market (to retrain adults or to keep adults out of the job market?) and the mortgage market (through the FHA, which is blithely giving 95 percent mortgages to questionable buyers) by implicitly guaranteed government credit.

This book is about the importance of credit and the way it drives the prices of just about everything that investors touch: equities, bonds, currencies, real estate. The evidence that shows the connection between consumption and credit during a cycle is obvious and will be laid out clearly and persuasively. A quite reasonable starting point for investment strategy—or even portfolio construction for a high-net-worth individual—should begin with grounded knowledge of the credit cycle for a country.

Equity valuations, house prices, bond prices, and currency values are derived from the credit cycle of a country. Income, inflation, capital formation, and other economic data sets come from credit, not the other way around. Looking at economics without regard to credit is a flawed experiment. The science of economics did not predict in any way, shape, or form the crisis of 2008. Furthermore, it claimed that the crisis of 2008 could not happen. So much for the modern school of economics! Something else must now be tried.

As an investment strategist and bank analyst for more than two decades, I have met with thousands of fund managers globally, and I contest that there are only a handful who understand the credit cycle and its implications. These are often current or former bank analysts or CIOs who have a mixed mandate for both equity and credit. Oddly, bank analysts, for instance, are seen as "separate" from corporate analysts in money management firms and are seldom utilized in asset allocation decisions. This is an astounding phenomenon. Indeed, the bank analysts should form the foundation of the portfolio allocation. Too often their work on credit and liquidity is left alone in the "too difficult" pile, and many corporate analysts are left with examination of such secondary and derivative trivialities as economic variables, revenues, costs, and price-to-earnings ratios (P/Es). These come after liquidity and solvency—not before! If an investment firm can have only one industry analyst, it should be a bank analyst. The rest is superfluous in comparison.

This book will show that trends in credit have an overwhelmingly powerful effect not only on stock prices but also on asset prices (houses and buildings) as well as the price of currency. In other words, when the credit cycle is on the upswing, the prices of equities, real estate, and currencies tend to appreciate at the same time. They are just as driven by these movements in credit as the moon is driven to rotate around the earth. Economic data pour forth from credit dynamics.

The phenomenon we see today is one where new forms of technologies are being created to allocate capital more efficiently. It is that simple. Banks have shown themselves to be out of touch when it comes to the allocation of capital and the management of risk. So, in a world where the cost of capital is zero, firms are attracted like a magnet to inefficient organizations that cannot change with the times and that mismanage their own core businesses. Furthermore, these institutions are so big that they are arguably incapable of change. Banking is a glaring example, although these titanic changes are occurring in education, retail, and many other industries.

While this disruption is happening, there is a great deal of debt from the last cycle that still needs to be warehoused until it matures. Central banks are accommodating this deleveraging (think of deleveraging as shrinkage) of credit by allowing loans that can no longer be held by banks to drop onto their balance sheets. This is contractionary. So, people who say that central banks are printing money are deluded. It is simply not true. In fact, the opposite is the case.

In similar fashion, when the curtain comes down on the credit cycle, equities, real estate, and currencies almost always tumble at the same time. The United States is closer to the end of the cycle, while Europe has a long, long way to go. This is why Euroland growth is so anemic. This book will dissect the various stages of credit trends and show how various asset classes react at these various stages. We will provide a kind of timetable for getting in and out.

These trends in credit have a particularly important effect on the prices of equities. We will see how at certain stages in the credit cycle within a country, equity prices tend to accelerate to the upside and form bubbles at precise moments. We will show that this is a repeatable phenomenon and, therefore, relevant as a powerful starting point in forming a new way of thinking about markets. And we will do this without any equations.

Conversely, the trends in credit will also tell us when to "get out of Dodge" as bubble conditions become unsustainable. There is a consistent and easy to measure marker for all countries in the past two decades that is a highly accurate indicator of a bubble about to pop. Without an understanding of the credit cycle, it is my strong belief that equity investors will consign themselves to a fool's errand of a guessing game.

The second part of this book is all about the new financial architecture. It is not just coming from Silicon Valley but also from London, Frankfurt, Tokyo, Beijing, and throughout Scandinavia. It is truly a global phenomenon in which countries are escaping from the grasp of a banking system that they all too often see as an old-boy's club of poorly managed, overpaid, and incompetent bankers who do not have their customers' interests at heart and are poor at managing risk.

Furthermore, astounding technological advances have been achieved in the past four years, allowing powerful applications to be implemented for the first time. Wide-reaching and powerful programs developed by PayPal, for instance, have migrated to companies like Palantir and are now being used for mass solutions for storage, security, research, applications, and computation. In short, capacity is expanding now at a 2× rate, as predicted by Moore's Law. It is actually happening at a rate that is dozens of times faster.

Companies like Alibaba, Palantir, Intuit, Mint, Indinero, and Tencent, among dozens of others, are at the forefront of new forms of funding, analysis, research, credit checking, trading, and lending that are causing banks deep anxiety. These same banks, however, are so big and have so many entrenched interests to protect that they seem institutionally paralyzed from acting. The resulting tug-of-war is a fascinating phenomenon; in short periods of time, new industries are developing that can offer efficient and inexpensive financial services in a timely, legal, and fair way. These same institutions are also gathering around them the younger people who are disenchanted by institutions they perceive as engaging in criminal activity.

This book asks the question that was posed to me in discussions with Fred Feldkamp while he reviewed the final draft of this book. Fred is probably one of the best financial lawyers I have met and author of *Financial Stability: Fraud, Confidence, and the Wealth of Nations.** Fred challenged

---

*Fred Feldkamp and Chris Whalen, *Financial Stability: Fraud, Confidence, and the Wealth of Nations* (John Wiley & Sons, 2013).

me as follows: Does the new world of algorithmic "bots" of financial technology end the ability of banks to extract artificially high spreads forever? Will the world will be better for it? Does the discussion of the toxicity of high LDRs in Part One of this book reveal just how much we let governements and universal investment bankers dupe us into losing trillions of dollars by generating what was, in hindsight, a system that thrived on picking off investors and businessmen, seriatim, by pretending there was a magical myth to the business of banking? We need to ask ourselves this question and whether regulators will allow a new form of finance to thrive and bloom in the face of global universal bankers who are seeing their worlds being swept away—gone with the wind.

Lastly, too much of the intellectual framework of modern finance has been shown up as either insufficient or out of touch with the realities of a broken credit system. I tell my students to explain their ideas as if they are talking to their grandmothers. I do the same when I teach. This book is about credit for grandmothers. We keep it simple. It is a simple "how to invest in multiple asset classes using the credit cycle" and is a useful guide for those who are in the business of political risk analysis. And we can get a front row seat in this technological slugfest as new and exciting upstart companies compete head-to-head with monolithic financial institutions, a few of which may just collapse under their own weight.

Paul Schulte
November 2014

How Bank Credit Drives Economics (Not the Other Way Around) and Why

CHAPTER 1

A Few Simple Concepts That Anyone Can Understand

After 25 years of writing equity and fixed income research for a wide assortment of investment banks (Swiss, American, Dutch, Chinese, and Japanese), I became baffled by the way in which the vast majority of professional institutional investors who were my clients displayed a blind spot when it came to trends in credit. This is because they were fed volumes of analysis from economists who were almost all trained in the modern economics of the dynamic stochastic general equilibrium model. This is especially true for any economist who has worked for a central bank and then jumped ship to work for a bank. They assiduously look at inflation, valuations, capital formation, consumption trends, interbank rates, and the like.

This model adapted macroeconomics to microeconomics and tried first and foremost to discover where prices allow markets to clear from the point of view of the firm in a near-perfect world of pure competition. It assumed that all agents are identical. It assumed that markets are rational. It assumed that everyone is acting in their best interest and that this interest is best for all. It assumed that people essentially borrow from themselves.

There was *no* room for banking in this model. There was no room for Fannie Mae (which happens to control 50 percent of the mortgages in the country). There was no room for rationality. And as Nobel laureate Joseph Stiglitz pointed out, "Finance is uninteresting if the person can only borrow from himself.... There can't be information asymmetries (apart from acute schizophrenia)."[1] In other words, people do not borrow from themselves. They borrow from banks.

Alas, we are not the same. We are not rational. People do not behave the same way as a firm. Governments always create inefficient oligopolies that they can manipulate and control (i.e., telecom companies, defense contractors, banks, energy companies, port authorities, etc.). These oligopolies create distortions in wages, credit, growth, and the allocation of capital. Central banks are a great example of a government-manipulated oligopoly. And we borrow from others, often way too much.

THE ERROR OF OUR WAYS

So, we see that the model did not take into consideration credit excesses, the blind greed of bankers, irrationality, and behemoth mortgage entities like Fannie Mae. It did not take into consideration the many senior executives in banks who had no interest in the common welfare and were merely creating leverage in order to create revenue that they could turn into profits. It did not take into consideration the vast swell of frenzied irrationality that has persistently shown up in financial bubbles throughout history.

No wonder I was baffled in dealing with many economists who seemed blind to the dangers I saw coming over the horizon. I was looking at the world from the point of view of the banks and the financial system. Economists were looking at the world through the lens of income, output, inflation, and rationality. It was clear in my mind that the underlying capacity of a country's banking system to create credit is *the* cause of all the other variables mentioned above. These other variables are a mere outcome of the ability of governments and central banks to create credit.

This blind spot exhibited by so many money managers—and the erroneous information they received from the community of economists—made me wonder if I was wrong. And then I started to discuss the issue with very smart MBA students who had economics degrees. As I mentioned earlier, these discussions with economics majors in my MBA classes reinforced my suspicion that credit as a means for causing a structural shift in demand was absent not only from the formulas taught to economics majors but also from the investment process of most global investment houses.[2]

Why is this? It may come as a great surprise to many that, according to a recent paper by the IMF, "most (economic) models currently used for macroeconomic policy analysis ... either exclude money or model money demand as entirely endogenous, thus precluding any causal role for reserves and money."[3] How can something as fundamental as the way in which credit and money interact be left out of economic models? This is a question that Joseph Stiglitz has been asking for the past several quarters. His point is that standard economic models provide a grossly insufficient model for anticipating credit crises because of "the lack of attention to credit and the institutions providing it."[4]

To put a fine point on the failure of economics (in the crisis of 2008 and, in my experience, many other crises) because it ignored credit growth, Raghuram Rajan of the University of Chicago said:

> *The fault of the economics profession ... was to ignore the plumbing. Economists could afford to do that ... because the plumbing didn't back up. Now that the plumbing has backed up, you find that loans aren't really made in a pure, pristine market. Things can break down.[5]*

THE MECHANICS OF ECONOMICS

And things did break down. Let's boil down the problem to its fundamental parts and see what caused the breakdown. Economics is a study of how markets clear. It is the study of the scarce allocation of resources by seeking out theorems and proofs about how the price of goods and services relates to the quantity to be produced at a given price. This equilibrium price determines how supply of goods meets demand for the same goods. These inputs try to model income, demographics, technology, tastes, money supply, leading economic indicators, and such to predict supply and demand, and *voilà*! Here's the problem. These modern models that try to predict a clearing price for goods and services in an economy do *not* take into consideration the way in which credit affects demand.

The field of economics only took into consideration a small subset of conditions and dynamics that affect demand. As a result, there was a large blind spot, which has been causing a wild overshoot of demand—and a resulting slingshot of collapsing demand in the aftermath of a credit downturn. This is the so-called *black swan* event, which seems to "come out of nowhere" and happens once in a blue moon. In this book, we will show that these black swan events:

1. Are predictable in that there are very definite and repeatable circumstances that can foretell credit crises
2. Happen like clockwork, in that there is a time line in which the behavior of bankers (local and international) brings about a chain reaction of events that affects multiple asset prices with similar patterns
3. Are a direct function of the credit cycle and have little to do with the concept of an economic cycle
4. Can be seen a mile away if credit conditions are given "primus inter pares" status with other traditional economic indicators

As an example, bank stock prices are a pretty good indicator of problems to come, yet these have never been included in any model. Take the case of Citi. Its stock price peaked in 2005 and was falling a full two years before the crisis became a full-blown meltdown. Similarly, Lehman Brothers peaked in 2006 and was falling for 18 months before the implosion. No one was talking about that. The equity market was giving us a very good signal of the coming problems, yet none of this was factored into any economic model.

If the reader is still in disbelief that so many of these models that were designed to predict dangers in the economy did not even consider credit as a central parameter, let's look at the analysis of Bill White, the chief economist for the Bank of International Settlements. Considered the sanctum sanctorum (the Holy of Holies) of the international banking community, Mr. White makes the case loud and clear that the model used by the Federal Reserve does "not see debt as a source of danger." He goes further with a savage comment and says that "in most of these models, debt isn't even there." He takes a swipe at the academic community (which presumably includes the Chicago School) and says that "in academic models, the financial sector isn't even there."[6]

The growing groupthink was that if the "important" people say that it is not there, it must not be important. And if it is not there, it can't do any harm. This is like a child who put his hands over his face. What he can't see because his hands are over his face is not there. It is dangerously naïve, but this description is absolutely accurate in my 25 years of experience of being inside banks. This is a classic example of Rule #1 in leadership: Don't walk into water over your head! The psychological weaknesses of the human mind are as important as the mathematical issues are when it comes to debt-fueled bubbles and all their destructive power. (Please see Chapter 8, in which we explore the psychological weaknesses of humans and why we seem to get suckered into all kinds of absurd financial bubbles over and over again.)

This is precisely why it was understandable for then–Fed Chairman Greenspan to have said that we are in a glorious and everlasting "Great Moderation." However, he forgot to look at the explosive growth in mortgage debt, which was funded with highly volatile offshore funding from German Landesbanks, central banks, and other large institutions that could pull their money at a moment's notice. And they did.

ECONOMIC BLINDERS

If you still find it unfathomable why many of the economic and policy elite failed to see the crisis of 2008 coming (or for that matter the Asian crisis of 1997, the Russian default in 1998, the meltdown in Turkey in 1999, etc.), there is more evidence. Not only did major economists and policymakers not see the oncoming crisis, but also they did not detect the recession that was *already* underway in 2007. One study by the IMF, for instance, shows that not one official economic forecast anticipated a recession in 2009. Yet there were recessions in 49 countries in 2009—almost one in four countries in the world.[7]

In late 2007, there was even some noise from the Fed about inflation creeping back up. This is astonishing, since I was at Lehman Brothers in the Asian Research department and there was deep anxiety about the situation. By the end of 2007, anyone with half a brain in any investment bank knew the implications of the leverage unwind that was inevitable. In a book that he edited called *Essays on the Great Depression,* former Fed Chairman Bernanke said that the number-one cause of debt-fueled deflationary depressions is that policymakers do not understand or appreciate the very large levels of debt that lurk underneath an ostensibly healthy economy prior to the onset of the unpleasant deleveraging process. In this context, it is all the more surprising that he did not hit the five-alarm button to warn his colleagues of the coming problems.

By the middle of 2008, there was still a kind of delusional sense that we were out of the woods, and some in the Fed thought about actually raising interest rates just before the real collapse came a few months later. Some of the members were actually concerned about inflation. Dallas Fed Chairman Fisher was raising the alarm bells on inflation only a few months before the worst collapse in the banking system since the Great Depression in 1929.

The Greenbook, which came out in September 2008 when all the evidence of a coming meltdown was obvious, said growth in 2009 would be 2 percent and growth in 2010 would be 2.75 percent. This is all the more delusional when they could have picked up any research on credit from any of the Wall Street banks (including Lehman Brothers Credit Research, which was raising alarm bells all over the place) and seen that credit spreads were blowing out all over the place. They could have seen that (widely traded) credit default swap prices for auto loans, mortgages, corporate debt, high-yield debt, and commercial property had all collapsed to levels never before seen in modern financial history. Why didn't anyone at the Fed raise alarm bells on this?

To their credit, people like Governors Yellin, Bernanke, and Rosengarden thought that the economy could weaken more than people expected. But the overall consensus was for more growth and a possibility of inflation. Few if any thought of lowering rates below 2 percent in the summer of 2008.

Like a cup of scalding hot coffee being knocked off a table onto someone's lap, the financial crisis fell into the lap of the Fed with suddenness and pain. Fed Chairman Bernanke acted quickly by offering credit guarantees and the TARP program. By December—only three months after saying growth in 2009 would be 2 percent—the Fed Greenbook forecast a collapse in growth of 4.7 percent for 2009. All along policymakers consistently underestimated the pernicious effect of deleveraging throughout the economy. Banks had to call in loans for homes, cars, commercial office buildings, and businesses. Without liquidity and leverage, the economy could no nothing else but shrink.

Again, what is the core intellectual blind spot that caused all and sundry to get it wrong? Modern economics looks to a supply-and-demand curve that explains how markets clear at a certain price. They have as an assumption that credit (the right amount of credit for all occasions, by the way) is just there. Markets will clear because they are rational. But they do not take into account the fundamental notion that virtually all important choices in human life (when to marry, buy a home, go on vacation, go to university, expand a business, go to the hospital, have children) are predicated on the availability of credit. How can economics just leave this out? For decades, the science of economics has treated financial markets as a "harmless sideshow."[8] MIT economist Olivier Blanchard said, "We thought of financial regulation as outside the macroeconomic framework."[9]

THE CORPORATE EXAMPLE

Credit creation can make or break the balance sheet of the corporate sector and, therefore, the income statement. We should call the income statement the "outcome" statement, as it is a derivative of underlying trends in credit. In this way, the price-to-earnings ratio (P/E) and earnings per share (EPS) of a stock are meaningless and tell us nothing (we will see later that they may be a contra-indicator for investment timing and cause people to lose money!). To focus on earnings and EPS without an eye on credit and the way that credit affects national liquidity and the balance sheet of a company is to miss the big picture. Furthermore, focusing on GDP data, money supply, leading economic indicators, and fiscal positions is a waste of time without proper attention to the extent to which an economy is stretched too thin when it comes to the availability of credit and the savings that funds that credit.

People borrow from a banking system whose capacity to lend is determined by how much these same people save. People go to banks to borrow their savings. Corporations do the same thing. Borrowings are loans (assets of a bank) and savings are deposits (liabilities of a bank). The savings of people and corporations create credit, and credit creates money supply. The ratio of bank loans to deposits (or savings) is the loan/deposit ratio (LDR).

This can reach a low of 0.5 ($50 of loans for $100 of deposits) or so. This is the beginning of a credit cycle that makes for glorious asset price appreciation for a considerable period of time, usually for four to six years.

A country that has its foot on the accelerator and is allowing credit growth to far exceed savings growth is running large current account surpluses. Domestic liquidity is sloshing around at an accelerating rate. This country can gun the engine of growth with credit up to an LDR of about 1.1 or 1.2 until they encounter trouble because the growth in credit has far exceeded the growth in savings. Examples today of highly liquid banking systems are the Philippines, Thailand, Indonesia, Singapore, Hong Kong, China, and much of Africa.

When countries have low LDRs (and accompanying current account surpluses), it is hard for companies to lose money because there is plentiful _future_ credit available. This is the same thing as saying that savings can easily be turned into loans. These loans can in turn become more deposits and a virtuous cycle occurs, as long as central banks prevent sudden spikes in credit growth.

When this happens, foreign wholesale lenders want to get in on the act and fill the gap as domestic savings are exhausted and a country is required to look for overseas borrowers to keep the party going. Bankers inside a country see foreign money as "other people's money." Foreign bankers see a country that is liquid as a "low risk, easy pickings" lending spot. The combination of these two characteristics creates circumstances in which domestic bankers look to exploit "dumb" foreign money (joint ventures) and foreign creditors (capital inflows) are looking to "make a killing" in a credit-rich environment. This creates a boom. This is the same thing as saying that capital inflows from international banking sources are pro-cyclical.

These foreign bankers make good developments really good—and they make adverse developments become really bad. These international flows are not a balancing mechanism. Rather, they are steroids for an aging athlete, because international money, when it comes in, usually arrives late in the game when the cycle is aging. We will see that it allows for an unnatural extension of a cycle.

When this happens, stock markets will tend to have good rallies and housing prices begin their rise. Politicians can do no wrong in this kind of environment. When savings has been consumed through borrowings, the loan/deposit ratio is 1 ($100 of deposits has been turned into $100 of loans). The current account is almost always in balance (by definition). Figure 1.1 explains the idea. It shows a line of best fit in a snapshot of the world just after the crisis. The United States is at the upper left, since we included the government-sponsored enterprises (GSEs) in the total LDR. This is something economics forgot about.

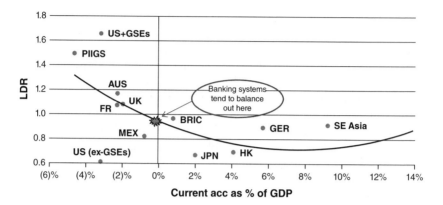

FIGURE 1.1 Global Credit System in 2010: United States Deleveraged and BRIC (Brazil, Russia, India, China) Releveraged
Source: China Construction Bank

The GSEs (Fannie Mae and Freddie Mac) were *not* funded by deposits, but by mortgage-backed securities, some of which were issued to overseas financial institutions (mostly foreign central banks). This caused a massive mismatch of assets and liabilities in the housing market. And this was the stealth rise in the LDR, which at its peak rose to above 115. In this case, central banks were the "foreign banks" that were lending to the United States in a way that aggravated the upside rise of asset prices. The situation suited them because they needed to buy dollar assets in order to keep their currencies undervalued and export cheap goods for Pier One Imports and Walmart stores in the United States.

PAINFUL REALITY

Another example was the countries of Southern Europe. Being used to rates above 10% for years, they were all forced to bring their rate structures to 3% to match Germany when they entered the European Union. So their LDRs shot up spectacularly since these countries could now get money in a sudden "half-off" sale. So the LDRs went to dangerous levels, far surpassing the usual danger zone of 1.2–1.3. At the worst, they went to 1.8. No wonder the depression in southern Europe (and subsequent unemployment rates of 50 percent for youth) was so severe.

The important point in Figure 1.1 is that the line of best fit finds its way through the Y-axis at exactly 1 while the X-axis is at 0. The natural resting place of credit is an LDR of 1 and a current balance of zero. This is a country that does not borrow from anyone else and that has deployed its entire savings into loans. It is a self-contained world that funds itself and is not reliant on or a slave to fickle and flighty wholesale funding from foreign banks who can leave tomorrow at 9:00 A.M. if they so please. This may sound like pie-in-the-sky thinking, but I think there is a groundswell of activity among regulators to: (a) restrict the absolute LDR level to below 1; (b) restrict the amount of lending a bank can do to its capacity to raise deposit liabilities in the country (subsidiarization); (c) restrict the amount of funds to be used in leveraged mortgage activity; and (d) force banks to capitalize in-country and not allow the capital to leave for an extended period of time. Does this sound like capital controls? It is absolutely not. It is called prudent banking policy.

As this LDR approaches 1, liquidity tightens a bit and there is a tendency to see rates getting tight and rising slightly. We will see later that many central banks are catching on to this phenomenon and are now capping their own country's LDR to 1. There is always a tendency to increase the LDR in any way for one simple reason. It seems to be a human trait that "more is better than less." And as things get going in a boom (as the LDR climbs toward 1 and credit is being deployed to make asset prices increase), no one wants to stop the party. Humans seem to favor chance over prudence. We all love to live on a chance. Credit fuels this tendency.

The opposing force here is central banks and governments who are— one by one—imposing a cap of 1 on the LDR. Examples of this are South Korea, Hong Kong, Singapore, and China. This is not autarky, and it is not a form of capital controls; it is prudence. At this point, however, bankers have had the bright idea to escape these lending caps and try to borrow from other countries that have excess savings. Then the local loan/deposit ratio can go to 1.1 or 1.2 or, as in the case of Spain before it blew up in 2008, a staggering 1.7 at the peak. This means that Spain was borrowing 50 percent more offshore than it had locally through its banking system. It should come as no surprise that, at the time, Spain was using one tonne of cement for every man woman and child for real estate development. On a per-capita basis, this was more than a third larger than China and multiples larger than the United States, Japan, or Korea. (No one was asking any questions.)* Australia and Brazil are current examples of countries whose LDRs are 1.2–1.3 and that are now encountering trouble with growth as

---

*This data comes from the 2004 World Cement Report. https://books.google.com.hk/books?id=Tsv9PkeV9iYC&pg=PA8&lpg=PA8&dq=global+cement+report+2004&source=bl&ots=PiSkyFNxLy&sig=VX52evRwWHMoXuFgf6GHRH8MQ7w&hl=en&sa=X&ei=nUXWVNfGJcOBuwTd4YHgDw&ved=0CBoQ6AEwAA#v=onepage&q=global%20cement%20report%202004&f=false

their savings pool is tapped out. Australia has a better history of prudential regulation, while Brazil is getting deeper into the red. How on earth will it pay for the Olympics? The current troubles with Petrobras, the Brazilian national oil company, are symptomatic of the excessive dollar borrowing. Petrobras has USD 91 bn of dollar debt, two times larger than the average dollar debt of the seven largest oil companies.

Incidentally, similar LDR numbers of 1.2–1.4 were seen in Thailand in 1997 prior to the crisis and Turkey in 1999 (before it blew up). The United States and Ireland also shared a similar situation in 2007. How come people *never* learn? An LDR of 1.2–1.4 is usually the endgame for a country, since this is where we tend to see ratings downgrades, financial scandals, excessive greed, and foreign banks that, as usual, react as lemmings and pull their money at the same time.

If the presence of credit can change our decision-making process for weddings, homes, and universities for our children, then the absence of credit can also have catastrophic consequences for basic life decisions. Why do governments over and over again allow wholesale banking (excessive foreign borrowing by domestic banks) to derail an economy and wreck millions of lives? Why don't they use simple regulatory guidelines to extend a cycle by moderating numbers like the LDR? Why do we *never* hear about these simple criteria in the discussions on Bank of International Settlements (BIS) rules designed to keep the banking system afloat and healthy?

HOW POLITICAL CHAOS IS CREATED FROM RUNAWAY GREED

Governments have a clear incentive to do this because we will show that governments that end up with banking systems that overheat with LDRs of 1.4 almost invariably are kicked out of power when the financial system finally overheats and blows up. Or they are forced to implement violent tactics and implement various forms of martial law in order to stay in power. Furthermore, chaotic political change has a tendency to slip into civil war or wars with neighbors. Politicians, bankers, and central banks allow this devolution into chaos to happen over and over again because they refuse to create a few simple rules of the road to manage the credit cycle.

David Shambaugh talked about this in his interesting book, *China's Communist Party*. He shows that one of the major reasons for the fall of the Soviet Union was the collapse of the financial system.[10] (See the accompanying PowerPoint documents, which summarize Shambaugh's thinking on this topic on the Wiley website). Banking systems that turn insolvent invite economic stagnation. In turn, budget deficits are created to accommodate the financial system as it tries to right the boat. Societal issues are impacted, such as when unemployment rises. Governments do not have room for extravagant subsidies and people become angry as the quality of life dwindles. Life becomes harder and there are fewer opportunities. When young people do not see a way out of their unemployment, they can turn to religion for comfort and they simultaneously abandon political parties. The rise in the Religious Right in the United States is a very understandable phenomenon in this regard. Another example is of the Brazilian financial system, which has been stuck in recession given that its LDR is 1.30 and there is just no credit left to distribute. There has been a large movement in evangelical Christianity in the country as young people give up hope of any progression in society. This is being exacerbated by the collapse of the Brazilian oil company Petrobras, whose shares have plunged more than 75% in 2013–14.

Let's get a sense of this cycle in historical terms to see just how long it takes to turn off (and then reduce) the excess leverage once the LDR gets to catastrophic levels of 1.3–1.4. Let's take a look at the timeline for the Asian crisis. The LDR of the Far East peaked in 1997 at 1.25 (The U.S. LDR peaked in 2007 at 1.16 and the U.K. LDR peaked in 2007 at about 1.2. The pattern repeats itself over and over again.) It took many years for the LDR to get back down to safe levels of around .75. In the case of Asia, it took about seven years. In the case of the United States, it also took about seven years. In the case of Europe, banks are a very big part of the economy, and southern Europe reached extremes that are almost unsurpassed in modern times. We put GIIPS (the five countries of southern Europe—Greece, Italy, Portugal, and Spain—plus Ireland) on Figure 1.2. We can see that the credit excesses of these countries make the Asian crisis pale in comparison.

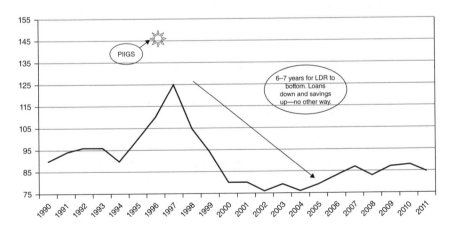

FIGURE 1.2 GIIPS LDR: Deleveraging Process of GIIPS More Severe Than Asia in 1997
Source: China Construction Bank

The trends in loan/deposit ratios need to be put into a global context because this folly we call wholesale banking is a global redistribution of money in which countries with low LDRs (China in 2005) can lend money to countries with high and unsustainable LDRs like the United States or Spain in 2006. Asset prices of the lenders will almost always do better than the asset prices of the borrowers, especially when the LDR is in the area of 1.2 to 1.4 (i.e., when the party really starts going and the "hard stuff" is brought out just before the crashing hangover).

Indeed, it is a perverse phenomenon that asset prices seem to accelerate *faster* between an LDR of about 1 to 1.3. This is usually a time when sane investors who understand credit would become alarmed and sell, probably too early. Asset markets seem to be happy to ride the tiger of wholesale bank funding from overseas fickle financiers, often without realizing they are driving at full speed toward the canyon of exhausted credit. The ride from an LDR of 1.0 to 1.2 tends to be glorious. But the ride from 1.2 to 1.4 is disastrous. Why governments—for their own sake, and one would think more importantly, for the sake of their people—do not step in and restrict excessive wholesale borrowing is a staggering mystery.

TANGIBLE LEVERAGE IS THE OTHER VITALLY IMPORTANT FACTOR

On top of this, there is one other simple number we will look at and that is tangible leverage. Tangible leverage is simply assets minus intangibles divided by capital minus intangibles. Intangibles usually arise when banks make an acquisition and have to put the value of the bank above and beyond the cash price on the balance sheet. The actual value of this "intangible asset" is zero and is usually a high number when a bank paid too high a price for another institution. You cannot buy a cup of coffee with an intangible asset—it is a filler. For instance, Deutsche bank has a great deal of intangible value because of its acquisitions over the years. These tangible leverage levels can range from low and healthy levels like 10× (a healthy $10 of capital for $100 of assets) for Thai banks and Indonesian banks in 2013 to the Swiss bank in 2008 at 50× (a suicidal $2 of capital for $100 of assets).

When a country's loan/deposit ratio is at 1.3× and the tangible leverage is at 30–40, I submit (and will prove it) that corporate earnings do not matter one whit. The stock market will be doomed and all stocks will fall, with better companies outperforming the worse ones. Few will see positive stock price movements. When the banking system cracks at levels of 1.3× on the LDR and 30–40× on tangible leverage, everything will be damaged as the deleveraging process unwinds. It gets very ugly, indeed.

When a country has a high LDR of 1.3 or so and tangible leverage north of 30–40×, the fuse has been lit and the macroeconomic explosion is only a few months away. Governments in these countries will be out of power within 24 months or so of the explosion of the banking system. Banking systems like those in Indonesia with a low level of leverage and low LDRs have a free ride for a considerable period of time. In fact, the deleveraging of Western banks had an effect of speeding up the deployment of leverage in places like Indonesia (for the simple reason that Western countries had to lower rates to zero and Asian countries with linked dollar exchange rates were forced to accept lower rates). The politicians in these countries can do no wrong. President Yudhoyono of Indonesia has been riding a virtuous wave of credit growth. But their wave may be cresting about now, seven years after the global financial crisis.

While the LDR for the West was at an unsustainable level of 1.2, the tangible leverage for the West was at a dangerous level of around 30. We showed earlier that the solution to a lower LDR was either lower loans (default, liquidation, or inability to renew loan agreements, all of which are painful) or raise deposits (save more or spend less, both of which involve painful decisions). There are no good solutions for banks or people when the LDR comes down. The reduction in the LDR is more of a public event between the bank and the public. The bank must force pain on the public by forcing property prices to fall. It must force pain on the public by repossessing cars, houses, jewelry, vacation condos, and other valuables.

The public must do something that is very difficult. It must force an increase in savings just to stay even. Costs must be cut with no discernible benefit. This involves great pain, including pulling children out of good schools that their parents can no longer afford. It requires cancellation of credit cards, postponement of vacations, willingness to accept humiliating unemployment benefits, cancellation of health clubs, and a general lowering of the lifestyle to which one has become accustomed. It may even cause a couple to decide not to have a child. These decisions cause embarrassment, loss of face, and sometimes outright poverty. Hence, we often see the wrath of voters who throw out any government that contributed to the banking crisis. They also have second thoughts about traditional political party affiliations. Alternative parties (often extreme) gather interest to vent the rage of people who see themselves slipping backward helplessly with no hope of regaining the old wealth.

WHEN *DEBT* BECOMES A DIRTY AND DANGEROUS WORD

The solution to a lower tangible leverage is slightly different but also requires painful solutions. It is a shared pain between bank managers and shareholders. And it often requires secret deals between the government and the bank. These deals often involve sweetheart deals, corruption, criminality, and the illicit use of public funds to bail out what is considered a "systemically important" institution. Lowering assets means reducing loan books by turning away past customers, writing off bad debt, shuttering a loan book for new customers, adding more low-returning cash, or liquidating securities holdings. These are all bad choices because they involve a very dangerous phenomenon we do not often see, and that is an outright shrinkage of debt.

Shrinking debt is very dangerous for a society because it involves deflation. Deflation causes asset values to fall and the real value of debt to rise, so people incur higher debt payments in real terms as their home value falls and their income falls. In response, they spend less. Deflation causes wages to fall, so people feel less safe and spend less. Deflation builds up expectation of falling prices, so people delay purchases and spend less. If deflation is allowed to take root, it becomes a phenomenon like in Japan in the last few years, and people keep on saving more and spending less and saving more and spending less. A sense develops that prices will always be lower tomorrow, so there is no need to hurry and buy anything. The only economic actor remains the government. This is very dangerous, as it leads to a buildup of debt that requires low interest rates to service. Low interest rates create an incentive for governments to generate low levels of growth and implement policies, knowingly or not, that reinforce deflation.

So governments are faced with the problem as identified in Figure 1.3. If tangible leverage is to fall to avoid an economic collapse, governments need to prevent a violent shrinkage of the loan book (assets) in the midst of a crisis. They must also prevent the capital base from getting too small. So, they need to do two things. They need to renew confidence *and* find buyers for more capital for the bank. This is complicated by one important factor. In the midst of a crisis, loans on the book are going bad because, ironically, the banks have stopped lending to their customers to repay debt (is the world anything other than an ever-greening of old loans by new debt?). When this debt starts to go bad, it must be written off the balance sheet. At the height of most crises, about 8 percent to 10 percent of a bank's balance sheet needs to be written off. This must be written off against capital. So, while the bank managers, shareholders, and government officials are huddling to find new capital, the capital itself is shrinking due to losses from bad loans.

Figure 1.3 shows the gargantuan problem that was staring policymakers in the face back in 2009. Global leverage at the time was about 30× (of course, leverage should *never* have been allowed to get this high, but that is a discussion for a later chapter). This means banks had about $100 of assets and about $3 of capital. This was a buffer to cover losses of 3 percent—not

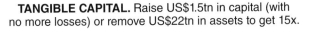

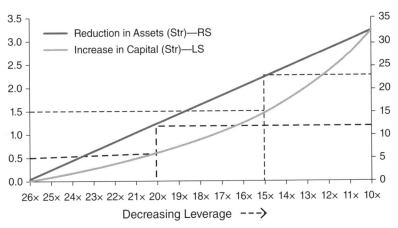

FIGURE 1.3   Methods to Decrease Leverage: Sell Assets or Increase Equity—Both Are Painful
Source: Nomura

the 8–10 percent that was to come down the pike as the crisis really got going. So, the system had to be backstopped. If the dam was about to break, a stronger and higher dam needed to be constructed quickly or the system would stop functioning. Figure 1.3 shows just how big the "new" dam needed to be if the world was going to keep functioning.

It was apparent that the world needed to see leverage fall to a minimum of 20 in order to become sustainable again. There is a simple formula: Assets have to fall and/or capital needs to rise. There is *no* other way to do this. It needed to happen *quickly*, and it needed to happen in the midst of large losses from the write-off of incrementally new bad debt. So, the math was simple. We pick two levels of leverage. One is 20× and the other is 15×. As it turns out, the United States chose a far more painful route and got its leverage below 15×.

Europe is taking its time and does not have the political will (or structure) to implement quick and painful measures. In the case of the global banking structure, we can see that getting to leverage of 20× (the left axis) requires that banks find about $600 billion. Hence, banks like Deutsche Bank, BNP Paribas, and Société Générale have high leverage seven years into the crisis. In fact, in the first half of 2014, the asset size of Deutsche Bank is above the level of 2009.

Indeed, the United States was able to bring down leverage quickly through the TARP program provided by the U.S. federal government. This was smart, but it was one of the major reasons that the Republicans lost the White House and the Senate in 2008.** European banks have not been able to get this capital either from the federal governments or from the European Central Bank (ECB); it took another route. On the right axis, we can see the reduction of debt needed to reduce leverage. The ECB did a smart thing by not taking this debt on its balance sheet (which would be against the law). Instead, it guaranteed trillions of dollars of this debt and allowed it to remain on the balance sheet of banks throughout Europe. *So,* the United States chose to recapitalize the banks *and* write off bad debt. And the European banks chose to attack the problem by way of the assets. In the midst of this extreme pain, every major government in Europe was brought down (except Germany, which still holds the purse strings).

EUROPEAN BANK WOES

The U.K. government took a midpoint solution. It nationalized the Royal Bank of Scotland (RBS) and took an 80 percent stake in the bank after its collapse. It forced RBS to close many businesses and shrink its balance sheet. It has had a strong voice in the background of Barclays and has been using moral suasion to get Barclays to give up on its unprofitable investment banking business (Barclays balance sheet is *still* one of the largest globally, and years of painful deleveraging are ahead.)

The crippling torpedo to the U.K. economy came from the real estate lender Northern Rock. It was mostly funded from wholesale borrowing. The cost of the collapse of Northern Rock to the U.K. people was a whopping 6 points of government debt as a percent of gross domestic product (GDP). This equates to tens of billions of dollars in government bailout funds (which caused the Labour Party to lose to the Tory party in a devastating electoral defeat). All too often, the general public concludes that the government is in bed with the "banksters" and does not care about the "little people." They take the view that the interest of a small and incompetent elite pay off the government for private favors. This opinion spreads not only to the federal government (parliaments and congresses) but also to the central bank. The bankers get bailed out for being reckless. They keep their wealth. And the middle class ends up paying higher taxes. They feel like they are subsidizing

---

**According to the website www.bailoutsleuth.com, 36 TARP supporters in the House and Senate were defeated in the 2008 election. These numbers explain the lion's share of the large political shift in the U.S. Congress.

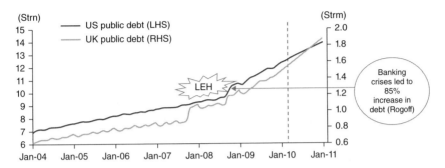

FIGURE 1.4 U.S. and U.K. Public Debt: Government Debt Levels Rose Precisely to Bail Out the Banks
Source: Nomura

reckless behavior, poor risk management, and outright corruption as the increasing debt level in Figure 1.4 shows. It is no surprise that governments fall after they support bailouts.

Ken Rogoff's book, *This Time Is Different*, is valuable because he articulates a very important point.[11] His extensive research shows that each time there is a financial crisis, government debt/GDP rises by an average of 50 points of GDP. This matches my research, but as we will see, there are extremes where a much higher LDR of 1.5 to 1.7 will cause an inordinately large increase in debt/GDP. On average the LDR of a country in a banking crisis will get to 1.2 and then snap back to about 0.75, with a resulting rise in government debt/GDP of about 50 points.

So, this sharp rise in government debt, nationalization, moral suasion— and very substantial increases in central bank purchases of government debt to keep rates down—have all contributed to a midway solution to the problem. The U.K. government would like to exit the RBS ownership with a profit, but this remains to be seen.

FOLLOWING THE NUMBERS

We will also notice that there is a kind of natural resting place historically for banks. We showed that from the point of view of "liquidity," the natural resting place for the LDR was 1.0. Historically, there is also a resting place for leverage. In our statistical work, there is a place where the stock prices of banks continue to peak and fall, and that is tangible leverage of around 20×. After a bank reaches 20× in its tangible leverage, the stock price seems to fall. The market sniffs out trouble and sees that every incremental dollar of

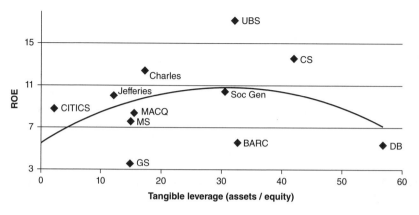

FIGURE 1.5 Return on Equity and Tangible Leverage: The Rule of 1 and 20: Maximum LDR of 1 and Tangible Leverage of 20
Source: China Construction Bank

income with leverage above 20 is not worth the risk. That said, the summary of this chapter can be seen in Figure 1.5. Consider it as a snapshot of 2012.

Interestingly, Deutsche Bank has been one of the worst performing banks globally, as it has been forced to roll back leverage and raise capital. It has made great progress getting its leverage back to a safer level in the 20s compared to suicidal leverage of almost 50 in 2008. But that means it has had to reduce assets (surrender businesses, shrink loans, retreat from geographical regions) or increase capital (have very expensive rights issues that irritate shareholders). Its capital increase in mid-2014 was a rights issue that alienated investors.

Barclays, too, is in the same boat and has been a terrible performer, as it has tried to cut costs and reduce leverage. It has been forced to essentially give up its investment banking business and reduce its geographical presence. Additionally, both banks (and many others) have tried to make up for lost revenue by engaging in questionable business lines for which they have been forced to pay significant penalties to regulators and prosecutors. These questionable business lines include fraud, high-frequency trading (which is tantamount to front running), tax evasion, smuggling, trading with the enemy, and many other felonious activities. In 2015, John McFarlane will assume the reins at Barclays and very likely take a knife to many divisions. McFarlane was chairman of Aviva when it was in crisis. He closed divisions, fired top management, suspended bonuses, and implemented a housecleaning from top to bottom. The same thing will happen to Barclays, and it is likely a foretaste of things to come for many global universal banks.

Learning Tools: 01_Credit_Master.pdf

This file includes a presentation that explains the dynamics of leverage, loan/deposit ratios, and calculations, using simple language.

Endnotes

1. Joseph Stiglitz, "Stable Growth in an Era of Crises: Learning from Economic Theory and History," *Ekonomi-tek* 2, No. 1, pp. 1–39, 2013.
2. One exception is the very talented Simon Ogus, chairman of Dismal Science Group (DSG), who has an acute appreciation for the influences of credit (especially derivatives) in economic models.
3. Seth Carpenter and Selva Demiralp, "Money, Reserves and the Transmission of Monetary Policy: Does the Money Multiplier Exist?" IMF Working Paper, 2010–41.
4. Stiglitz, "Stable Growth."
5. John Cassidy, "After the Blowup," *The New Yorker*, January 11, 2010.
6. Bill White, chief economist of the BIS from 1995 to 2008, in the documentary *Money for Nothing*.
7. Ahir Hites and Prakash Loungani, "'There Will Be Growth in the Spring': How Well Do Economists Predict Turning Points," *Vox*, April 2014. This is from an article in *The New York Review of Books* called "Why the Experts Missed the Recession" (September 25, 2014). The article also makes the point that the famous Fed Greenbook cannot make accurate predictions even one quarter out. A key reason for this is that these economic models, astonishingly, cannot accommodate credit data.
8. Ibid.
9. Ibid.
10. David Shambaugh, *The Communist Party* (University of California Press, 2008).
11. Ken Rogoff and Carmen Reinhart, *This Time Is Different* (Princeton University Press, 2009).

CHAPTER 2

Differences between Liquidity and Solvency Are Thin

Financial systems are always seeking equilibrium. This equilibrium is found when there is enough liquidity to fund growth through non-inflationary wage growth accompanied by productivity gains. When people are earning good money and efficiently making things the world wants at a good price, there is ample prosperity. This prosperity results in deposit and savings and is accompanied by confidence in the future. This confidence leads to a willingness to buy homes and invest in expensive education for their children. Alas, these moments are few and far between.

These moments are found when lending growth is about equal with the growth in savings and income. It is found when the demand for international goods abroad is about equal to the demand other countries have for this same country's goods. The problem lies in the abuse of wholesale funding as countries with excess liquidity (too much surplus in the current account) are looking for a quick buck by lending to countries with a deficit of liquidity, countries that cannot get their act together to create enough wealth to fund the future. When this happens, surplus countries lend too much money, usually at the wrong time *and* at the wrong price. It almost always leads to excess and implosion. This willy-nilly spilling of wholesale funding to unsuspecting countries has a strong tendency to create destabilizing financial conditions, default, government bailouts, and social chaos.

Figure 2.1 shows the relationship between the sustainability of the banks to create liquidity and credit in a country (the loan/deposit ratio, or LDR) and the sustainability of macroeconomic growth. We want to know for how long a time a country and its corporate actors can safely generate cash flows. We want to know whether there is a crisis looming around the corner, especially if everything looks rosy. Indeed, disasters often come just after everything looks the rosiest. The relationship between the LDR and the current account deficit is the nexus of this question of sustainability and safety of credit.

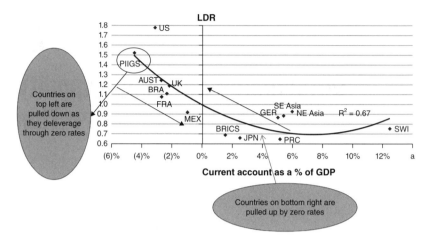

FIGURE 2.1 LDR and Current Account: The World Is Seeking Equilibrium at (0,1)
Source: China Construction Bank

The X-axis shows the current account. Basically, this figure shows which countries are living beyond their means (and are dependent on foreign borrowings) and which countries are liquid. Buyers of financial assets should seek out liquid countries, as these assets are not bogged down by leverage. Investors should only ever seek out the assets of the leveraged countries (ones in the top left) during a period of debt restructuring and the subsequent rebuilding of liquidity when the cycle begins all over again.

Notice the curved line. It is a line of best fit, which gives the trend for all of the countries in the set. It has an R-squared of almost 70 percent, a quite compelling correlation to explain the way a country's LDR and current account work together. It is also interesting that if we go up the Y-axis at zero, we meet the line at 1. In other words, when the LDR is 1, the world's current account balance is zero. At that point, all is bliss. No one is borrowing money from another country, and no one has a bloated trade surplus for reasons fair or foul. Alas, this world of stasis never lasts. We are not saying that balance is an ideal to be achieved. All we are saying is that countries should avoid either of the extremes on the chart—either on the right or the left.

CURRENT ACCOUNT VERSUS LDR

The current account is comprised of three simple items. The first is exports minus imports. The countries with high trade surpluses are, like Southeast

Asia now, competitive and offering goods to the world that are of sufficient quality and at the right price. The current account includes interest income from overseas assets. And it includes transfers from citizens living abroad. This is a country's savings. The more, the merrier. As we shall see, however, these surpluses are mostly good, but only up to a point.

The Y-axis is the LDR. The LDR and the current account can be seen as two sides of the same coin. The more savings a country has through the current account, the lower the LDR tends to be. These are the countries in the lower-right-hand corner. The higher the current account deficit, the more dependent a country is on foreign borrowing. This foreign borrowing is the "filler" above and beyond an LDR of 1.0. By definition, an LDR above 1.0 must always come from foreign savings. This is wholesale banking—recycling of foreign savings into a local economy that is short on savings to fund growth. Or so the theory goes. We will show, however, that these LDRs of 1.2–1.3 will almost always lead to catastrophe for a country, since it is relying on the kindness of strangers for its growth. Statistically, this is a very bad way to grow.

Why do these high LDRs lead to such pain? Let's take a snapshot of the situation in 2010 and see just how dangerous the situation was at the time. In addition, the fact that the economists out there were ignoring leverage meant that they were blind to an exceedingly problematic issue for national growth for most of the world. Table 2.1 shows this in spades.

In short, countries with yawning current account deficits and high LDRs in excess of 1.2× are doing something that our grandmother told us not to do: They are living far beyond their means. Greece, Italy, Ireland,

TABLE 2.1   Tradeoff: Pain through Shareholder Dilution or Asset Sales

Tangible Capital World gearing is 26×. Europe gearing tops at 37×. Asia is the lowest at 14×. All others over 20×.

Region	Tangible Assets ($BN)	Tangible Capital	Leverage (×)	Assets to Reduce for 15× ($bn)	% of GDP	Equity to Raise for 15× ($bn)
Japan	5750	241	23.8	2132	48%	142
Asia ex-Japan	5250	366	14.3	−239	−3%	−16
Australia	1470	63	23.4	529	59%	35
United States	14241	622	22.9	4908	36%	327
UK	9142	267	34.2	5134	183%	342
Europe	16557	444	37.3	9895	59%	660
Global	52409	2003	26.2	22358	48%	1491

Source: Nomura

Portugal, and Spain (infamously known as the GIIPS countries) have the greatest imbalances globally, with exceptionally high current account deficits. We can also see that the United States is in the top left as well *if* we include the government-sponsored enterprises (GSEs; that is, Fannie Mae and Freddie Mac) in the equation.

We should include them, as these two institutions own almost *half* of all the mortgages in the United States and do not have one dime in savings in their balance sheets. By law, the GSEs cannot charge interest on deposits and must fund themselves with securities. They are (or we should say, were) completely beholden to domestic and foreign buyers of their bonds (mortgage-backed securities) to fund their mortgage purchases. These two institutions are now insolvent and in receivership by the Department of the Treasury. These two institutions *must* be considered as part of the savings equation of the United States.

BAD CREDIT KARMA

Figure 2.2 shows how Fannie Mae and Freddie Mac contributed to the excesses. In the space of just two years from 2004 to 2006, the amount of mortgages that were not backed by any kind of deposits (and were almost entirely funded by foreign money) *doubled* from US$3 trillion to US$6 trillion between 2004 and early 2007. Most of these mortgage originations came from the GSEs and were funded by foreign central banks. Many of

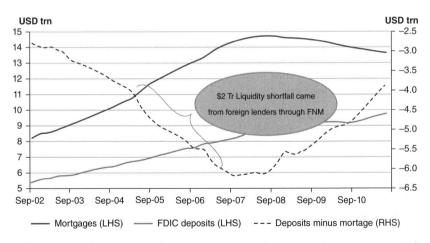

FIGURE 2.2 Mortgages and Deposits: Government GSEs Quietly Hijacked the System and Funded It with Overseas Money
Source: China Construction Bank

them were forced through the system at lightning speed and were rife with fraud. This all came to an end in mid-November 2007.

In fact, while at Lehman Brothers, I and a senior mortgage salesman from New York met investors in Hong Kong. He told a group of them in November 2007 that "it was possible" that the entire vintage of 2006 and 1H 2007 mortgages were fraudulent. I believe these smart people in central banks like the PBOC, HKMA, and the Bank of China in Taiwan did their homework and had their eyes wide open. They were hoodwinked. *But*, it is important to remember that many people warned policymakers in countries like China, Japan, Taiwan, and Singapore that they were running ruinous mercantilist policies that are caused by undervalued currencies generating huge trade surpluses. These surpluses necessarily had to be recycled into dollar assets to prevent the currencies from appreciating and damaging the export engine. These policy makers were forewarned, but it is eminently clear to me that these policymakers, many of whom I spoke to on a regular basis, were absolutely hoodwinked by the vast hidden leverage in the dollar financial system. So, they were warned about icebergs in the water, but kept their ships moving at full steam. For instance, One sovereign wealth fund was very close to buying HBOS in the UK in the summer of 2008 before it collapsed.

This boom in Fannie Mae mortgages was a disguised and stealthy explosion in the LDR. There is just no getting around it. Break the LDR rule and you can take five to seven years to pay for it. The United States is only now getting back into some kind of equilibrium, and it looks like Fannie Mae may emerge from receivership in some form or another. Back in 2011, it was a sure bet that Fannie Mae would be taken out back and shot in the head. Recent activity in Congress indicates that it may be resurrected, but in a much smaller and less powerful role.

During a financial crisis, it is a common tactic to corral the toxic bad assets (defaulted loans on houses and buildings) and separate them from the still-healthy parts of the economy. These toxic assets go into the "bad" bank and the "good" banks can then try to regain health. The Federal Reserve and the U.S. Treasury were smart and basically turned the GSEs into *the* bad bank. As a result, these toxic mortgages are largely in the GSEs, and the "good banks" (if we subscribe to the useful fiction that the GSEs can really be hived off and be allowed to restructure their obligations) can go on their merry way. So far, this has worked.

THE "GOOD" BANKS

If we look at the good banks by themselves, they have low LDRs and are now capable of lending once again. In general, banks with low LDRs often have low leverage, and vice versa. We shall see in the chapter on central banks, however, that there is a catch. Much of the savings is unfortunately but understandably being channeled to the bad banks (GSEs). The cash piling up on the balance sheets of the banks is being deposited into the Federal Reserve at 25 basis points and not being lent out. The Federal Reserve then turns around and uses this cash to buy the mortgage-backed securities of the GSEs, as well as purchasing government debt, part of which was used to fund the losses of the GSEs. There is little choice, but we can make the case that the Federal Reserve is serving the commonwealth in that it is causing a stabilization of house prices. Without this effort, it is almost certain that U.S. house prices would continue to fall and stagnate at best.

At a certain point, the banks will detach from the Federal Reserve and, as they feel better about the economy, they will direct their savings into risk assets. It takes a long time for this to happen. Banks in New York are not only looking at the situation in the United States but also at the fragility of the financial system in the United Kingdom and in Europe. It is a scary world out there, and the Federal Reserve has in the past kept rates low for a long period of time to accommodate dangerous dynamics in the European or Asian financial systems. This is the price the Federal Reserve must pay for being the reserve currency of the world.

So we ask ourselves, what on earth the Federal Reserve was doing when the overall LDR of the United States (if we include the GSEs) was at a staggering level of 1.7? The Fed allowed the external borrowing of the United States to reach levels that the International Monetary Fund (IMF) would have declared unacceptable to any developing country under their aegis, especially at a time when the budget deficit was also out of control. There is no other way to describe the fiscal and monetary policy of the United States from 2004 to 2007 except as out of control.

What were they thinking? On September 11, 2007, Chairman Bernanke addressed an audience at the Bundesbank on the topic of savings and current account deficits. He noted the current account is equal to investments in factories, buildings, and houses minus the savings of households, corporations, and governments. The total stock of savings as a percent of GDP was about 14 percent of GDP, and the total investment was about 20 percent, so this deficit was about 6 percent of GDP by 2007. This was mostly a deficit in household savings. People did not have the savings to buy a home, so they basically "borrowed" the savings from China and Japan through the GSEs.

Bernanke made the point, of course, that the capital account (the other side of the current account, which includes the "foreign" savings) was flowing like a river. Of course it was. And he made the point that "the increase in the current account was matched by a similar expansion of net capital flows."*

---

*Ben Bernanke, "Global Imbalances," Bundesbank Lecture, September 11, 2007.

A WELLSPRING OF DEBT

By 2007, the current account deficit was US$800 billion. Bernanke was wondering why it was so high and why there was such a bonanza in refinancing and house purchases at that point. Of course, the free capital flows of the United States meant that if the U.S. economy was growing beyond its means, capital flows from abroad could add more booze to the punch bowl. If we add the fiscal deficit at this time to the current account deficit, the numbers would have exceeded US$1 trillion, or more than 10 percent of GDP. Given this staggeringly large number, it is shocking that Bernanke did not offer a prescription that would have been blindingly obvious if the United States was under the aegis of the IMF. U.S. policymakers at the time were behaving like inexperienced politicians in a developing country and running a growth trajectory that was wildly unrealistic.

If any developing country were running a similar policy of profligate and unsustainable growth, the IMF would have forced the country to implement policies to halt real estate speculation, reduce consumption, and increase savings. The number-one suggestion would have been to raise interest rates. Had the United States raised interest rates more aggressively starting in 2004, the catastrophe we have on our hands today could have been averted. Raising interest rates would have caused a decrease in consumption, a reduction in real estate speculation, and an increase in savings. When I was working with the Ministry of Finance in Indonesia in 1991, I remember the IMF coming down like a ton of bricks onto the government to rein in growth and raise interest rates when the current account deficit reached 3 percent of GDP. The U.S. deficit was *double* that of Indonesia in 1991. (It helps that the United States is the controlling shareholder of the IMF. Remember the Golden Rule: He who has the gold makes the rules!)

Instead, Bernanke opined that the excessive growth in the United States in 2006 and 2007 funded by foreign inflows reflected the "attractiveness of both the U.S. economy overall and the depth, liquidity and legal safeguards associated with its capital markets."** (This seems like a throwaway line, as we must believe someone at the Fed was aware of the shenanigans in the leveraged CDO market and the systemic fraudulence that has been uncovered en masse in many of the largest mortgage brokers in the United States.)

Bernanke made the point that running current account deficits "can reduce tendencies toward recession" for countries in need of savings. He did say that, at the time. The current account deficit was not sustainable, but he also said that the foreign borrowing by the United States was not "putting an exceptionally large burden on the American economy." This was simply not true at the time and there were numerous voices saying that there was great

---

**Bernanke, op cit.

danger. In fact, at that very time the ratings agencies had awakened from their slumber and had *already* begun to ring the alarm bells on the excessive leverage in the system, much of which was funded by foreign entities in Germany, China, Taiwan, and Japan. "An adjustment must take place," he warned. There was one sure way to force an adjustment and that was to jack up interest rates.***

As long as there were foreign inflows to fund the excessive growth, there wasn't a problem. A country can have growth that is deemed excessive by one and all as the current account is hemorrhaging, but as long as it is "funded" by wholesale borrowing, there is no problem. This is the same thing as saying that a heroin addict does not have a problem as long as he has his next fix. This insane logic seems to infect one country after another until it is too late. The endgame of high current account deficits and LDRs of about 1.2 to 1.3 is governments that are thrown out of power and years of social pain. Over and over again, no one seems to see it coming.

This is the same trap we see one crisis after another. Capital account inflows in the form of credit enter and offer pro-cyclical momentum to countries that, by definition, are *already* growing too fast and are very likely to have had the best quality growth already. These pro-cyclical flows (when the LDR moves from 1 to 1.2) will tend to be the "real" party, as this wholesale money enters the economy quickly and is deployed quickly to purchase real estate and other assets. It is an "easy come, easy go" type of capital, which a growing number of countries are finally realizing is destabilizing.

So, the United States fell into the same trap in 2005–2007 that countries in Southeast Asia fell into during the Asian crisis in 1996–1998. Current account deficit and LDRs were way too high and had reached 1.3–1.5 if we correctly include the GSEs. In many ways, the GSEs were the poison in the U.S. economy, yet few were aware of it. This really was happening under the nose of the Fed, since the GSEs' national headquarters are within a few miles of the Federal Reserve. The same was true of Turkey in 2000 before it blew up. The same has been true of so many Latin American countries in the past. And the same is true of *all* of the countries in the Olive Belt today—every single one of them!

And we could go further and submit that France, Australia, and Brazil are in peril, since they are stretched beyond their means and global liquidity continues to shrink at the margin. What is Brazil doing to solve its problem of stagnant growth due to insufficient savings? It is *lowering* interest rates, so people can consume *more* and save *less*. This seems like a recipe for trouble. Brazil should be doing the opposite and raising interest rates.

***Bernanke, op cit.

LESSONS IN ASIA

Let's look at the progression of East Asia in the run-up to the Asian crisis in the years 1994–1997. The line shows nicely what this book is about. For three years of boom, East Asia paid a dear price, since the unwind of the boom of 1994 to 1997 lasted until 2003—seven years of bad luck. There was a bonanza of credit during this time, and there were all sorts of absurd justifications for the foreign credit pouring into these countries. There always are. Every country in Southeast Asia was going to become a financial hub. Thailand was going to become a lending center for Indochina. Malaysia was going to be a center for Islamic banking. South Korea was going to take on the Western conglomerates in every industry. The stories of excess were endless.

At one point, one could go to Thailand and look out of a hotel window and know something was amiss. It was easy to count dozens of buildings under construction within a two-mile horizon. Yet, few investors were ringing any alarm bells. All one had to do was to look at the loan/deposit ratios for a few Thai banks and see that they were exceeding 1.20. For every $100 of savings, the country was borrowing $25 of foreign savings and pouring it into the economy. When the ratings agencies emerged from their splendid isolation and actually began to do some homework, they began to downgrade these countries. Foreigners got itchy and left, as usual, en masse. It seems they only know how to leave in a group.

As John Maynard Keynes said, "A sound banker, alas, is not one who foresees danger and avoids it." He is the kind of man who "is ruined in a conventional and orthodox way along with his fellows, so that no one can really blame him." It seems bankers always go over the cliff together, because they can never resist the dangerous profits brought about by fickle wholesale money from foreigners. Alas, when these foreign bankers in London, New York, and Amsterdam withdrew their money at the same time, bankers in Thailand, South Korea, and Indonesia were ruined overnight. International bankers and local bankers were operating at cross-purposes because both ignored the dangerous LDRs that were building up. And central banks did nothing to prevent the oncoming catastrophe. Without a local deposit base, banks who rely on foreign wholesale borrowing to fund long-term local currency assets very often implode when the going gets tough. Northern Rock was a good example in the Great Recession. So was Allied Irish Bank. Iceland's collapse also falls precisely into this category.

If we look at the dot in the top-left-hand corner of Figure 2.1, we can see where the countries of the Olive Belt in Southern Europe are. Once again, we had a group of five countries that went on a foreign borrowing binge, and central banks just stood by and watched. For three years of boom, these countries in Southern Europe, like many Asian countries in the 1990s, created vast suffering for their people in the form of political chaos, public spending cuts, high unemployment, and social upheaval. In the case of Asian countries, they were all able to devalue their currencies and at least recover some degree of hope in the form of cheaper exports. In the case of the Olive Belt, however, they are locked into the euro and cannot devalue their way out.

So, these countries have been forced to bleed out their excesses through a devaluation (or a depression) of asset prices in local currency terms. This is happening at the same time as foreign banks are demanding all of their money back while budgets are being cut to the bone. We need go no further than the words of John Maynard Keynes to see the potential for a poor outcome in this circumstance. He said that the father of revolution is the banker who refuses to offer some forgiveness of debt in the face of economic catastrophe of a country that has borrowed more than it should have. The bank, by definition, lent more than it should have.

How do we know when the lending boom is too much? If bankers in the home country and also in the lending country were paying attention to the LDR of the borrowing country, and if authorities in the borrowing country applied the brakes when the LDR reached 1.15 or so, then catastrophe could have been averted. If people apply the same argument that Bernanke in 2007 did and say that it does not matter how high the LDR goes as long as it is funded with healthy capital inflows from overseas "investors" because they see good opportunities, this is missing the point. At an LDR beyond 1.15–1.2 or so, credit becomes a dangerous narcotic and should be regulated. History tells us over and over again that a country with an LDR of 1.2 and rising is a runaway train. When these trends develop, it is virtually impossible to avoid catastrophe—for politicians, rich people, bankers, and the middle class. If all parties are affected so badly and no one is left unscathed, why does this keep happening over and over again?

Lesson Tools: 02_Banks_Master.pdf

The presentation shows the dynamics between current account and credit and how, where, and when problems start to show up. We can use the example of Brazil and India in 2013–2014, whose respective currencies devalued sharply.

CHAPTER 3

Anatomy of a Credit Crisis and Examples in the Real World

Economies have an uncanny ability to create spectacular booms as the country deploys savings from a loan/deposit ratio LDR of about 0.6 up to an LDR of 1. Those in power are lucky, as they ride a wonderful gravy train of credit creation, rising asset prices, and rising productivity (we will see later that new calculations of productivity are mostly predicated on credit creation; this is one of the dirty secrets of the modern age). A modern example of this has been the spectacular rise of Lula in Brazil. He rode a great wave of credit creation in the 2000s in Brazil and could do no wrong. He became a darling of the developing world.

Now that Brazil's LDR is at a dangerous level and there is simply no credit around, President Roussef is having a harder time. The Brazilian fiscal deficit at the end of 2014 is heading to US$10 billion. And the current account deficit is heading to US$80 billion, one of the highest globally. The same was true of President Yudhoyono when he became president of Indonesia. When the credit cycle is in your favor, you can do no wrong as a leader (for example, President Reagan in 1980–1988). When the credit cycle stalls and asset prices fall, you can do nothing right (President George H. W. Bush in 1992). President Lula was a hero in a great wave of credit, President Roussef is hanging on by her fingernails, and their policies are very similar. President Clinton's reign was one of spectacular credit growth from a base of a low LDR. President George W. Bush's second term was (and will be) cursed by the greatest implosion in credit in modern history as the LDR reached multiyear highs by 2008. Credit makes and breaks national leaders.

It is important to remember that within 12 months of the Asian crisis, every leader was voted out of office or chased out of town on a rail. And several political parties in power for decades collapsed overnight. Examples of political parties or persons who were gone within 24 months of the crisis include Golkar and Suharto in Indonesia, the KMT in Taiwan, and President Y. S. Kim in South Korea. Thailand's government collapsed. Opposition parties that had been out of power for decades rose to power. In Malaysia, deputy PM Anwar tried to assert his leadership but was thwarted. Mahathir was gone by 2003.

The 2008 global financial crisis was a repeat of this political turmoil. President Obama came to power in a landslide in 2008. The Labour Party was thrown out of power in the United Kingdom. In a 24-month period, governments throughout Europe collapsed, including Spain, Greece, Ireland, Italy, France, Iceland, and Holland. Right-wing parties were born and are on the rise in many of these countries. As the cost of capital falls to zero and labor wages remain sticky, there is an irresistible urge to replace labor with capital. This phenomenon always aggravates a financial crisis. Young unskilled labor, which is not ready for the technological booms that always follow a financial crisis, rebels when it finds itself uncompetitive and out of work. We will follow up on this in the chapter on financial technology.

CAPITAL CYCLES

The world is fundamentally unbalanced. When Asia's LDR was rising from 0.6 to 1.2 in the period from 1992 to 1996, the United States was recovering from the worst recession since World War II. It was digging out from the mess of the savings and loan (S&L) crisis. George H. W. Bush was defeated and Clinton came to power in 1993 with much to do—but the worst was behind. In 1998 to 2003, when Asia was collapsing, the West embarked on a very impressive boom, which culminated in the real estate bubble of 2006–2007. When the West collapsed in 2008 to 2011, the emerging markets embarked on a spectacular boom as these countries received zero interest rates from an exhausted Western financial system.

Figure 3.1 shows the interplay between the emerging markets and the developed markets over time. It has been a toxic relationship in which one reinforces the excesses of the other because both were rapidly attached to the idea that unfettered capital flows—no matter how overwhelming and ultimately destructive—were *the* ideal. So, the wholesale funding of one part of the world with excess liquidity poured it into the other part regardless of whether the recipient was ready or able to digest the flows in a healthy manner. In the 1990s, Western banks with little demand poured excess capital into Asia and then withdrew it just as things were getting tough. This made the situation that much more violent when the credit cycle stopped. This is a classic example of how capital flows—the other side of trade flows—are pro-cyclical.

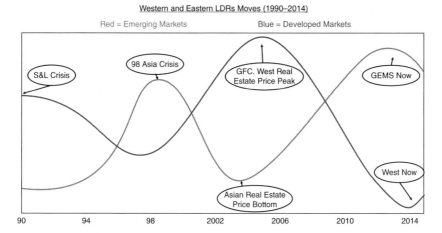

FIGURE 3.1 Western and Eastern LDRs: If LDRs Can Go as High as People Want, Systemic Instability Will Rule

Similarly, in the early 2000s, when Asia was on its back, banks like HSBC bought into Household Finance only to sell out at the top of the market in 2009 and 2010, thus aggravating the situation in the United States. Never mind that the United States was peddling fraudulent collateralized debt obligations (CDOs), which were funding the real estate boom. Many central banks with excess liquidity (including the central banks in Japan, Hong Kong, Taiwan, and China) bought these CDOs only to discover that these were problematic. They were doing this to keep their currencies under-valued (buying dollar-related assets to pull the dollars out of the system and prevent these dollars from buying local currency and increasing its value).

Figure 3.1 shows the problem. Only in the past three years or so have some countries awoken to the fact that it is okay to slow down capital flows and not be named a capitalist heretic and burned at the stake. More countries are restricting wholesale funding by refusing their own LDRs from exceeding 1. They are forcing banks to become wholly owned subsidiaries inside the country and allowing them to lend only what they collect in deposits. This is a healthy trend. As we will see later, when the LDR blows out to 1.1 to 1.3, the resulting crisis always falls on the taxpayer. And the government in power is almost always thrown out. Politicians and taxpayers, then, are peas in a pod when it comes to preventing excessive wholesale funding from blowing up an economy.

Before we go into the individual examples of countries and their fall from grace through credit crises and balance sheet recessions, let's try to lay out the anatomy of a crisis as it applies to just about any country. There are clear and unequivocal similarities among and between countries, whether in the developed or the developing markets. It goes something like this:

1. *Corporates grab for stand-by facilities.* At the beginning of a crisis, the LDR actually rises after the crisis is in a full-blown stage. We see this most of the time. This is because as corporations realize that the party is over and pain is ahead, they quickly scramble to exhaust lines of credit. These lines of credit are contractual obligations between the bank and the corporation to provide funding on request. So, the corporations and financial institutions scramble to draw down as much as they can for the tough times ahead.

2. *Receivables/payables squeeze, followed by a sudden drop in growth.* Following this period of drawing down as much credit as possible, the real squeeze starts when corporates try to extend their payables and take as long as possible to make payments. And they call around and browbeat their customers to cough up money. This is the process of "getting blood out of a turnip," and it is usually the earliest sign of the crisis. The early signs appear at first in the short-term part of the interest rate structure. There is a tug of war, with corporations both demanding money from everyone else and at the same time delaying their own payments for as long as possible. This causes a squeeze and the scarcity of money to go around causes rates to spike.

3. *Banks pull lines of credit.* This spreads to the other parts of the economy quickly. Banks finally wake up and begin to pull lines of credit. The old adage of bankers that "they give you an umbrella when it is sunny and take it away when it is raining" is too true. The scarcity of money to cover business costs and make interest expenses on an even larger pile of debt (after lines of credit are drawn down) becomes aggravated as banks withdraw lines of credit. When it rains, it pours. Many forces coalesce to worsen a situation if banks only could act to counter a liquidity squeeze. All too often, they tend to either cause it or aggravate it.

4. *Wholesale banks withdraw lines and things worsen fast.* Then it gets really nasty. A short-term liquidity squeeze spreads into the economy, and the supporting cables of the financial bridge snap one after the other. At first it is worrying, but people (forever optimistic, for what choice do they have?) just assume the bridge will hold. After a few months, however, the wholesale banks (forever behaving like a knitting club and passing along the local gossip) act in unison to pull large lines of international credit. As we have seen over and over again, the pulling of these very large lines of international credit (which are present only after the LDR exceeds 1 and only after asset prices have been bid up by the exhaustion of local savings) causes significant and sudden damage.

The pulling of large lines of credit—often hundreds of millions of dollars at a time—has a pro-cyclical effect and worsens the liquidity squeeze. Governments that signed up for unfettered and free flows of capital have no choice but to see this capital walk out the door overnight.

5. *Domestic confidence tumbles and deposits exit.* The next part of the crisis is the loss of domestic confidence, as the crisis in the short-term part of the financial system spreads to the long-term part of the funding structure by way of the exodus of wholesale funding. At this point, a few things happen. Some wealthy individual depositors and corporates decide that they want out completely and withdraw their deposits, convert them to foreign currency, and move them to another location. It is a well-kept secret that in the case of Thailand, domestic entities all the way up to the top of the government were also converting their local deposits into foreign currency deposits *before* the Thai baht was devalued on July 3, 2007. In the case of Russia today, it is the locals that are also causing the currency to collapse as they are exiting into dollars. (It is a fascinating mark of our times that many of the people looking to get their money out of Russia are doing so through bitcoin!) While it is all too convenient to blame foreigners, it is often the locals who initially trigger a capital outflow event that leads to currency collapse. This was also particularly rampant in both Greece and Spain at the height of the global financial crisis. In the case of Greece, more than 20 percent of local currency was converted into foreign exchange and left the country to places like London and New York. The same was true in Thailand in 1998. The fact is that the United Kingdom decided not to be a part of the euro that saved it. London was one of the biggest winners globally as capital from the Olive Belt exited Spain, Greece, and Italy and went to London deposits, houses, apartments, and other Sterling assets.

6. *Bankers try to protect their fiefdom and cover up.* At the early part of the crisis, local bankers do not see it coming. As someone who worked *inside* some of the biggest wholesale banks globally, I promise you: They never see it coming. A few might, but they do whatever they can to squash the naysayers or research analysts who want to warn the group. At first, these bankers honor their commitments to draw down lines of credit. As time passes, their internal financial controllers begin to see a tightening of conditions and then see a marginal withdrawal of credit. Bankers themselves panic and add to the problems. They make poor decisions and try to protect their fiefdoms only to make matters worse. They try to deceive their internal auditors, doctor documents, and tell their colleagues to keep their mouths shut. They try to push the problem under the carpet and do anything to keep the central bank or regulators from knowing the truth.

7. *Lending falls, and savings and lending fall more—the vicious cycle.* This is the chain reaction of spiraling as the withdrawal of credit causes an automatic reduction in lending, which causes a reduction in deposits. Increasing withdrawals of deposits to be used either to cover financial problems or for the purposes of capital flight aggravates the problem. When deposits stop coming in or recede, there is an automatic cessation of lending—for lending comes from deposits and vice versa. Panic generally ensues, and bankers try to do what bankers do best—cover their own behinds. They have stern conversations with their customers to "come up with the funds" or else. Bankers inadvertently cut their own throats, because they force their customers to use up savings to repay debt. Pressure is exerted and threats of pulling all credit lines ensue. If available liquidity is used to repay debt and future debt is stopped, the liquidity squeeze intensifies as less savings leads to less lending and less lending leads to less savings. This is a vicious cycle from which it is hard to emerge.

8. *Currency collapse.* This part of this unwind of the excess credit buildup is the collapse of the currency. As local depositors see the exodus in wholesale funding, and the liquidity squeeze causes paralysis in the financial system, it becomes hard to conduct business. Activity stops because the leverage machine has suddenly come to a halt. If it is hard to fund (pay for) inventories of tires, textiles, sugar, and payroll, business slows down and people are fired. Confidence begins to unravel, and after a few months, panic sets in and corporations (domestic and international) decide to leave the country. At this point, strikes may occur and there may be some violence. People lose their homes, cars, businesses, luxury items, and the like. Bitterness and recrimination rule the roost, and the political system becomes dysfunctional, since all there is to do is point fingers. Politicians are hopelessly confused by the unwinding of the financial system and often resemble deer in the headlights. It is interesting to see in so many crises how long it takes for the currency to finally crack. The currency can go sideways for a year to 18 months before it suddenly falls apart.

9. *Central bank intervention.* This part of the crisis is the need for the federal government and the central bank to replace the liquidity that is leaving at a rapid pace. This is where we go back to the all-important quotation of Alan Greenspan. Asked what the most important role of a central bank is, he once basically said that central banks buy time. At this point in the crisis, central banks enter and first try to stop the bleeding. They intervene in foreign exchange markets to stabilize the currency. They intervene in the interbank market and try to introduce liquidity. Often, they need to intervene and backstop the credit system

by buying assets, which would otherwise contribute to a spread of panic. The Federal Reserve did this by actively intervening in the mortgage-backed securities market and buying more than US$1 trillion in mortgage-backed securities. We will see in the chapter on central banks that once a crisis is in a full-blown stage, it becomes necessary to step in. Of course, the central bank can do much to prevent the mess in the first place, but—alas!—central banks actually work for the bankers, and not for shareholders or taxpayers.

10. *Government collapses.* The tenth part is the collapse of government. By the time a financial crisis reaches full-blown proportions, the central banks have intervened to stop the bleeding and provide some normalcy in credit markets, but the economy is a mess. As a result, governments are forced to both engage in deficit spending for public works and other projects and also help to recapitalize the banks. Inevitably, however, politicians can't help themselves and get involved in sweetheart deals as a quid pro quo for helping the bank. Of course, taxpayers are disgusted that those politicians are helping the very same people who have been busy repossessing homes and cars. But when they find out that the bankers and the politicians have been scratching each other's backs by allowing such things as predatory lending, deceptive mortgage practices, sloppy or nonexistent appraisal processes, or outright fraud, the electorate goes berserk and throws out the entire party. We will discuss this in the chapter on lending and politics.

At this point, confidence is shattered, the banking system is at a virtual standstill, and the population is burning mad. Arrests at this point are common. The point is that expectations are so bad that anything will work. At this point, the smart politicians and central bank governors will step up to the plate. At this point, no one cares about anything except "trying anything." This is where greatness comes from. It is a matter of the right timing and right place; it is not a matter of the right person. From here, there is nowhere to go but up. A new government does not have the taint of scandal, so it can make bold moves.

THE WINNERS AFTER A CRISIS

Here are a few examples. President Obama's administration in the early days of 2009 and 2010 made some very bold moves by passing a huge stimulus package and deepening the policies imposed by Secretary of the Treasury Paulson. He kept on the same people against popular pressure. He created continuity, but brought creative people in who were not afraid to "try anything." David Cameron's government made very aggressive and bold moves and succeeded as well. Ireland's government made very brave and painful moves at first and these have paid off in spades. Ireland was the first to exit the deep recession and has been rewarded by investors. France's new government did not make any bold moves, and there has been a series of bad governments. The same goes for Italy and Spain. The political choices are all bad, but the politicians who make the boldest moves at the bottom often reap the greatest benefits. Those who dilly-dally are soon out.

Thailand

Thailand is a terrific example of a country that has had among the most remarkable boom-and-bust scenarios in the world over the past 15 years. I was in Asia in the early 1990s, and there was a great love affair with Thailand at the time. Investors poured billions of dollars into the "Land of Smiles" in the early 1990s through equity markets. The credit market took off, as we can see in the left side of Figure 3.2. The LDR peaked at 1.15, meaning that Thailand was being forced to look for international lending from wholesale banks in order to cover the deficit internally. (Any LDR above 1 means that all savings has been deployed into the economy through credit, so the country must resort to outside activity.)

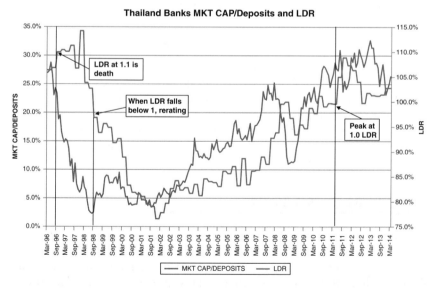

FIGURE 3.2 Thailand Banks Market Cap/Deposit and LDR: The More Extreme the LDR, the Greater the Pain

The problem here is that by 1996, the LDR had already passed 1 and the listed banks smelled a rat. As the U.S. banks did later in 2006, the Thai banks peaked in the summer of 1996, a full year before the whole crisis got out of hand and the Thai baht collapsed. At that time, a host of Pollyannas said that everything was okay and a minor economic downturn was underway. Again, this prognosis by economists was the right call *if* they completely ignored the extent of the credit creation relative to savings (both individual and corporate).

By the early spring of 1997, the listed banks had already fallen 40 percent and, remarkably, there was an air of calm. I know of one large fund that made a US$500 million bet on the banks at this point. They thought the banks had fallen enough but were also blind to the realities of the credit cycle. This was a very expensive lesson, for this fund walked out of Thailand with a US$400 million loss. They did not understand the extent of the deleveraging required. The lesson in the unwind of leverage cost them an 80 percent loss. Leverage bites!

As the bank stocks kept falling and the LDR hovered at 1.15, the pressure on the currency was too great. Why? We see over and over again that by the time all of the savings of a country (both corporate and individual) have been deployed, all of the assets of a country have generally been scooped up, and there is little value left over. This makes a lot of sense since locals would have used the boom to purchase plant, equipment, houses, vacation homes, urban condominiums, agricultural tracks of land, and other assets such as jewelry, luxury cars, and boats. By the time the LDR passes 1, the excesses are already baked into the cake with credit. The suckers, wholesale funders who entered Thailand after the LDR exceeded 1 (banks like Standard Chartered, HSBC, Citi, Bank of America, among others), did so when prices had *already* been bid up and all of the domestic credit had been disbursed.

By the summer of 1997, the currency could not take it anymore. Think of the currency as the price tag of a country. In mid-1997, Thailand was a low-end manufacturer with a Switzerland price tag. The currency had to give. When it gave, a chain reaction of mass destruction was set off. In this type of situation, three things happen.

First, cash buyers are the only ones left when the credit window shuts. When I give a loan of $90,000 for you to buy a home and you put down $10,000, the value of that loan directly relies on the loan to keep the price up. If credit is suddenly cut off, the only other person who can buy my home from me is someone with cash. So, this person without leverage can only buy my home from me at a fraction of the price—hence, the destruction to asset prices when credit is cut off. Economics fails to take this into consideration.

Second, a devaluation of the currency destroys people who have borrowed foreign currency. Take this further and say that the person borrowed

$90,000 in U.S. dollars and did not hedge it. They converted this $90,000 into local currency (the Thai baht at the time had a prevailing rate of THB 25/US$1). They bought a home with THB 2.25 million. They put down THB 250,000 (US$10,000) for a total of THB 2.5 million. When the Thai baht finally collapsed under its own weight (the price tag of the country could not in any way justify the underlying fundamentals of industrial output), it finally went to THB 50/$1. This meant the person had to pay back the mortgage in dollars, which had become THB 4.5 million when the devaluation of the currency had been taken into consideration. The unhedged foreign debt payments for all obligations ballooned.

Third, as and when the currency falls, wholesale lenders into a country, like rats, leave the sinking ship. At the same time, the devaluation of the currency caused a panic (as all sudden devaluations do) and foreigners pulled out their money. Economic activity then slowed (after the fact), and it became harder for individuals and firms to create revenue. On top of this slowing activity, the absence of credit caused a fall in prices (after the fact) for goods and services, and people had a harder time creating revenue to service debt.

This chain reaction caused by excessive domestic credit (and high levels of foreign credit) brought about a chain reaction that was mostly blind to all—except to bank stocks. Banks' stocks had seen this coming a long time before. By the time the crisis was a full-blown implosion in the late summer of 1997, the combination of the dynamics above (difficulty in creating revenue to make interest payments, higher principal repayment given the absence of future credit to prop up assets, and the need for more cash to repay foreign exchange obligations loans at a dramatically lower rate) caused a total meltdown in the economy. It is all predicated on credit dynamics, which are missed by basic economics.

What Happens in Thailand Does Not Stay in Thailand The aftermath of this catastrophe is that bank stocks finally stopped falling (not surprisingly) when the LDR fell below 1. At this point the savage devaluation did have *some* benefit. Thailand became very competitive again, and there was a lot of new trade as well as inflows of equity to buy cheap assets. This is what is known in common parlance as a "reset." Bank stocks like to see the LDR below 1. What happened after that is a common phenomenon (currently happening in the United States) where people have an economic form of "shellshock" and lack confidence to start a new firm with debt. They pay down existing debt. They are trying to wiggle out of bankruptcy. They distrust banks. And as we shall see in the chapter on politics and banking, there is almost always a change of government that is populist in nature and that has to raise taxes to pay for the banking crisis. These tax increases tend to discourage investment for a period.

Furthermore, interest rates tend to fall dramatically after the crisis dies down (as they did in the United States from 2009 until now) and the cost of capital falls dramatically *relative to* labor. Wages do not adjust down as quickly as capital does, so many people find themselves underemployed or out of work. The smart ones can reinvent themselves and, for example, close the overpriced beauty salon and open a toy exporting company to take advantage of a weak currency. Too many people are stuck in a "middle-class" trap and have a wage level that is not matched by a level of expertise appropriate in a new economy. This dynamic always brings resentment and bitterness, especially from young men and women who have had a taste of the good life and are now suddenly cut off from the upward climb of wealth.

From 1997 to 2003, Thailand was in a mess very much like Europe today. This is because during a period of deleveraging, banks not only do not have any new credit to distribute, they are also withdrawing credit from the system; therefore asset prices are falling. Businesses are shrinking. And consumption is flat at best. The only parts of the economy that were growing were the government (by deficit spending) and exports (after a savage devaluation of the baht). Growth was sluggish and unemployment was high, especially for youth. By late 2003 and early 2004, after a seven-year belt-tightening experience, the country had replenished its savings and the banking system could begin to lend again. Bank stocks began to move and the LDR was rising. Banks make money by lending a quantity of loans at a price that is the difference between the deposit rate and the lending rate. This spread was high, and the quantity of lending was high. So Thailand was once again in "fat city." The economy and the stock market were on a roll. What happens during a financial crisis, however, is that between five and seven years go by, and a generation of young people either drops out of the workforce or cannot afford school—or both. This generation suddenly finds the economy booming again, yet lacks the skills to engage the system and find solid employment. This disenfranchised class of youth can create a problem for governments. It happens all the time and is happening currently in Spain, Greece, and Italy.

This dynamic started in 2005 in Thailand and has been smoldering for many years. The new economy of Thailand favored the asset holders, who still had access to credit when the economy imploded. These are usually the wealthy urban established families. The rest will tend to slowly drift away as the economic iceberg cracks apart. We will see in the chapter on politics and banking that this rich/poor gap must be addressed through creating new industries, new sources of productivity, better education, or some direct or indirect form of redistribution through taxation. Otherwise, the pocket of youths who have been cut out of the economic future of a country will turn to violence; hence the ongoing violence in Thailand. This very definitely had its roots in the 1997 crisis. Thailand has not been the same since 2005, when an increasingly violent populist impulse across the country began to raise its ugly head. A sudden absence of credit to the middle class causes all sorts of nasty problems for a society.

Brazil

Like Thailand in the early 1990s, investors had a passionate love affair with Brazil when President Lula came to power in early 2000s. Investors were initially uncertain about just what kind of industrial policies he was going to follow. It was unclear whether he would lurch to the left and pursue protectionist, socialist, collective policies to support the poor and move toward economic nationalism. It turns out that he was pro-markets and pro-reforms. In that sense, he welcomed private enterprise and entrepreneurialism.

What he had up his sleeve, however, was a banking system that at the time was one of the most liquid systems in the world. See Figure 3.3, and notice that the LDR was 0.7. This means that for every R$7 of loans there

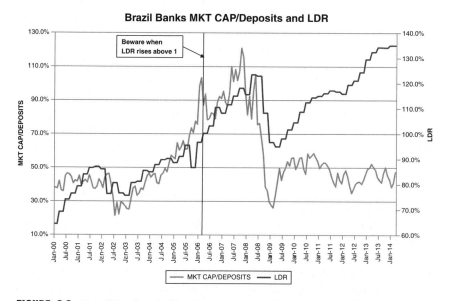

FIGURE 3.3 Brazil Banks Market Cap/Deposits and LDR: In Definite Danger Territory

was R$10 of deposits. To get to the ideal target of an LDR of 1, the banking system could conceivably double and still be in the safe zone. This is exactly what happened.

Between 2003, when Lula came into power, and 2010, at the peak of his power and popularity, the banking system reached an LDR of 1.2. Brazil had generated a spectacular credit boom and was also a beneficiary of the demand for iron ore, coal, and commodities from China. Since 2012, however, Brazil's economy has been sputtering, despite the torrent of activity for the World Cup in July 2014 and the Olympics in July 2016.

In addition, look at the red line. We see over and over again that the greatest rallies in banks always occur as a country is deploying its savings and creating credit from the level of 0.6 or 0.7 all the way up to 1. See in the case of Brazil that bank stock prices kept on increasing as the LDR increased up to 1. It was almost the same line. It is wise to use market cap/deposits (a more pure form of the price-to-earnings ratio, or P/E) to remove the noise that many book values of banks contain. Market cap is the pure form of price. Deposits are the pure form of value for a bank. After all, a bank's value is kept only insofar as it creates confidence for depositors to conclude that their money will be safe tomorrow.

By 2008, however, the Brazilian banks smelled a rat, like Thailand did in 1996, and peaked when the LDR breached the safety zone of 1. They rallied for a bit after that, but fans of technical analysis will notice a perfect "head and shoulders" formation, which the banks formed throughout 2009–2010. The banks have never been the same and have traded in a sideways, choppy manner ever since. The banks have been dead money—and for good reason.

Brazil now stands as one of the major economies that have the largest LDRs globally. And this does not count the debt levels in the national development bank (BNDES). The LDR currently stands at 135, far higher than the LDR at the height of the Asian crisis in 1997. Furthermore, the BNDES went on a lending spree in early 2014, presumably to fund construction for the World Cup. The institution lent out more than US$20 billion in one quarter between January and March 2014.

As of this writing the 2014 World Cup, hosted by Brazil, has been a success, but the country is sorely cash-strapped and it is increasingly clear that it does not have enough resources to finish the facilities for the Olympics, which are to be held in two years' time. There has been discussion of moving the Olympics to another country, but it is too late in the process to do so. In addition, the Olympics has tended to be a kiss of death for a country. There is a long tradition of post-Olympics recessions/downturns.[1]

The banks are very likely to be a bad investment for a considerable period. This may prove to be a period of plenty in capital markets as Brazil is forced to liberalize the listing process and remove the multi-decade cobweb of bureaucracy that covers the stock exchange. We can be hopeful, but my experience is that the country is now controlled by a powerful party apparatus that has given birth to an extreme form of bureaucracy bordering on psychotic. In addition, there are levels upon levels of corruption that may hamstring the country for years to come. Brazil may need a new government that can break up the monstrous bureaucracy and tackle corruption at all levels. Let's not hold our breath for this one.

Indonesia

Indonesia is an exceptional example of a country that not only weathered a severe storm in 1998, but came out of the crisis with its democracy intact. We cannot say the same about Thailand. It is difficult to overestimate how severe the damage was when Indonesia hit the wall in 1998. The currency went from IDR2,500/US$1 to IDR25,000/US$1. The economy came to a halt and shrank more than 15 percent. If one tries to collect the data to reconstruct the banking system in 1998–1999, it is virtually impossible since the banking system came to a complete standstill and most of the banks in the system collapsed.

When the country emerged from the economic ashes in 2002, banks like Bank Niaga had 90 percent of their assets in central bank notes. Think about it. It had *no* loan book for the private sector, and its lifeblood depended solely on the sovereign credit rating of the government. The currency slowly began to appreciate and the economy slowly began to recover. If we look at Figure 3.4, it is remarkable to see that the LDR for the banking system by 2003 was 0.3. I have been looking at banks for 20 years and I have never seen an LDR of 0.3. This tells us that Indonesia in 2002 was pretty much a cash economy and the credit system (five years after the crisis) was still virtually nonexistent.

The United States

As noted above, while Asia was recovering excess liquidity found its way into the United States in 2002 and peaked in 2007. The banking system was full of wholesale lending. Banks like J.P. Morgan lent money through the wholesale market to Lehman Brothers in order to fund the enormous CDO machine. Lehman was creating obscure real estate securities and then selling them to central banks with too many dollars. Lehman was its own country within the United States and was entirely dependent on wholesale funding. This dependence was an imbalance far worse than anything that we saw during the Latin American debt crisis in the 1980s. All it took was one phone call from J.P. Morgan in September and Lehman was gone.

FIGURE 3.4 Indonesia Banks Market Cap/Deposits and LDR: Bumping up against a Ceiling

It is here that many people say that the banks don't really matter because of the size of the corporate paper market and disintermediated credit products. The facts do not bear this out. By 2008, the corporate paper market was indeed large, but credit generated by the banking system was just shy of US$4 trillion. At the time of the crisis, this was one third of GDP—a very sizable portion. The proportion of bank debt to total debt for most countries globally is about 70 percent to 80 percent of GDP. These bank debt numbers matter!

Figure 3.5 shows that the United States in 2008 was a carbon copy of Asia in 1997. First, it is interesting to note that at the peak of the boom in credit, most banks have a market cap/deposits of about $.35 to $.40. The United States had exactly that. Second, the U.S. banks also peaked out at an LDR of 1.15, similar to Thailand and other countries who experienced economic downturns. Third, when the LDR of the U.S. banks passed 1, this was in the second quarter of 2007. Arguably, this was the last quarter of the old normal before the system cracked. By the summer of 2007, strange noises were heard as the financial ship began to creak under its own weight and began to list. The ratings agencies woke up from their corrupt slumber and began slashing ratings on CDOs. Many economists—including economists within the Federal Reserve—said everything was okay.

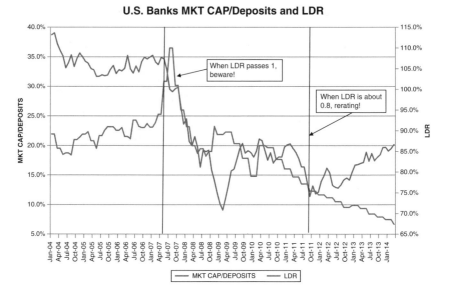

FIGURE 3.5 U.S. Banks Market Cap/Deposits and LDR: Turning a Corner for a Multiyear Credit Run?

During this time, bank stocks were doing what they do when the LDR breaches 1 and rises to 1.15–1.2: They fell, and fell hard. By early 2008, when many economists were still saying everything was all right, the LDR was peaking and bank stocks had fallen 30 percent to 35 percent for many banks. Then something strange happened, which is a hallmark of any financial crisis. Just before the worst of the damage hits, the LDR will have a spike. This is because many corporations will see trouble suddenly hitting and will start to feel like water is coming in over the deck. They all have standby facilities that banks are obligated to grant given certain conditions. Smart banks and corporations exhausted these facilities to gather liquidity before the real problems hit.

After these standby facilities are exhausted, companies are forced to act and the real pain starts. This is the balance sheet recession that my old colleague Richard Koo talks about. When individuals, corporations, and banks are all hit with an exhaustion of credit given the exhaustion of the domestic savings system, this is the time (and it is precisely *the* worst timing possible) when wholesale institutions reserve their right to pack up (literally) overnight and bring their money back home. The United States was no exception and endured a quality of pain similar to that experienced by the Thais and South Koreans in 1997.

At this time, all institutions that are entirely dependent on wholesale funding have an instant-death experience. In Thailand, it was a famous company called Finance One. Finance One in 1996 had one of the largest market caps of any financial institution in Asia and was a real estate darling of Thailand. It had not one cent of deposit liabilities and was completely funded from wholesale funding from banks. By 2009, it was no more. Anglo Irish Bank in Ireland was also a real estate darling and had few if any deposits. It was a foreign-funded bank. In 2008, it collapsed. In the United States, the victim of the withdrawal of wholesale funding was Fannie Mae. Fannie Mae was completely funded from mortgage-backed securities, many of which were bought by foreigners. It did not matter whether the portfolio was good, bad, or indifferent. The point here is that underlying property can only hold up if there is adequate liquidity (or funding or deposit liabilities, for they are all the same meaning). We can all have a view of value, and it is often said that beauty is in the eye of the beholder. But beauty and value are only as good as the liquidity that stands behind them. When that liquidity disappears (and wholesale liquidity disappears faster than any form), real estate values will fall apart, especially when the LDR is about 1.15–1.3. This situation happens over and over again, yet people never learn. We will see in the chapter on LDRs and asset values that there are uncanny relationships between property and the trends in the LDR.

In the case of the United States, the Federal Reserve was smart and stepped in to provide a new kind of "wholesale funding" that had never been tried before. It used its balance sheet to buy the mortgage-backed securities that foreigners were selling in order to prevent a complete meltdown in property prices. It backstopped Fannie Mae's balance sheet, which at the time was more than US$4 trillion. It owned more than one third of the U.S. housing market and was in danger of completely collapsing. The Treasury guaranteed the creditworthiness of Fannie Mae, and the Fed stepped in as a wholesale lender and backstopped the balance sheet. Federal deficits then exploded to the highest levels since World War II. We will see in the chapter on federal deficits and the LDR that the reduction and burn-off of the LDR down to about 0.8 is almost matched dollar for dollar in an increase in federal deficits. The fact that only a few governments globally restrict the LDR to 1 after myriad evidence of the damage to economies when the LDR exceeds about 1.15 is evidence of the folly of man.

Replicating the figures of the emerging markets above, the U.S. financial system collapsed from a value of market cap/deposits of $.35 to a low of about $.05. This tends to mark the low for a banking system, and the U.S. banks were no exception. This number of $.05 is not a special number, but it seems to be where the collapse stops and government intervenes to keep the ship from capsizing.

The United Kingdom

In the case of the United Kingdom, we again see in Figure 3.6 the same phenomenon with the trends in LDR and the way in which the peak and trough in the LDR virtually dictates a high degree of accuracy. In addition, the LDR trends are clearly a leading indicator of signs to come for banks and for economic activity. The LDR and tangible leverage are not on the radar screen of any modern school of economics, so we clearly conclude that economics do not tell us much about the effects of a balance sheet recession brought on by a banking crisis. Economics does not seem to give us any leading indicator of the problem, let alone any signs that the problem is worsening or ebbing.

Stop me if you have heard this one. The LDR in the United Kingdom peaked at 1.2 when the market cap/deposit of the banks was about $0.25/$1 of deposits. The U.K. banks were trading in a choppy manner prior to this event and were giving negative signals. There was a blowout for a few months when irrational exuberance got out of hand. The market cap/deposits indicator collapsed to about $.05/1 of deposits. There was a 100 percent rally from the $.05/$1 level to about $.1/$1 or so, and then the banks tended to retest the old lows. This happened within 24 months, and then the banks slowly crept along the bottom until the bank stocks sensed that the LDR was falling below 1. At that point, there had been extreme

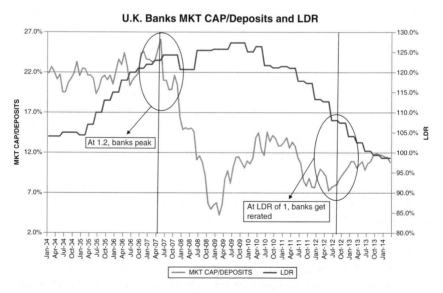

FIGURE 3.6 U.K. Banks Market Cap/Deposits and LDR: More Pain Ahead with Asset Sales and Deleveraging

pain in the economy as banks shrank lending and people saved more. This dual process caused the banking system to reliquefy so that the banks could lend again. Economic activity could stir. Confidence could return. The government could stand back from economic activity and reduce deficits.

For all that to happen, the U.K. government had to come in and recapitalize the banks through nationalization. The government became the largest shareholder of RBS. In addition, the government had to pump the economy with deficit spending to compensate for an absolute shrinkage of credit. It had to create economic activity where there was an outright shrinkage of economic activity caused by a recession (a receding) of credit. This recession of credit is now commonly thought of as a balance sheet recession. I simply ask: Is there any other kind? The answer seems to be no. But since economics does not include credit in its calculations of counting economic activity, someone like the esteemed Rickard Koo of Nomura has to come along and develop a new name for something that has *always* been there as a root cause of economic downturns, but which was never counted. This is absurd but true.

We have seen these developments in the previous examples. I wanted to use the United Kingdom to bring home the point. It is all like clockwork, and there are few exceptions. In this way, the economic implosion of advanced economies like the United Kingdom or the United States in the 2000s was a carbon copy of the economic implosions of developing economies like Thailand or Indonesia in the 1990s. The Asian crisis and the global financial crisis were one and the same. It seems that the developing and developed world take turns bringing each other down because of the total absence of discipline or order in the wholesale market. One causes the other to have an LDR that explodes above 1 to 1.2 or 1.3 at the wrong time when asset prices are too high. Then that system implodes and rates collapse. This causes a boom in other parts of the world, and money in the part of the world that is on its back with a broken system goes to the other, healthy part of the world, causing asset prices to blow out by way of unrestrained wholesale lending, which causes the LDR to blow out to 1.2 or 1.3.

THE ABSURDITY OF WHOLESALE LENDING: THIS IS A B-A-D BUSINESS

The complete willy-nilly movement of wholesale lending allows one part of the world to enjoy a good time through an asset bubble and unsustainable LDRs. This situation is brought on by other parts of the world with excess liquidity (given that they have a broken banking system), who dump their money into assets in a madcap and ill-thought-out strategy to make money.

The absurd thing about wholesale funding is that, by its very nature, it comes in at the top of the market. People only ever need wholesale money from international banks when the domestic savings base has been exhausted and all of the assets within a domestic economy have *already* been bid up.

Wholesale banking is a bad business pure and simple. Look at the lumps that Standard Chartered has taken in South Korea from lending to the Republic of Korea in the 2000s, when the LDR was already tapped out and asset prices were already high. How does Standard Chartered expect to make money on lending into a red-hot economy when there is very little additional marginal leverage to drive up asset prices? Demand is one thing, but it is clearly leverage that drives up asset prices. We will see this in the chapter on the effects of leverage on property and currencies.

Learning Tools: 03_Trading_The_LDR_Cycle.pdf

The presentation can be used for discussion on the relationship between bank stock valuations and loan/deposit ratios.

Endnote

1. There were serious economic downturns and/or stock market crashes after the Olympics in Calgary, Barcelona, Los Angeles, and Beijing. The excessive spending on physical infrastructure has many knock-on effects, but many of the physical buildings have no use after the Olympics. In the case of Manaus, Brazil, and a few other cities, the relatively small populations will never be able to sustain stadiums that can accommodate 60,000 or more.

I Am from the Government, and I Am Here to Help Your Broken Banking System

Socialization of Debt after Mismanagement by Bankers (or, Why Keynesian Economics Doesn't Work)

In this chapter, we will focus on one salient point. When bankers try to fund their balance sheets with wholesale funding and create loan/deposit ratios (LDRs) of 1.2 to 1.5, the unwind and the resulting deflationary spiral can and must be stopped or reversed only by governments, which step in to run deficits that are designed to:

1. Recapitalize the banks, which are running losses from bad debt
2. Stimulate an economy that is otherwise going down a deflationary sink-hole
3. Buy or subsidize assets from the private sector banking apparatus

The best way to see how this phenomenon plays itself out over and over again in nearly identical fashion is to use examples. The first example is one in which we have full, complete, and accurate data of the "before and after" in the Asia crisis. This example is Thailand.

THAILAND

Thailand can be seen as the eye of the storm, in that the devaluation of the Thai baht on July 3, 1997, seemed to trigger the whole crisis. There was no profound meaning to the events surrounding the devaluation of the baht, other than it was a tripwire that set off a great economic and human catastrophe that was years in the making and that destroyed the financial well-being of millions of families throughout Asia. The factors that contributed to the

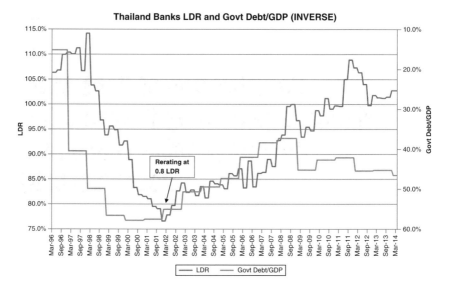

FIGURE 4.1 Thailand Banks LDR and Government Debt/GDP: Debt Is Still Quite High—Leftover from Crisis

Asian crisis were similar to those that set off World War I: cronyism, mismanagement, hubris, economic backwardness despite repeated warnings, fixed ideas, and no imagination.[1]

Figure 4.1 shows what happens in the aftermath of a large debt blowout. Recall that when a country's LDR is 1.15, all of the domestic savings have been deployed into loans. Furthermore, the amount of debt that has been accumulated from the outside world (by definition) is 15 percent larger than the existing savings base. Savings rates around the world differ for different reasons (demographic, cultural, historical), but suffice it to say that for our purposes, the absolute amount of credit above and beyond the domestic savings rate is a vitally important number and the data support this conclusion.

Thailand is a classic case of how governments are forced to offer relief to a collapsing economy in the face of a deleveraging banking system. The LDR peaked at about 1.15 by late 1997. This means that all of the domestic savings were *already* deployed through leveraged purchases of stocks, bonds, primary residences, cars, vacation homes, honeymoons, university tuition, and other activities. And it means that Thailand borrowed from the outside world an amount in excess of tens of billions of dollars in foreign purchases of stocks, foreign direct investments (FDIs), and other speculative purchases.

When this world of excess credit unwinds, ratings agencies are often the common trigger point. They usually downgrade a country at the height of the excesses, which is of little help as it is difficult to exit a trade when there is so much downward pressure on asset prices. Nonetheless, the ratings agencies stepped in and warned about the sustainability of the boom as well as the value of the currency. At this point, the façade began to crack and the excess debt load was revealed. Peeling back this excess debt showed an economy that was overheating and in an unsustainable asset boom that bore no resemblance to reality.

As a result, domestic banks began to call in loans, and foreign bankers got spooked by the warnings and began to decamp from Thailand. As both of these phenomena occur (they almost always happen at the same time), economic growth slows and asset prices start to fall. As foreign money leaves, the value of the currency drops. As it drops further, the value of the foreign debt owed by Thais went up, causing a painful squeeze. All of this causes a sudden and excruciating economic slowdown that requires some degree of countermeasures to arrest the slowdown, which is where government deficits come in.

In the case of Thailand, the country had a debt/gross domestic product (GDP) of 15 percent, a very small number, when the crisis began. Notice that Thailand has the same pattern as so many other countries we will see, and that is the way in which the government debt/GDP replaces the LDR almost 1 for 1 as the LDR falls. This means that either savings must go up in a painful way as consumers are forced to tighten their belt (in this case, government spending comes in to compensate), or loans must go down, in which case banks are pulling in loans, writing off bad debt, or putting it into a bad bank (in this case, the government must create a bad bank, which is expensive; help the banks recapitalize, which is also very expensive; or act as a kind of lender to businesses that are deprived of credit from banks).

In this way, we can see that the government debt/GDP rises in lockstep with the drop in the LDR. So, the debt/GDP for Thailand rose from 15 percent of GDP at the beginning of the crisis and peaked out at 60 percent, a rise of 45 points. At the same time, the LDR (a ratio of the loan assets of a banking system relative to a flow of savings into an economy, which is created by corporate and individual savings) fell from 1.15 to about .75, a fall of about 40 points. We will see this pattern over and over again.

The cardinal rule we see here is simple to understand: The more extreme the blowout in the LDR, the higher the deficits to prevent a catastrophic deflationary depression as the banking system unwinds. In the case of Thailand, the economy shrank by more than 10 percent, and millions of people were out of work. Asset prices collapsed; you can drive around Bangkok today and see hundreds of buildings whose half-finished concrete foundations lie among the weeds.

It took Thailand almost seven years to recover from the disastrous financial policies that allowed a debt buildup that was so easy to quantify and articulate. It is just one of several examples we will see in the following pages. Putting in place a financial speed limit—or at least financial guardrails—would have spared Thailand and many investors a lot of pain. Imposing a cap of 1 on the LDR and a cap of 20 on any bank's leverage would have gone a long way. We will see later that this is finally starting to happen in some jurisdictions.

It is important to point out here that many people have a deep misconception about what governments can realistically do in the aftermath of a debt crisis. In the case of Thailand, and other examples we will see throughout this chapter, the government response is primarily aimed not at bringing about a recovery or stimulating growth. It is aimed at accommodating a deleveraging of the banking sector (reducing loan assets and building up savings), which can take five to eight years. Government debt merely accommodates the deleveraging of the banking system by replacing the bank debt with government debt in order to avoid a deflationary collapse of asset prices and wages.

This is what many interest groups are now beginning to figure out. The main activity of central banks in their "stimulation" of the economy is nothing more than removing assets from the bank balance sheet that would otherwise have forced a bank's collapse. Alternately, it is the purchase of government debt that is used to recapitalize banks or to somehow clean up the wreckage caused by excessive leverage. In this way, "Keynesian" economics does not—and cannot—work to stimulate growth during a period of bank balance sheet reduction because the so-called stimulus is not stimulating anything. In fact, if we think of the economy like an athlete, Keynesian economics is not anything like steroid shots for a good athlete. It is more like a painkiller for a severely ill athlete. Recovery cannot be expected. It is only a palliative until long-term therapy and repairing of the credit system can be achieved. By the time Keynesian stimulus can work, it is, frankly, no longer needed.

In the case of Thailand, this is was absolutely true. Deficit spending kept a terrible problem from becoming a terminal problem. In fact, the devaluation of the Baht had more to do with a recovery than the deficit spending. To bring this point home, look at Figure 4.1 and notice when the deficit/GDP began to bottom out and improve. In the second half of 2002—a full six years after the crisis began—the deleveraging of the banking finally came to a halt. In the case of Thailand, it came to a halt when the LDR reached about .75%. In other crises we shall examine, the crisis peaks and a collapse occurs when the LDR reaches 1.15 to 1.3. And a recovery comes when the LDR reaches a low of about 70 percent to 75 percent. Thailand's recovery was like clockwork.

In another chapter, we will see the effect this deleveraging process has on the price of the currency and the price of real estate. It is interesting to notice that the banks bottom out and begin to rally about six months before the deleveraging process bottoms out. And, the currency has a strong tendency to bottom out and begin to rise about the same time that the LDR bottoms out. This happened in 2002 and in the first half of 2003. We will see that there is too much similarity from one country to the other for this to be a mere coincidence. In addition, these phenomena make intuitive sense that our grandmothers can understand. When a banking system is ready to lend again, the price of real estate can again rise. Real estate values do not for one second rely on wages or income. They rely on leverage. Without leverage, they cannot rise. Similarly, we should think of the price of the currency as the price of the country. As the value of this land goes up (houses, buildings, secondary beach homes), the value of the country goes up. Hence, it is entirely logical for the FX to rise as well.

THE UNITED STATES: IN MANY WAYS, A CARBON COPY OF THAILAND

Figure 4.2 shows the journey of the U.S. financial system from the height of the boom in 2007 to its depths in 2013. This unwind has many uncanny similarities to Thailand:

- Both had a banking system that peaked out at about 1.15 in the LDR, the usual level where crises tend to begin.
- Both countries had current account deficits of about 4 percent of GDP.
- Both countries, from the point of the beginning of the crisis, had large devaluations of their respective currencies.
- Both had complex non-bank financial structures that at the time were considered sound.

Some considered them brilliant and cutting edge. The United States had Fannie Mae, which had *no* local deposit funding and which was largely funded by foreign purchases of mortgage-backed securities. It completely imploded and disintegrated when foreign funding stopped. The heads of Fannie Mae and Freddie Mac were highly respected and well-connected to the center of power. These two had a national mandate to provide homes for all of the middle class. Thailand had Finance One, which had one of the largest market caps in Asia in 1996. It had *no* local deposit funding and was largely funded by foreign investors. It had a national mandate to provide funding for Indochina through the BIBF (Bangkok Interbank Funding

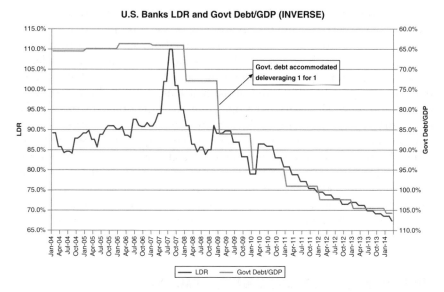

FIGURE 4.2 U.S. Banks' LDR and Government Debt/GDP—A Very High Price for the Crisis: 45% of GDP Addition to Debt

facility). This idea was as cockamamie as providing a home to anyone who could fog a mirror.

The result for both was a savage drop in equity prices and a drop of about 30 percent in property prices. The U.S. dollar fell about 25 percent; the baht fell about 50 percent. Fannie Mae became worthless, as did Finance One. A few core banks survived, but many were swallowed up or closed. The stock markets went down more than 60 percent for both countries.

The debt of both countries went up by about 40 points of GDP. The only difference here is that the United States began with a much higher stock of debt, or about 60 percent of GDP.

Another interesting similarity is the way in which inchoate political rage formulated in the wake of the crisis. Thailand got Thaksin. The United States got the Tea Party. Both movements became extremely distrustful of banks and the center of government. Both felt like the government had sold the middle class down the river to save the elites. Both movements had as their center a jingoistic and antiestablishment message that appealed to the lower middle class. It will be fascinating to see how the political struggle in the United States plays out.

It is uncanny to see that the recovery in the equity market and the property market is taking place as the LDR makes a turn at about 65 percent to 70 percent. At this point, it is likely that the banking system can begin to recover and risk appetite should return. Many people at this point ask me if this is an accurate way to look at the United States, given the large proportion of corporate debt. My response is that the U.S. banking system is still a US$6.5 trillion balance sheet, very sizable and capable of making a very large impact on funding. I heard the same thing in the 1990s on Thailand. People said that the LDR of the banks did not matter because of new funding structures like Finance One. Indeed, people made the same arguments about Fannie Mae. This is all the more absurd because people who point to new and interesting leveraged structures that are reliant on bonds or foreign funding are making the fundamental mistake that is the theme of this book. If a banking system exceeds its own capacity to fund, it *must* fund itself from foreign money. This foreign money tends to come into the country as wholesale borrowing *after* local savings has been put to work into loans to drive up the value of everything. The foreign money coming in gets the leftovers (i.e., high-priced assets that are being sold by savvy locals). So, companies like FNM were a time bomb waiting to go off. So was Finance One in Bangkok in exactly the same way. Another finance company we need to watch out for is Pactual in Brazil. The country is highly leveraged with an LDR of 130. And Pactual relies almost entirely on bond funding with no local deposits. Let's see.

SPAIN AND IRELAND: THE MOST EXTREME EXAMPLES OF IRRESPONSIBLE LENDING IN MODERN HISTORY

The examples of Spain and Ireland in 2002–2007 make the Asian crisis look like a garden party. When the euro was introduced in 1999, it was imperative for one currency to be backed up by one interest rate structure. Germany had low rates, and Spain, as well as Ireland, had high rates. As a result, all rates were forced to adjust downward to the 3 percent level of Germany. Germany has a pristine postwar track record. Spain and Ireland did not, but all of these countries—responsible or not—were mandated to share one interest rate structure for the currency to work. (Otherwise, money would always flow from one country with low rates to another with high rates.)

Imagine when the cost of credit in Ireland and Spain (with a history of poor growth rates and high default rates) suddenly became the same as Germany's. This sounds astonishing, but there were also political imperatives to include as many countries as possible in the euro to give it financial, economic, and political critical mass, so the political imperative was, "The more, the merrier! We can deal with the consequences later." Suffice it to say that rates in Spain and Ireland were in the double-digit range, and suddenly these rates became three. Anyone who could read a newspaper knew that

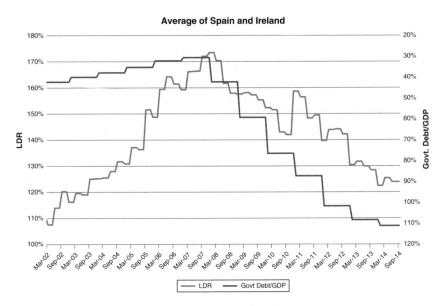

FIGURE 4.3 LDR and Government Debt/GDP (Average of Spain and Ireland): The Crisis Broke the Bank for Both Countries

an asset bubble would come out of nowhere as rates fell by about 700–900 basis points (BPs) in a short period.

So, Figure 4.3 shows what happened. The Celtic Tiger and the Spanish Miracle (it should have been called the Spanish Mirage) were born of sudden and large drops in interest rates that allowed U.K. and German banks to fund vast real estate projects (literally building thousands of homes at a time). The LDR was already above 1 when the interest rates collapsed to 3 percent. In this way, Spanish and Irish credit risk became German credit risk. In other words, their credit risk was priced the same as far more conservative and disciplined credit risk. I used the average of both because the trajectory of each of them alone was uncannily similar. They both took off like missiles and did not look back until it was too late. They were both foreign debt–fueled rocketships, and this fuel was designed to leave the atmosphere but had no mechanism for returning.

The move in the LDR to 1.7 occurred in a relatively short period of time. The race to 1.7 started in earnest in the second half of 2002 and peaked in the second half of 2007. In my 25 years of looking at banking systems, I do not ever remember seeing an LDR that high. Of course, both Spain and Ireland had current account deficits in excess of 6 percent of GDP. Even Thailand and Korea in 1997 had LDRs that were only about 1.2–1.3. The debt levels achieved by Spain and Ireland via wholesale funding from Germany and the United Kingdom, among others, was quite impressive. To give an example, why did no one bat an eye when it was discovered that Spain had used one tonne of cement for every man, woman, and child in the country in real estate development? This is 30% more than China at the boom in investment in 2012–2013. Wouldn't this kind of excessive demand for cement cause alarm bells to go off?

Now, let's move to the unwind of this financial bubble that began in the summer of 2007. Recall that at this time, the ratings agencies finally woke up and began to downgrade slews of real estate–related securities. This caused the funding machine to come to a halt. Spain and Ireland were by this time two of *the* most leveraged economies globally. Recall the earlier chapter on the 10 steps to financial tragedy; these happened very quickly in the case of Ireland. The rule at hand here—and the maxim for this chapter—is simple: The higher the LDR, the larger the bailout.

There is an uncanny similarity in the order of magnitude of the bailout relative to the order of magnitude of the LDR. Notice what happened when it came time for the government to step in and accommodate the monetary contraction in credit. When the LDR for these two countries had reached about 1.7, the debt/GDP was very low. In fact, the "miracles" were so powerful that the debt/GDP was actually falling in the mid-2000s. This was because economic activity was booming and the government was receiving all sorts of taxes from property-related transactions. Therefore, bank lending was offering a slight reduction in debt/GDP, but only about 4 percent to 7 percent of GDP. Furthermore, as was said earlier, the bank financing of this property boom was a rocketship that could blast off but had no way to reenter the atmosphere.

By the end of 2007 and early 2008, it was clear that the jig was up and the bill for the party was delivered to the government in Dublin. Rather than default on the debt, the government agreed to make the system whole through taxpayer money. Spain did the same thing. So, government debt had to explode, and taxpayer money was exchanged for the real estate–related debt that was issued by the banks. In three years, the countries' debt went from 30 percent of GDP to 70 percent of GDP. To put this in perspective, this is the kind of debt load increase typically seen in a country that has fought a war.

By 2014, the debt/GDP of these two countries had already surpassed 100 percent of GDP. Unless a country has some new technology or reinvents itself in a dramatic way (or embarks on a severe devaluation), it is usually difficult to get out of this debt pickle. As with the United Kingdom and the United States, the debate about the effectiveness of Keynesian economics is a genuinely moot one. The "Keynesian" stimulus is *not* designed to generate economic activity. It is designed to bail out the banks. In other words, the deficit spending is not intended to stimulate spending and economic activity. It is geared to prevent the banks from disappearing as bad debt eats into the banks' capital to the point where the entire system becomes insolvent.

So if we want to discuss the merits of Keynesian economics, we need to change gears and not look at GDP growth or consumption growth or employment. We need to look at how many banks were saved by the stimulus. Some may say that this is heresy, and that stimulus programs are not related to the banks but rather are connected to employment. But the uncanny relationship between the reduction in the LDR and the increase in government debt/GDP must make us reassess the causality. There is great philosophical debate about the merits of using Keynesian economics to bail out the banks. Of course, this is what the stimulus is all about. Inflation is needed to keep asset prices afloat, so at least economic stimulus can try to do that. If the banks are allowed to fail one after the other, then economic activity will stop. If banks are bailed out, then moral hazard encourages bankers to go over the cliff together time and time again. Halting LDRs at 1.0 is one way to prevent systemic credit from getting out of control.

Furthermore, the bottoming-out process of an economy when employment does improve and when economic activity does accelerate (and when real estate prices seem to bottom out and begin to rise) always seems to correspond *not* to stimulus programs but to a return of credit from the banking system. We see this over and over again.

The discussion of the viability or success of Keynesian economics must move away from indicators such as employment or consumption and more toward bank viability. This will offer a richer dialogue. This is because those opposed to Keynesian economics usually say that the benefits go toward those who cannot make a big dent in the economy (the middle class or lower-middle class). If people look closely at how much of the deficit spending in Ireland, Spain, the United Kingdom, and the United States went to the banks, and not to the middle class, the tone of the discussion will change.

Stimulus programs in the postwar era are designed to accommodate an unwinding of bank balance sheets. Part of this debt is, of course, private consumption. But other parts of programs include recapitalization of banks, assumption of debt portfolios, creation of bad banks, purchases of certain types of assets by central banks, guarantees of international bonds by banks to other jurisdictions, and so forth. Some consider these vital to the future of an economy, but they have nothing to do with buoying consumption. They have everything to do with stopping an implosion. So, the measure of success is the extent to which the bleeding of bank balance sheets is stanched and not how much private consumption is created.

The vital question here is if there is a vital interest for a country in bailing out its banks. This is a different question altogether. Many savagely condemn men like Andrew Mellon, who was Secretary of the Treasury in 1929 when the Depression started, who said that a bloodletting of the banks is a healthy and desirable thing. His policies created the Depression. Others look at the Depression and say that banks need to be bailed out to avoid what would otherwise be a deflationary morass from which it is difficult to exit. This is a more appropriate starting point for Keynesian stimulus than mere consumption or employment, for without a functioning banking system, it is nearly impossible to get a rise in employment, asset prices, or consumption. The discussion of the banks is the starting point of whether Keynesian economics is worthwhile or not. A discussion of employment or consumption is a byproduct of the healthy banks—not the other way around. Until the discussion changes, there will be more heat than light about a concept that is so grossly misunderstood.

THE UNITED KINGDOM

The U.K. economy is an example where there is so much discussion around one issue: Government debt as a percent of GDP keeps expanding, but there is precious little to show for it in terms of consumption or employment. Why? This is another example of how the discussion about the effectiveness of Keynesian economics runs at cross-purposes. The debt/GDP was running steady all the way into the global financial crisis in early 2008, and then the deficit exploded. It has continued to rise since then. Figure 4.4 shows this yet again.

In the first quarter of 2008, the debt levels began to explode. A large chunk of this debt at the time was used to plug the hole that was created by the collapse of Northern Rock. Northern Rock was a bank that was largely funded through wholesale funding (stop me if you've heard this one). It had no depositor base to speak of. As a result, when the wholesale funders pulled loans to the banks, the U.K. government had to step in or the real estate market would have been in freefall. This was probably wise at the time, since the consequences of allowing the property market to collapse would have been catastrophic. (Northern Rock is a perfect example for this book, since it was a house of cards built on unsustainable level of debt from outside the system.) The net effect of the Northern Rock collapse is that a full 15 percent of GDP was added to the country's debt load when the government intervened and bailed it out.

From then on, much of the government debt issued at the time was purchased by the Bank of England to keep rates from exploding. As vast

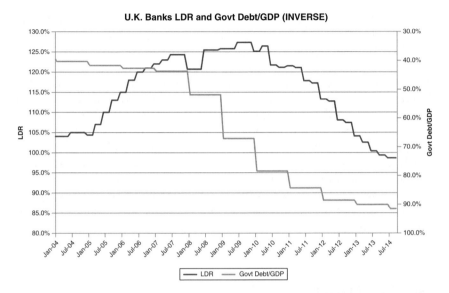

FIGURE 4.4 U.K. Banks' LDR and Government Debt/GDP: RBS and Northern Rock Broke the Bank

amounts of supply of government debt entered the market, it would have been natural for the price of this debt to fall and for yields to rise. I calculated that in 2009, the Bank of England had purchased 90 percent of all the debt issued by the government.

The bailout of Northern Rock (and the nationalization of the Royal Bank of Scotland, or RBS) was a result of government debt. The intention of this buildup of debt was, allegedly, stimulus. So, the debate is why the stimulus is not creating jobs and consumption. The fundamental error here, as is the case for Spain, Ireland, and other countries caught in financial crises, is that the debt issued by the government is largely used to *replace* the debt that is being offloaded by an overleveraged banking system. In the case of the United Kingdom, we can see that the rise in the U.K. debt/GDP has the same trajectory as the fall in the LDR of the U.K. banking system. Without a dramatic increase in government debt, it is virtually impossible for the banking system to shrink its balance sheet (retire loans, write off bad debt, offer over bad debt to the government-created bad bank, renegotiate debt) *without* an increase in government debt. My numbers show that there is something like a one-for-one *increase* in debt as a percent of GDP against a *reduction* in bank debt as the banks get out from underneath a pile of bad debts.

This means that the net effect of stimulus during a financial crisis is neutral until and unless the banks finish the process of shrinking leverage (loans) in the process laid out above. Also, the system is forced to find ways to increase its savings (deposits); this is usually achieved through devaluations. It is also achieved through government efforts to support new industries, encourage tourism, impose consumption taxes, create subsidies for job-creating investment and real estate purchases, and so on.

As banks clean up their assets and governments create more national savings (and also recapitalize the bank capital), bad debt can be written off or renegotiated and deposit liabilities can rise. Hence, the reduction in the LDR is achieved. *Deficit spending merely accommodates this process. It does not add a new layer of demand.* Indeed, the United Kingdom has come a long way, as the LDR is now just a shade before 1.0. In this way, the United Kingdom has moved out of danger, but its banks are still far too large. Further asset reduction is underway, especially at Barclays Bank.

In the wake of a banking crisis, Keynesian stimulus is useless to create jobs. It is not a kind of fertilizer to help the economy grow more quickly and to help create jobs more quickly. The analogy here should be that Keynesian stimulus is nothing but a safety net to prevent terrible accidents from occurring while the banks carry out dangerous deleveraging that would otherwise have toxic effects on an economic system. This is precisely the theme of a book like *Essays on the Great Depression*, which was edited by Ben Bernanke.

Another analogy for fiscal stimulus is that it is foam on the tarmac as planes are coming in for an emergency landing. The foam may not prevent the airplane from tumbling end to end, but it will go a long way to reducing dangerous fires that could get out of control and cause great damage. I think this is what Bernanke and others were thinking when they encouraged large fiscal stimulus packages in 2008. Bernanke's precise words were: "They can't hurt." In other words, deficit spending can help a great deal to prevent outright deflation, which would otherwise be the case if there were no countervailing measure to highly destructive debt deflation caused by all banks shrinking their assets at the same time. (This is the "paradox of thrift" that is a key part of Keynes's thinking. This states that if everyone saves at the same time in a prudent effort to replenish savings, then this effort backfires and causes prices to fall and the real value of savings actually goes down and hurts people.) It seems to me that deficit spending only keeps prices falling even further than they otherwise would without the stimulus. In this sense, deficit spending may have a great effect, but we will then need a new way to measure its effectiveness. The effectiveness comes from analyzing the fall in leverage versus the fall in prices. The effectiveness of stimulus packages will not be seen in consumption and employment, because these two dynamics may actually deteriorate for a long time while a more important intended consequence of stimulus—price stability—may actually be improving. Consumption and employment may be aided by stimulus, but we need to more effectively measure the ways in which deficits "plug the hole" caused by the withdrawal of bank credit. Deficit spending is a preventive prophylactic to aid in reducing the harm as leverage is withdrawn. It is not a curative.* The point here is not to debate the merits of Keynesian economics versus monetary economics. It is to suggest that we change the way we gauge the success of Keynesian deficit spending to reflect what is gained to offset the pain of deleveraging (a lower negative) rather than what is gained in terms of employment and income (a higher positive).

In the case of the United Kingdom, there has been a twofold process of stimulus. The Bank of England has kept rates close to zero for several years while the government continues to run fiscal deficits. In all this, the LDR is only now at 1.0, while the LDR of the United States is at a far healthier .65. Why? For many historical reasons, the U.K. government allowed the financial sector of the country to become a large multiple of GDP. At the height of the bubble in 2008, the U.K. financial system was almost 3 times larger than the entire GDP of the country. It is one thing for a country to want to become a financial center. It is another thing for the regulator to be asleep at the switch and allow a banking system to become more than 400 percent of the GDP of the country. This should never have been allowed to happen, especially in the case of the grandiose ambitions of a bank like RBS.

As a result of this, not only do the U.K. banks have an LDR that is still on the high side, the United Kingdom also has a size issue that will require banks to reduce assets for a considerable period of time. In the instance of Barclays, the new chairman John McFarlane will need to find a way for the bank to reduce assets by one-third. This is the equivalent of about $700 billion over a three-year period.

The net effect of this is a perverse bubble in London for two reasons. The first is that the Bank of England will need to keep rates low for a long period of time. The second is that many wealthy Europeans, who fear incompetent regulators or the tax man, are now relocating to London. This is fuel to a fire and is causing skyrocketing prices for flats in London. I presume this will continue for a period of time.

---

*For a more detailed and complete analysis of this, please see *A New Deal* by Michael Grunwald (Simon & Schuster, 2013). Also see Alan Blinder's *After the Music Stopped* (Penguin, 2013). Also see Robert Skidelski's *Keynes: The Return of the Master* (Penguin, 2010).

INDONESIA

In the case of Indonesia, let's look at a post-crisis economy after the wheels fell off as a result of excessive international borrowing and corrosive corruption by the Suharto family. In the run-up to 1997, Indonesia had an LDR far in excess of 1.15 and current account deficits in excess of 4 percent of GDP. I was in Indonesia in the early 1990s and saw the early signs of corruption run amok: an overheated economy being hijacked by the five children of President Suharto. Everything was for sale to the children. At one point, it was estimated that the Suharto family itself owned more than 20 percent of the economy. In addition, it was also thought that capital inflows were more than sufficient to cover the current account deficits.

Once again, it is surprising that it took so long to realize that capital inflows in the capital account are, in fact, pro-cyclical. They make everything look better when things are good. The capital account grows larger as the current account deficit grows larger, making things seem better than they are. And they make everything look worse when things are bad by having capital flows leave the country after the cycle peaks, exacerbating the downtrend. They are erroneously thought to be a counterbalance to high current account deficits. This was especially true for development aid. In thinking that has now been debunked by senior economists from the World Bank,[2] not only is development pro-cyclical, it covers up excesses that should never have been allowed to exist in the first place. They are also dangerous because these capital inflows—much of which are also private sector wholesale lending—can leave at a moment's notice and cause a sudden implosion in local currency asset. This is precisely what happened in 1998.

As the Asian crisis gained ferocious momentum, the rupiah tumbled and the stock market tumbled and local asset prices also began to fall. The worse it is when the LDR is above 1.2 or so, the saying goes, the worse it gets. It is a self-feeding mechanism. As this momentum gathered greater pace, there was a resulting political crisis, and President Suharto was forced to step aside. In the political tussle that ensued, Chinese entrepreneurs lost their political protection. As a result, development aid slowed, private wholesale borrowing reversed, *and* private Chinese capital, which needs to be counted in the tens of billions, also left the country. It did not help that a few savage military officers tacitly let Chinatown be burned down. So, there was a threefold reversal in capital in Indonesia—development aid, private sector international borrowing, and outflows of Chinese money.

The result was a total collapse of the economy, the banking system, and the currency. The rupiah was at about Rp2,500/$1 in 1997 and hit a low of Rp25,000/$1 by 1998. This is about a 90 percent drop in the value of the currency. The stock market in dollars fell more than 90 percent. The banking system all but ceased to exist. It is no surprise, then, that by 2003, when the smoke finally cleared, the LDR of the Indonesian banking system was about 0.4. This has to be one of the lowest LDRs in modern history.

In Figure 4.5, we can see that coming out of the worst of the country crises in Asia in the great Asian crisis, the LDR was at .3 percent. It is accurate to say that, for about four years, the banks' lending activity stopped. Recovery was a matter of confidence returning as Chinese businessmen were given assurances that they and their businesses were safe. As a result, deposits returned and the banks could resume lending.

By that point, of course, the government had to run large deficits to accommodate the sudden depreciation. So, the debt/GDP of Indonesia exploded from about 20 percent of GDP to a peak of 70 percent of GDP (along with a spectacular devaluation and a few impressive defaults on dollar debt). As the LDR began to rise and the banking system finally began to function, a number of things happened:

- Local property prices began to recover.
- The equity market started to move up in a sustained fashion.
- The currency began to recover and appreciate.
- Yields on government debt began to fall.

All of these are a response to the creation of liquidity and credit within the economy. Yes, there was economic growth and investment did recover.

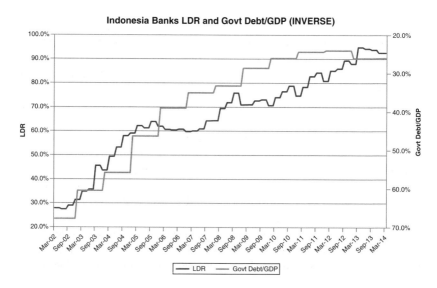

FIGURE 4.5 Indonesia Banks' LDR and Government Debt/GDP: Spectacular Improvement Postcrisis

But without credit, there is no lifeblood in any economy. In Indonesia, the dead Frankenstein economy sitting on a slab of cement received a lightning bolt of credit, and the creature came back to life.

As the banking system comes back to life, economic activity begins to create tax revenue. Growth begins to accelerate. Property transactions return and tax revenues from this property-related activity improves. As a result, the debt/GDP falls. This turns into a virtuous circle, since the more credit that is circulated in an economy, the better tax revenues becomes and the better the creditworthiness. Ratings agencies can come along and upgrade the country and individual conglomerates. As a result, more credit flows. The currency appreciates and local asset prices can improve. The result is a rising LDR and a falling government debt/GDP. Because Indonesia started from such a bombed-out LDR of a mere .30, the rally in Indonesian assets has lasted more than seven years. (Imagine! An LDR of .30 means that for every 100 dollars of deposits there was only 30 dollars of loans. Much of the balance sheet of the Indonesian system was simply government debt.) The LDR in 2014 is now about .9 percent, so Indonesia is far closer to the end of its cycle than the beginning.

The Indonesian government is doing something smart here. The collective national memory of policymakers is still in shock from the Asian crisis and so is fairly fanatical about the need to keep the LDR below 1. I think this is very wise, and I hope they stick to this policy. (Hong Kong, Korea, Singapore, and China all are sticking to this policy as well.) In forcing the LDR below 1, the country will no longer be beholden to pro-cyclical capital inflows, which can be quickly destabilizing. The country will not fall into fits of hypergrowth, which are hard to slow without damage. And the country does not need to talk itself into a higher trajectory of growth, which turns into a nightmare when capital flows reverse and the currency falls apart. Countries that run current account balances pretty close to zero and that cap LDRS at 1 and tangible leverage at 16–18× have a good shot at not falling into a cycle of boom and bust. They will not have to implement Keynesian deficit spending, which will not work. They will not be thrown out of power amidst a crisis. And they can sustain slower but more prosperous growth over longer period of time. This is all so simple, yet politicians all too often have the credit pixie dust thrown in front of their eyes only to, in the end, experience the wrath of the general population when the credit bubble bursts, property prices fall, and the economy falls apart.

CONCLUSION

The vital point of this chapter is the following: Keynesian economics says that deficit spending in the face of a debt-induced recession (we saw in earlier chapters that the credit cycle is the economic cycle) can help create employment and consumption as the economy adjusts. The examples of this chapter and many others show that deficit spending during a credit-induced recession can only ever act as a counterweight and as an accommodation to the shrinkage of credit as the system works toward equilibrium. Only after the banking system reaches a new and healthy equilibrium can credit flow, with the resulting improvement in employment and consumption. Without LDRs falling below 1 and leverage levels falling below 17–20, a system cannot recover. Therefore, any deficit spending only acts as a counterbalance to the activity that allows total credit to fall and total savings to rise. Until then, it is a moot point to discuss why and how Keynesian economics does not seem to work.

Advocates of Keynes who have reviewed my book make the following counterpoint which I think is legitimate and merits clarity here. Any tool that can allow an economy to go from a large negative growth trajectory to a smaller growth trajectory is a good thing during a devastating credit-driven downturn. In this way, deficit spending during a credit crisis does in fact help things to get less negative and is a good thing for a society. The cost/benefit tradeoff will always be debated, of course, but it must not be debated in terms of what it does in GDP points. It must be counted in what it does to *mitigate* a collapse of a banking system. This is what Bernanke meant when, upon asking if the country should engage in deficit spending, he said that it can't hurt. In this way, the success of how and why Keynesian economics can create economic benefits to economic downturns through the creation of growth should not be calculated in GDP contribution.

Most downturns are driven by the exhaustion of the credit cycle that is created over and over again by irresponsible wholesale bankers who create unsustainable LDRs. The recovery can only be achieved by inflation, time, debt forgiveness, devaluation, and renewed productivity. Keynesian deficit spending—in alliance with central bank intervention—is the tonic that buys time for a system to deal with engorged debt levels. First, it buys inflation that inflates away the debt's value. Second, it allows for the creation of new industries to improve productivity. Third, it creates economic activity, which in turn creates some savings, which replenishes bank deposit bases. It is only in alliance with central bank activity, then, that we can see if and how Keynesian spending programs make a real dent in credit-driven recessions. I think the answer is easy for all to see. In these conditions, Keynesian economics works without a shadow of a doubt. The same people in the Chicago School who say that government should get out of the way of the market need to incorporate these ideas into a new understanding of credit and the marketplace. Until then, the Friedman school of monetary economics has a lacuna squarely in the middle of the discipline.

Learning Tools: 04_Plus_Ca_Change.pdf

The file is the full report on how government debt levels are directly related to the unwinding of excess leverage. Several more countries are used as examples and all point to the same conclusion. Government deficits only replace the debt burned off by banks, and so can't affect real activity. It is only a counterweight and should be measured as effective in terms of how much *more* asset prices or employment would have fallen without the deficit spending. This is where the science of economics should go. Government bails out the banks after irresponsible wholesale borrowing over and over again. Will we ever learn?

Endnotes

1. See *The March of Folly* by Barbara Tuchman, which weaves together the human folly that leads to catastrophes. Many of these lessons are entirely appropriate for the financial sector, including a failure of imagination, pride and hubris, being locked into a fixed world from which it is impossible to escape, a refusal to question strategies and create a "Plan B," and so forth.
2. See William Easterly's *The Elusive Quest for Growth*, a fairly brutal indictment of capital inflows that are state-sponsored aid. He basically says that this is state-directed socialism and has generally been a failure for four decades.

CHAPTER 5

Why Capitalist Bankers Create Soviet Banking Models When the Going Gets Rough

One of the most fascinating conversations I had in recent years was with a banker who worked for one of the major global banks for 30 years. He agreed with my analysis and was perplexed by something. It was a profoundly simple problem. If the loan/deposit ratio (LDR) is seen as a reliable marker for excesses, and an ideal LDR for all countries to avoid economic catastrophe is about 1.1× maximum, then why doesn't the Bank of International Settlements (and other central banks) use the LDR as a standard marker for bank safety instead of some arbitrary capital measurement? So much damage has been done by tinkering around with capital ratios while ignoring the much larger issue of domestic liquidity and the dangers of foreign wholesale borrowing.

Like central banks, the Bank of International Settlements (BIS) is de facto owned and operated by the banks and is not directly accountable to governments. Indeed, its physical premises are legally sovereign territory and local police may not enter under any circumstances. (An excellent treatment of the history of the Bank of International Settlements is called *Tower of Basel* by Adam Lebor.) The BIS was originally set up in 1930 to monitor the egregious and eventually suicidal war reparations placed on Germany to pay for damage it had done during World War I in terms of destroyed land, property, and life. This payment system of reparations, as many predicted, ended up being a cause of German humiliation, hyperinflation, bankruptcy, and rearmament. This plan did not end well. Indeed, John Maynard Keynes wrote in his book *The Economic Consequences of the Peace* that the reparations plan in the Treaty of Versailles was a "Carthaginian Peace" and would ruin Europe. How right he was. He also stated that "The Treaty of Versailles was a peace treaty to end all peace." The BIS was set up in 1930 to monitor

German debt payments and Germany defaulted in 1931. This was not a great start.

In other iterations, the BIS was behind Basel I and II, and it is now behind Basel III. Banks have blindingly followed these prescriptions over the decades. Yet we have to ask ourselves whether the prescriptions of the BIS have themselves contributed to unintended consequences and perverse bubbles. Why didn't the BIS set down plain and simple rules to cap LDRs rather than tinker with capital rules?

BASEL I: THE JAPANESE FINANCIAL M&A BOOM AND BUST

Basel I was implemented in the late 1980s and allowed banks a great deal of freedom and latitude to incorporate cross-holdings of financial affiliates in their calculations of prudential capital. What could go wrong with this? If you own a subsidiary bank, why not allow the capital of this bank to be counted in your own capital? A bank holding company with many subsidiaries should be allowed to stand on its own two feet as a consolidated entity.

This is fine until any one of the smaller subsidiaries (a risky real estate financing entity, for instance) goes bust and potentially infects the holding company with a financial virus. After this, the unwinding of the whole entity could lead to a cascading descent for all of the subsidiaries, and this reinforces the fall of the holding company. The virus in a small entity ends up killing the whole financial institution. This precise situation happened in Japan, where the unwinding of the cross-holdings led to a financial meltdown. There were other causes, of course. But the cross-holdings accelerated a meltdown in a quick hurry. The unwinding was more toxic and more rapid than would have otherwise been the case.

An example of this is that by the early 1990s, when the bubble was deflating, the Japanese banks owned about ¥60 trillion in stocks of other companies. And this stock was used as capital. It was Tier 2 capital, but nonetheless was used as total capital calculations. This was all well and good as long as stock prices went up. This must have been the intention of the Basel Committee—to goose the stock market by allowing banks to use stock as capital.

In retrospect, this seems ridiculous. At the time, however, banks were up to their necks in "legitimate" Tier 2 capital, which was stock in companies in a deflating equity market. How much was ¥56 trillion at the time? It was more than US$400 billion, or about 25 percent of bank capital. In other words, one quarter of the bank capital to buoy the balance sheet of the nation's lifeblood of credit was predicated on the flimsy assumption that stocks always go up over time. Banks took a bath on these stocks at the same time that they were bleeding nonperforming loans.

The idea to use stock holdings as capital was a terrible one, but was brought to the banks by a sacrosanct organization with the international imprimatur of legitimacy—so it couldn't possibly go wrong, could it? The nonperforming loans in the Japanese economy, most of which came from real estate losses, caused a hemorrhaging of the capital structure of the banks, but the problem was made far worse when the stock market fell. The obvious question one must ask here is that even a freshman in an economics class could figure out that during an economic slowdown, nonperforming loans are bound to rise. At the same time, it is also clear that stock prices could just as easily fall. So capital is being eaten away at both sides at the same time. Why would the Basel Committee not see this coming?

This may not have been the direct cause of the Japanese meltdown of 1990, but many financial experts consider this cross-holding structure to be a contributing cause to the meltdown. To draw an analogy: An electrical short may have caused a fire, but the gasoline sitting next to a furnace on top of stacks of newspapers made it explosive. The cross-holding structure was kindling for the fire that started as LDRs for the banks rose dangerously above 1.0. By 1990, the LDR was pushing above 105 percent, and Japan had tapped out its extraordinarily large domestic savings base, a phenomenal sum of money created by an undervalued currency and the subsequent windfall in export earnings. This is mercantilism and is all too often present in these types of domestic liquidity bubbles.

At the same time, Japanese corporates were issuing bonds into Europe (euro-yen bonds) in order to fund a property market whose values were already sky high due to the exhaustion of domestic credit. Once again, we see that these forms of foreign borrowings to prop up a property market are especially dangerous, since they are, by their very nature, late to the party. They are Johnny-come-lately funders to a property party at three o'clock in the morning. Wholesale funding tends to end in disaster. For an excellent analysis of this, read Michael Lewis's September 2011 article in *Vanity Fair* called "It's the Economy, Dummkopf!" In it, he describes the poor wholesale funders in Dusseldorf who were left holding the bag at the end of the party. No one told them it was 3 A.M. and the party was over!

BASEL II: THE RISE OF THE AAA-RATED CDO BOOM AND BUST

Here's another example of how BIS rules on capital adequacy rules to ensure "prudential banking" backfired horribly and led to the blunder of the mortgage-backed security implosion in 2007–2009. In Basel II, another attempt to bring about prudence after the debacle of Basel I, the BIS laid down rules that basically said that banks can hold as many "AAA securities" as they like without any capital against them, as long as these securities maintained their AAA rating from two of the "big three" ratings agencies (Moody's, Fitch, or S&P). The end result is that bankers came up with so-called "AAA securities" in collusion with the ratings agencies to satisfy this quota system.

There is an interesting sidebar here. In all this mess, non-U.S. international ratings agencies cried foul. They said that this ménage-a-trois was a cartel that was, in effect, bringing about restraint of trade—a violation of the Sherman Antitrust Act. Furthermore, many clients of mine in China looked on in amusement as these ratings agencies made billions by rating any old paper being issued by banks as AAA. In fact, there were myriad stories of the ratings agencies actually handing over their own internal ratings programs (an astonishing breach of confidentiality) to the banks so that the banks could manipulate data. This created, in effect, a credit cooperative sponsored by the BIS. The BIS was saying that banks could produce as much of this paper as they wanted and have no capital against it in a mindless game of soviet quotas. This turned into a sham and earned the mock derision of many countries around the world.

Many policymakers watching from Asia and Latin America said, "What's good for the goose is good for the gander"—so countries in the emerging world decided to have their own ratings agencies that they could manipulate to their own ends, just as the U.S. system did. The breach of confidence by the West gave financial leaders in the developing world a sense of carte blanche to write their own rules when it came to ratings, regulations, and the like. It also makes Asian financial institutions groan a bit when they have to listen to yet another round of Basel III requirements. You can feel it in the room at Basel III conferences. Asian CEOs are less willing than ever to cooperate, because they have been witness to a corrupt and incompetent old-boys' club in the West, which has caused a calamity from which is has been difficult to escape. Why should Asian bankers cooperate in yet another hare-brained scheme?

In Basel II, the fundamental underpinning was that the AAA securities that were blessed by these ratings agencies happened to be mortgage-backed securities (real estate prices never go down, right?), which could be placed on the balance sheet of the banks as inventory and as investments without a single dollar of capital against them. This means that there was virtually zero chance that they would default and need to be written down at the expense of scarce capital. These were "bulletproof" mortgages from a diversified number of ZIP codes across the country that could withstand any small recession. Real estate prices *never fall in all ZIP codes in the United States at the same time,* right? The banks blindly went along with this charade, never asking a simple question: "How could there be more than 50,000 AAA-rated securities in the United States when there were only 7 companies in the entire country that had an AAA rating?"*

As a result, a bubble in AAA-rated securities emerged on the balance sheets of banks globally and at the same time. (Is it preposterous to say that this is similar to Stalin telling the whole country to plant wheat, or Mao telling the whole country to make a steel factory in their backyards? Think about it!) No banker needed to ask whether these really were AAA-rated securities, since the ratings agencies said so and since the BIS said it was okay to have as much as you liked. So, vast amounts—literally trillions of dollars' worth—of these AAA-rated securities were created and placed on the balance sheets of financial institutions without *any* capital against them. There was no need to do so, because the BIS said so.

These securities were placed all over the country and then went overseas to foreign central banks. These central banks were searching for safe yield, and these AAA securities offered security (they were AAA after all) *and* yields of 85 to 100 basis points over other AAA-rated government securities. When these securities were suddenly downgraded simultaneously in the summer of 2007, there was both a glut of not-unsold inventory on the balance sheets of banks and vast holdings that many institutions did not and could not hold any longer. Central banks in Taiwan, China, Japan, Hong Kong, and other countries found themselves with toxic assets. They simply couldn't tell which of these assets were good and which were more akin to counterfeit currency. Furthermore, these banks suddenly needed much more capital to hold against these securities, which were downgraded to junk.

So, the banks all went over the cliff together (once again) as they followed the Basel II rules. There is a bigger problem here. As the banks put more and more of these AAA securities (numerous variations of mortgage-backed securities) on the balance sheet, no one asked just how these would be funded. These were an asset of the banks—a product that was for sale. They needed to be funded on the liability side of the banks. Most of the banks that dealt in this toxic world were investment banks, which were barred from taking deposits. Only their commercial

---

*It is interesting to note that it was only in January 2015—eight years after the mess started—that several attorneys general finally reached a $1.4 Bn settlement with S&P regarding allegations of wrongdoing with regard to the thousands of AAA ratings it assigned to many types of securities that were eventually worth zero. One of the interesting stipulations for the settlement was a retraction by S&P that the government was going after S&P as a revenge tactic for downgrading the sovereign rating of the United States.

banking arms could take deposits. So, what did these investment banks do? They lobbied for the abolition of the Glass-Steagall wall between commercial banks that could take deposits and investment banks that could manufacture "AAA-securities." They lobbied the government to allow Federal Deposit Insurance Corporation (FDIC) deposits to fund these toxic securities and other dubious investment banking or proprietary positions.

One investment banker whom I know called it a kind of counterfeiting operation. By 2006 or so, many bankers who were manufacturing these securities smelled a multitrillion-dollar rat. It was hard for even the bankers inside these financial institutions to tell the difference between the good CDOs and the fraudulent CDOs; they were all mixed together. Almost 20 percent of these alleged AAA securities eventually became worth zero; in other words, one in five blew up. Who cares? As long as Basel II rules were being followed, the game was on. And the party continued. If the ratings agencies said they were AAA-rated, that was all that counted.

As long as this game continued, bankers could make vast fees and continue to generate these securities. However, when there was a hint of small amounts of counterfeit CDOs swirling around, the smart insiders became increasingly uncomfortable and forced the issue by complaining to the Federal Reserve, the ratings agencies, and the SEC. It is a good guess that the arm of the ratings agencies was twisted enough for them to start downgrading these securities in the summer of 2007. This was the beginning of the end for the house of cards. By the summer of 2008, one year later, the assumption was that everything was counterfeit unless proven otherwise. This is what hastened the collapse. No one—not even the smartest guys in the room—knew what was good and what was worthless.

So, these banks issued billions of dollars of debt and availed themselves of the balance sheets of their parent banks, which had (literally) trillions of dollars of deposits. These included banks like Bank of America, Citi, and J.P. Morgan Chase. Even this vast amount of savings was not sufficient to accommodate the mortgage-backed securities to fund the real estate boom.

Even though the numbers showed that the "capital base" of the banks was sufficient to accommodate losses, the LDR of the system was ballooning out of control, and no one was watching this because the LDR was not a remote consideration of the BIS. Indeed, Basel III does not envision any kind of loan/deposit cap.

Yet it is not the leverage levels of the banks that tend to show up problems. It is the LDRs that tend to be blood pressure indicators. LDRs are the purest indication of liquidity, and liquidity is everything. Liquidity in the form of deposit liabilities that can buy time during difficult periods is the key to survival. HSBC had a relatively prudent LDR during the 2008 madness and did not need a bailout. So did Standard Chartered. So did the Canadian banks. Those banks with liquid balance sheets were safe. Those with LDRs of 1.2 or 1.3 were all crushed, and the equity was wiped out. These banks include *all* Irish banks, *all* Greek banks, Spanish banks, many U.S. banks, and *all* of the U.K. commercial banks (which were taken over by the government). You get the point. Liquidity *is* solvency, and do not let anyone else tell you differently.

So, let's take a look at a perfectly fine document like the *Basel III Handbook*, published by Accenture (www.accenture.com/sitecollectiondocuments /PDF/Financialservices; registration required). It has dozens of pages of new arrangements for capital adequacy aimed at creating a prudential framework for banks in a new environment. Go through the document and you will not find one single paragraph on something as fundamental as the LDR. Deposit funding is all about what creates the liquidity to allow banks to remain solvent. The long-term debt that too many banks have used (as well as convoluted derivatives) does *not* belong to the bank; it belongs to bondholders. In this sense, Deutsche Bank has ended up with a balance sheet that is only one-third funded by deposits. Two-thirds of this balance sheet is funded by bonds. The same is true of other banks. What happens when regulators like the UK FSA (the financial markets regulator of the UK) force the commercial deposit–taking arm of the bank (with high-quality deposit funding) to be separated from the investment bank, which is largely bond-funded. The investment banks will undoubtedly be treated as a separate credit and will likely be downgraded. This is a problem for future funding.

In too many ways, capital adequacy ratios (CARs) are a shell game. They allow national banks to play a host of "risk management" games, which offer a sense of safety but which often ignore the ways in which these risk assets are funded. Liquidity (deposits) is the water that makes the assets of a bank grow. Capital is merely fertilizer for the balance sheet. It is vital, but cannot have an effect without the water provided by the credibility that causes us to deposit money in the bank and allow it to remain there. The water of this delicate financial ecosystem is savings (deposits liabilities of both individuals and corporates that can be turned into loans). Using assets/capital ratios ignores the liability funding issue completely. It has caused banks to ignore the vitally important role of deposit funding and instead has caused a focus on quasi-equity and bond funding, which introduces a higher level of risk because these bond portfolios are, after all, leverage.

This capital is very expensive. It must be rationed very carefully. Risk systems must be put in place to ensure that profits can be generated from the spread between the cost of savings (deposit liabilities) and the rate of return on loans (assets) that the bank receives. The spread between these two in turn creates more capital over time. The problem here is that lopsided investments in assets can become problematic when too many banks have too many of the same assets at the same time. This is likely to happen with government bonds as investments on the asset side are backed by too little real capital and instead are backed by long-term bonds on the liability side. This time is over, and this gargantuan monstrosity is very definitely being dismantled.

This is what happened with the global financial crisis—too many banks had committed their balance sheets to manufacturing or holding mortgage-backed securities because the Basel II regulations steered too many banks into doing this. And they were all doing so at the same time. The entire financial ecosystem was motivated to move toward a type of Soviet collectivization or mandated "crop rotation" for all entities all at the same time. The result was a windfall of one type of financial crop—the mortgage-backed security. This is akin to the entire Midwest of the United States deciding to plant only corn because corn prices were high and the CME (Chicago Mercantile Exchange) told the major agricultural producers in the Midwest that it was to their benefit to plant corn. The result in the next season would undoubtedly be a collapse in corn prices. This is why the price of mortgage-backed securities collapsed: Everyone was planting them because the BIS and Basel II said it was a smart thing to do. As we look at Basel III, let's see what we are now setting ourselves up for.

Furthermore, the new Basel III rules are astonishingly punctilious. There are a dizzying assortment of slices that make up the capital structure. The level of detail is unrealistic when it comes to the day-to-day functioning of banks. Many CEOs of banks find this level of exactitude laughable. It is as if those who are writing these rules are divorced from the realities of banking. In addition, as more detail is required for understanding the rules for what kind of capital applies to what kinds of circumstances, a great deal of wiggle room is created to search for exceptions and ways around the rules. In essence, the Basel III rules create quotas for capital. Quotas always create long queues, and long queues create corruption. Quotas make for corruption.

In this way, we can see that the BIS acts as a kind of central planning commission that decides which products the banks should hold as inventory and sell. It is a perverse form of central planning that tells all the global banks what to do at the same time. Surely this cannot be a good thing. And yet it continues through one financial bubble after another.

BASEL III: THE RISE OF THE GOVERNMENT DEBT BOOM AND BUST?

Now, we have Basel III being promulgated in the next year or so. What is this central planning commission steering the banks to do? It is now steering the banks to deal with one of the biggest problems globally. This problem is government debt. Since the global financial crisis, governments have been running up large deficits to deal with the catastrophe of the Basel II–inspired mortgage-backed securities collapse. These deficits have been running anywhere from 3 percent to 7 percent of GDP. In addition, governments like Ireland and the United Kingdom had to increase federal debt to fund the collapse of banks like Northern Rock and other financial institutions. So, governments were using deficits both to create a floor under growth by stimulating the economy and also to bail out financial institutions that got carried away by wholesale funding of real estate. This wholesale funding of real estate, as we have seen in Chapter 3, always ends in tears. And the additional exuberance came to us from Basel II, which encouraged all of these financial institutions to hold mortgage-backed securities for investments.

We can see that Basel III rules cause the boat to rock from one side to the other precisely because all banks must, in general, be compliant with these regulations. And who decides these regulations? The banks do—and the bankers occasionally consult with governments. At this juncture, government deficits to bail out the banks and restart the growth engine make both the governments and the banks happy—for now. The governments can continue to find a place to warehouse ever-growing deficits. And banks can buy government debt without any capital commitment and make a good spread without any risk—for now.

There is clearly mutual interest here. When financial crises happen, banks expect to be bailed out—and governments accommodate them. This happens over and over again, all over the world, in all times. One would be hard-pressed to find a government that just stood by to let the entire financial system collapse. As it is, the process of deflating a bubble and allowing financial ruin for even a few is so politically unacceptable that governments usually rush to the aid of banks as the process is in its early stages. Governments must do this to stay in power. And banks fully expect this to occur. Let's show one example. Figure 4.1 (in the previous chapter) illustrates Thailand's progress as the process of deleveraging occurred after the peak of its property bubble in 1997 and banks tried to unwind their lending orgy.

As banks unwind their excessive debt positions (from which they made billions of dollars in fees over the years), there is almost a one-for-one increase in government debt. Imagine a global system in place that allows the entire world to now act as a giant version of Thailand. The unwinding of the LDRs occurs in order to allow the banks to recoup stability and turn on the profitable credit engine. The unwinding of the LDR causes loans to be called in; homes are repossessed, vacations and credit cards are canceled, and jobs are lost as a result of the slowdown in consumption and investment. Governments can fall out of power and often do when populations are forced into austerity in a world where they do not understand the pain that is caused by the reversal of the credit engine.

Government and banks are always acting in concert. They are hand in glove. When the banks are lending, governments can do no wrong. When the bust happens, governments must intervene in order to stay in power, so they run deficits to prop up the banks and make the deleveraging of the balance sheet tolerable to an already angry population. Without these deficits, the financial system could and often does go down a deflationary spiral from which it is difficult to recover. So there is some rhyme and reason in this dysfunctional and symbiotic relationship.

The above explains why Basel III is evolving into a state planning commission in the small town of Basel, which is now saying that there must be a new crop. Banks must go from making only corn (mortgage debt) to only cotton (government debt). There is slight irony here, since U.S. dollars are actually made of cotton and not paper. The more government debt that banks hold, the less overall capital they need. This is because Basel Committee told them that this is so.

Here is the problem. In the same way that banks engineered counterfeit AAA-backed securities that were in fact an improbable financial hoax, how can all these countries that have government debt/GDP ratios of 90 percent to 120 percent have Standard & Poor's (S&P) ratings that are double-A? The answer is that they have these ratings because they belong to a special club that gives their members exclusive rights to a high rating even though they are irresponsible issuers of debt. This bad behavior and financial irresponsibility is like the teacher at the reform school for wayward teenagers, forced to grade on a curve to make sure that everyone passes. In the same way, these governments are offering each other grades of A and A– for work that is more like C.

The Basel committee is finalizing the list of countries whose government debt can be held without zero capital against it. This old-boys' club includes the usual suspects and blocks out those countries that are not traditional allies. Hence, this exclusive club of developed countries ensures its own survival even though they are engaging in irresponsible funding behavior that resembles that of third-world countries. In this way, there is a crafty political angle to government debt. The group of rich countries preserves their funding ability, and the debt of poor countries cannot be held by the majority of banks globally. If debt cannot be held, it cannot be issued. It is that simple.

The countries considered to be sterling issuers of debt have a zero weighting. These countries are basically the G-7 countries and a few other

Anglo-Saxon countries. If you look at the debt/GDP of some of these countries with Rolls Royce credit ratings and compare them to other countries that have far better credit profiles, it becomes clear that the decision about whose debt is worthy of ownership and whose debt is not worthy of ownership is somewhat arbitrary. (For instance, is Deutsche Bank really an A credit when it is trading at a price/book of 0.5, one of the lowest valuations globally?) Indeed, it appears to be a system rigged in favor of the incumbent, where it is hard for a challenger to move in and create pressure for change, reform, or another direction. The structure of the system is one of status quo. This is precisely the problem. In organizational theory, systems like this are called *closed systems* because they do not allow new thinking and new organizations to enter, challenge, alter, and transform existing systems into newer and more evolved systems. We will see in the next chapter how this can lead to a system that is brittle and incapable of rapid change. For countries like China, this creates tension, because structures that were put in place 80 years ago seem too archaic and troublesome. Many senior government representatives in China, Indonesia, and Hong Kong have told me they are indifferent to many of these organizations because they are seen as arcane, brittle, corrupt, and somewhat inept.

In conclusion, we can see that the Basel Committee acts as a kind of soviet (the precise meaning itself is a kind of "council" or "committee," not unlike the structure of the Basel Committee). This committee creates rules with all kinds of unintended consequences. One of the most evident and yet rarely discussed consequences is that Basel rules create a fundamentally unhealthy global concentration of risk over and over again. The underlying foundation of all investment theory is diversification of risk. This is the idea of not putting all your eggs in one basket. Yet, the Basel committee has been telling the banks precisely to put all their eggs in one basket.

In Basel I, the unintended consequence was that banks were all buying equity in cross-owned companies. When the unwinding happened, the equity fell apart just when the banks needed it most. When a financial crisis starts, the equity of the banks is the first to go down. In a financial crisis, the banks need the capital more than ever as a buffer against losses. So a perfect storm occurred, especially in Japan, which made the situation much worse than it needed to be. Imagine a further disaster when all of these banks had to sell this equity at the same time into a falling market, which made the situation worse, and so on. The unintended consequences of this concentration of risk created a self-reinforcing downward spiral. In retrospect, it sounds ludicrous to think that there was any rationality at all. It gets better.

In Basel II, the committee told all the banks that all banks at the same time could hold as much AAA-rated paper as they wanted with no capital against it. This led to a very dangerous concentration of risk in hundreds of billions of dollars of paper that had an AAA rating. No one bothered to ask how is this was possible if the United States at that time had only eight companies that had an AAA rating. As long as Basel II said it was okay, there was no problem. Imagine the problem, however, if one of the ratings agencies came along and said that the paper was not AAA-rated anymore but was BBB-rated. Suddenly, two things would happen. The first is that covenants would be triggered in pension and insurance companies, forcing them to sell the paper. Prices would fall, and banks holding this paper suddenly would have large losses that would have to be absorbed by capital—but wait, there is *no* capital against this paper! So the banks themselves would be forced to sell it precisely at the wrong moment. This concentration of risk led to a catastrophe, since the prices of these securities (which were connected to the highly politically sensitive mortgage market) collapsed and brought down Fannie Mae and Freddie Mac, not to mention several banks, including Bear Stearns and Lehman Brothers. Again, this fairly obvious concentration of risk was not questioned. And again, the unintended consequences of this concentration of risk caused the worst recession in 75 years.

Now, we are entering Basel III, and the Committee is saying that it is perfectly acceptable to hold a concentrated portfolio of government debt without any capital against it. And it is all right to do this for the debt of the G-7 countries. By the way, the average debt/GDP of these countries is rapidly approaching 100 percent. (See Appendix A for the layout of the debt structure.) If Basel I and II are anything to go by, this is likely not to end well.

Author and practitioner Satyajit Das also comes to the same conclusion. Basel III and other regulations have conspired to create more and not less instability. Soviet-style quotas and collectivization schemes, which demand that banks "hold" (let's call it *harvest* to keep in sync with the idea of agricultural collectivization) more government securities, "are now the potential source of problems."[1] These new powerful incentives to hold ever more government securities increase bank exposure to sovereign bonds, adding to existing exposure to government securities via repurchase transactions, investments, or trading inventories. A ratings downgrade of a sovereign, Das asserts, results in a fall in value of bonds, triggering losses. Banks would then face calls for additional collateral, which would drain liquidity, which in turn would require additional capital. Where would the capital come from? Very likely, the government would have to fund it. How would the government fund it? Of course, they would fund the recapitalization through government debt. The unintended consequences, therefore, of this Basel III zero-weighting of government securities are highly problematic in the event of sovereign downgrades. More bankers and market participants are sounding the alarm bells *before* Basel III is even fully implemented.

Something else happens as an unintended consequence of allowing so much harvesting of government debt. Das makes the point that market participants need to hedge against the large holdings of government securities and so short stocks, currencies, or insurance companies. This transmits volatility throughout markets. The net result is falling liquidity and rising volatility in the event of any downgrades. Furthermore, governments that are downgraded have further problems with funding and may even see their funding costs rise.

Lastly, a growing chorus of institutions in the developing world is not so keen on Basel III, especially because many of the Asian banks are in such better shape than the Western banks. The full implementation of Basel III will take several years in the European banks, in particular, because of the parlous shape of their balance sheets. So many Asian banks are frowning on the litigious carving up of the capital structure into so many basis points of this and so many of that, and they're wondering what's it all about. There is very definitely a low-grade fatigue among many banking institutions I visit when it comes to international institutions like the BIS. BIS I and BIS II both ended badly, they say. With Basel III, is the third time the charm? Maybe not.

An alternative is to create capital requirements whose intellectual foundation is the same as any book in investments: diversification. The best way to get to a diversified portfolio for a bank is to have an equal weighting for all portions of the balance sheet. The risk of trade finance should be given the same weighting as a mortgage. Why? The bank should be in a good position to gauge this. Otherwise, they should get out of the business. This is a somewhat disturbing idea, given how much time and energy has gone into parsing the Basel III requirements. But the idea is a profoundly simple one. Allowing local authorities to decide what is best for them in some form of consortium (and having all elements of the balance sheet of a bank have equal weight) would undoubtedly create a far more diversified system that would not implode simultaneously every time there was a crisis. I think it is absurd to have no ratios that take into account the rate of growth of credit relative to the rate of grow in savings (any form of the LDR!). This is a key variable, and it is not only absent in economics, it is also absent in Basel III. This is astonishing.

Learning Tools: 05_Credit_Bubbles_And_Catastrophe.pdf

The book called *Tower of Basel* by Adam LeBor is a good tool to understand the origins and incentives for the BIS. *Lords of Finance* by Liaquat Ahamed is a classic "behind the scenes" book describing the workings of central banks and their relationship with the BIS.

Endnote

1. Satyajit, Das, "'Coffin Corner' Threat to Financial Stability Now Ever Present," *Financial Times*, October 30, 2014.

CHAPTER 6

Central Banks Are Carrying the Greatest Load and Will Dominate Outcomes

One new phenomenon in this crisis is the role of central banks. On top of negative credit growth, massive central bank intervention is another phenomenon that no one who is alive in the West has seen before. For 20 years, Asia analysts have been watching as the Bank of Japan has tried in vain to alter asset prices by expanding the balance sheet. We submit that central banks cannot alter the path of asset prices; they can only slow the path. As Alan Greenspan said many years ago when someone asked him to define the role of a central bank: "Central banks can only buy time." We will look at how central banks enter the picture and act as a kind of quasi-banking entity to stabilize asset prices. We will show that without active and aggressive "writing off" of bad assets and bank recapitalization, central banks are simply too small to have any real effect on the financial assets.

WHY HAVE CENTRAL BANKS BECOME SO INVOLVED IN THE SOLUTION OF THE GLOBAL FINANCIAL CRISIS?

A loan is like a tube of toothpaste. Once the toothpaste comes out of the tube, it is impossible to put it back in. So it goes with a loan. When a loan of $100 is given to a borrower, only two things can happen. Either the borrower pays it back in full with principal of $100 and interest of 6 percent (which is $6), for a total of $106 after one year, or the banks have to write off the loan below its initial value of $100 and try to collect some collateral that the borrower has offered up. The banks needs to find something else of value equal to $100—property, cash, stocks, or similar. The banks can also sell the loan to someone else, but the loan still remains someone else's obligation. It does not go away. Someone is always on the hook for a loan.

Here's the problem with the 2008 global financial crisis: All of the debt that was distributed to borrowers (mortgages, corporate loans, individual loans, margin lending) was so vast that there was not enough cash, stocks, property, and so forth to repay the banks. The Western banks had obligations in excess of US$55 trillion of debt. The gross domestic product (GDP) of the United States and the Eurozone combined is about US$30 trillion. As this unwind of leverage came apart, the amount of collateral being called in (with the result that prices were being pressed down or depressed as things were being sold all at the same time) was in danger of creating a deflationary catastrophe similar to the Great Depression.

Since there is no one on Mars or Venus to buy these assets, banks called the central banks and told them of the problem. If the central banks did not buy these assets, a deflationary spiral would have been created that would have become hard to pull back from (figure 6.1). This is because if loans were called in, the underlying assets would have fallen in value because there would be no one else around to buy them with leverage. Only cash buyers would be around. What you can buy with cash and what you can buy with a loan are very different. A cash buyer would only be able to afford to buy these assets at a fraction of their value. Also, it is very likely that the major central banks in the United States and the United Kingdom, the European Central Bank (ECB), and the People's Bank of China (PBOC) were all talking

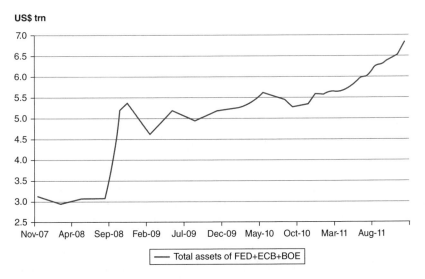

FIGURE 6.1 Central Bank Total Assets: They Had to Absorb Assets Being Thrown Overboard by Banks
Source: China Construction Bank

to each other at the same time, probably in the summer of 2008. They needed to provide standby credit facilities in the early summer of 2008, but it was becoming clear that other means would be necessary.

If some other entity did not buy the loans (we can think of buying a loan as "funding" a loan, for this is the same thing), it is likely that banks would have been put out of business because of the write-offs of bad debt that would have resulted. It is also likely that systemically important institutions such as Fannie Mae would have collapsed and caused a spiraling down of property prices, bringing about a collapse in the U.S. mortgage market. So, the Federal Reserve, the Bank of England, and the ECB all huddled together to find a solution. They needed to find a way to embark on a major extraordinary bailout of the financial without creating panic and a downward spiral of depression.

To give you an idea of how big central banks are in the scheme of things, Figure 6.2 shows the total assets of central banks relative to other assets. For instance, as of mid-2014, the assets controlled by central banks were almost US$15 trillion. Contrast this to other assets and we can see that the central assets are six times larger than all of the hedge funds put together. They are also six times larger than all of the sovereign wealth funds put together. In fact, if you put all of the private global private equity funds, the global hedge funds, and sovereign wealth funds together, they would still be one-half of the central banks' assets. So we need to consider that these central banks

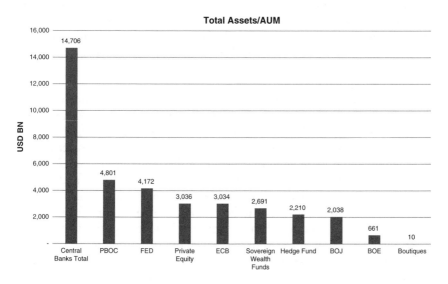

FIGURE 6.2　Total Assets by Industry. Central Banks Are Still *the* Heavyweight. Could Private Equity Morph into Investment Banks?

decide the course of assets for some considerable period of time. The problem is that these central banks, whether we like it or not, are fickle political creatures and respond to the flotsam and jetsam of political demands. This makes the art of investing in this age of financial crisis very difficult.

The way that central banks got so large was by purchasing two major asset types. The first was risk assets that could not be bought or "funded" by banks. The risk assets that were most at risk were mortgages. So, the Federal Reserve bought more than $1 trillion in mortgages. The second type of debt that did not have sufficient numbers of buyers was government debt, which was being issued both to stimulate the economy and to assist in the bailout of the banks. If the Federal Reserve did not do this, there was a risk that the supply of government debt being forced onto the economy would have caused a collapse in prices (and a spike in yields), given that the supply of debt available would have swamped any reasonable demand. A spike in yields would have been another shock to the already damaged real estate market.

The point is that a new source of demand was needed outside of existing market players, since the existing players had too much debt and insufficient collateral and were in no condition to absorb even more debt. It was mathematically impossible to solve the problems without a new source of demand for all the debt. So the central banks stepped in and acted in ways that were historically unprecedented. A purchase of debt on this level had never been tried before. Central banks had to act, or the entire banking system would have imploded. And the central banks of the United States, the United Kingdom, and the Eurozone had to act in concert, because the financial system was a complex global web of transactions in which Bank of America was trading with the Royal Bank of Scotland (RBS) and Deutsche Bank at the same time. An unwinding of one system in one country would have brought down the entire system.

As it turns out, former Fed Chairman Bernanke envisioned such a scenario in a book that he edited, called *Essays on the Great Depression*. Bernanke is considered an expert on the Great Depression, and he also contributed a chapter to the book. In this chapter, he outlined exactly what he thought should be done in the event of a debt buildup that could result in a depression if it were not handled correctly. Bernanke was pretty clear on what informed his views on depressions. The main cause of deflationary episodes, he surmised, was that policymakers tended to underestimate the level of debt in an economy when trying to implement measures to clean out the system or to allow excesses to be cleaned out or written off. If the levels of debt are larger than anyone thinks, the process of purging the system of bad debt and "resetting the clock" can backfire and result in a wipeout of bank capital and a freezing of the credit system. Indeed, this is exactly what happened in the Great Depression.

TABLE 6.1 Bernanke's 10 Commandments from *Essays on the Great Depression*

	In order to prevent debt deflation, THOU SHALT …	Start Date
I	Raise capital through government	October 2008
II	Guarantee assets, deposits	October 2008
III	Run large fiscal deficits	March 2009
IV	Guarantee GSEs	September 2008
V	Slash rates/commit to low rates	January 2008
VI	Purchase long-term assets/treasuries	March 2009
VII	Depreciate the U.S. dollar	Ongoing
VIII	Guarantee and purchase high-risk assets	Ongoing
IX	Offer explicit (asset) inflation target	Ongoing
X	Renegotiate debt between banks and borrowers	Ongoing

Source: Nomura

In Table 6.1 we outline Bernanke's 10 Commandments to avoid deflationary depression, as derived from the book (indeed, the actions he and others implemented were a carbon copy of those from *Essays*). These are the *thou shalts* of policymakers in order to prevent a collapse in land values, the wages of labor the bank capital required to fire the engine of credit. In his writing, he errs on the side of regulatory forbearance (or liberality) when it comes to debt forgiveness. Others on the right side of the ideological spectrum (for the sake of simplicity, let's call these the "Austrians") prefer quick and sudden pain to clean out the system. Bernanke would say that this is naïve, because it would cause an automatic shutdown of the system and create a self-perpetuating downward spiral from which it would be difficult to exit.

The 6th and 8th commandments, which we discussed above, are only part of the whole plan; these involve not just buying government debt but explicitly buying risky assets to help put a floor under the private sector credit system, in particular, the real estate market. All of these measures are designed to prevent deflation in the event of a debt meltdown. The other commandments serve as a means to restore confidence and allow economic activity to resume:

- Guaranteeing deposit liabilities in order to allow depositors to have some relief about keeping their cash in the bank
- Running deficits to restore confidence and create jobs
- Offering a long-term commitment to low rates to reassure investors
- Offering an explicit inflation target to allay the fears of those who were afraid of deflation

The all-encompassing philosophy of these actions of the past six years is to avoid deflation at any cost. Deflation has insidious effects on debt. The simple reason is that if I owe 100 dollars in 12 months, and I also still need to pay 6 dollars in interest, deflation means that my wages go down and the value of my house goes down. I am poorer and I feel poorer. In addition, I have a harder time paying back the same amount of dollars, because the 100 dollars does *not* go down in value. It actually goes up in "real" terms in deflation, producing a perverse effect of making debtors get poorer just by standing still. This is what happened to the United States in 1929 to 1934. It got poorer just by standing still because policymakers allowed a debt-laden economy to endure deflation without providing any support or relief to debtors. This was suicidal and proved to be utterly destructive to land, labor, and capital. Arguably, the deflationary depression lasted until December 8, 1941, when the war effort ramped up and unemployment fell dramatically. On Friday, December 5, 1941, the unemployment rate in the United States was 20 percent. Deflation is a nefarious animal and should be avoided at just about any cost.

Where are we in 2014? Table 6.2 shows where we are now. The amount of debt purchased by the combined central banks of the Federal Reserve, the Bank of England, and the ECB are now about 30 percent of GDP. This amounts to about US$13 trillion. Consider that before the crisis, each of these central banks had puny amounts of risky or government assets. In the specific case of the Federal Reserve balance sheet, it was a mere 6 percent of GDP. It now stands at more than 30 percent of GDP. On the asset side of the balance sheet, we can see a picture of a swelling of government bond holdings as well as risk assets, almost all of which are mortgage-backed securities. (It is important to mention here that the "real" definition that Bernanke envisioned was *not* merely buying government bonds but buying risk assets such as mortgages. Some pundits say that one of the reasons that

TABLE 6.2 Central Banks and Their Weight as Percent of GDP

Country	GDP ($BN, IMF '14 EST)	Central Bank Balance Sheet ($BN)	Central Bank Balance Sheet/GDP	Reserves/ GDP	Currency in Circulation/ GDP	Bonds/ GDP
United States	17,438	4,172	23.9%	15.6%	7.0%	12.5%
China	9,761	4,801	49.2%	32.0%	10.1%	13.5%
Japan	5,228	2,038	39.0%	18.4%	15.6%	31.3%
Europe	13,203	3,034	23.0%	4.2%	9.9%	0.0%
UK	2,627	661	25.2%	18.8%	3.7%	23.7%

Japan never recovered from the morass of debt deflation was because the Bank of Japan was not quick enough to engage in the outright purchase of risky real estate assets. Since history never reveals her alternatives, we will never know.)

The liability side of the Fed balance sheet is slightly harder to understand. It is the way in which every single nickel of the assets must be funded or "paid for." In the past, the liabilities of the central bank were almost entirely composed of notes and coins. All of the money pouring forth from an ATM is a liability of the Federal Reserve. Prior to 2007, there were almost no other liabilities. Table 6.3 shows the composition of the Federal Reserve in mid-2014.

In 2008, when the bank bailout package was passed by Congress, there was one vitally important sentence that made all the difference to just how large the balance sheet could become. The one sentence said that for the first time in the history of the Federal Reserve, it could pay interest on deposits. As such, for the first time, there was an incentive for banks to deposit money in the vaults of the Federal Reserve. These are called voluntary deposits or voluntary reserves. These are deposits that are mostly electronically deposited. They are, for all intents and purposes, used by the Fed to buy government debt. In fact, the growth in money supply is in sync with nominal growth, so the vast majority of the growth in the balance sheet of the Fed has been caused by customer deposits in banks (which are cash on the asset side of the balance sheet of the bank) to be transferred into the liabilities of the Federal Reserve balance sheet. It is just cash going through a lot of machinations without doing anything except funding a buildup of government debt.

It is important to remember that the voluntary deposits that received interest did not exist (they were not legally capable of existing) before the global financial crisis. So, before 2008, 90 percent of the liabilities of the Federal Reserve were nothing but "notes and coins in circulation." This is basically money in the ATMs. Now, we can see that notes and coins (1) are less than 30 percent of the entire balance sheet and (2) have been

TABLE 6.3 Fed Balance Sheet: Voluntary Reserves Is "Unused" Money; Fed Owns 15% of Housing Market

Federal Reserve Balance Sheet (USD BN)

Bonds and notes	2,181	Deposits	2,720
MBS	1,570	Money in circulation	1,215
Premium on securities held	193	Others	180
Others	227	Total capital	56
Total assets	**4,172**	**Total liabilities and capital**	**4,172**

growing only slightly higher than nominal GDP in this entire period. So, the notion that the government is printing money to buy government debt is wrongheaded and muddy thinking.

Because the money used to "buy" government bonds is actually voluntary deposits from banks, which would otherwise have that money sitting on their own balance sheets collecting virtually nothing, the ability of an *extra* dollar to make a difference in additional GDP growth or credit activity is actually falling. This is the idea of the money multiplier effect. Cash that is doing nothing in a bank is transferred to the Federal Reserve to buy government debt, which is being used to accommodate a deleveraging of the financial system and stabilize asset prices. Hopefully, the activity caused by government debt has some auxiliary effect in creating activity through infrastructure buildup or defense activity. The point here is that the Fed is not creating money out of thin air. It is borrowing existing cash from banks that are scared to lend. In this way, the activity is understandably neutral at best and deflationary at worst. The cash is just "round tripping" and not creating an extension in the private sector.

This is a slightly more elaborate argument, similar to the chapter discussing loan/deposit ratios (LDRs) and Keynesian economics, that demonstrates why deficit spending during financial crises does not work. The excess cash available is pushed into buying treasuries while the balance sheet of the bank shrinks back to a sustainable level. Until this is done, the ability of an extra dollar to generate activity is hampered, because the real power to drive up asset prices and wages comes from leverage. Until the banks reach an equilibrium (an LDR below 1 and leverage below 16), the system will limp along; government debt simply is a bandage for the bleeding caused by the exit of leverage from banks. As and when banks resuscitate their balance sheets, the system can return to normal. At that point, deficit spending will no longer be needed. In fact, deficits will tend to drop and turn to surplus precisely because banks are now driving up asset prices, consumption, and employment. Government spending is very definitely second fiddle. We can see here that the banks are definitely the dog wagging the federal tail. It is not the other way around.

To drive the point home further, while the banks are offering over deposits to the federal reserve (of the Bank of England or the ECB for that matter), they are offloading debt (shrinking assets) by:

1. Closing out the loan to a creditor and telling them to look somewhere else for credit;
2. Writing off the loan against income or writing it off against capital in the case of losses; or

3. Restructuring the loan and selling it to another bank in the form of a securitized loan or some kind of financial product; and

4. Placing bad assets in a bad bank that is to be auctioned off in a safe and stable manner. This is, of course, capitalized and managed through the beneficence of government debt.

Banks are also trying to find new ways to lend money, but they are in defensive mode and are trying to cut costs, so they often spin their wheels. (We will see in another chapter that while the banks are spinning their wheels, entrepreneurs enter and find new ways to allocate capital, lend money, or manage risk.) Once a loan is distributed, either the borrower pays back the money, or his assets are seized, or the bank writes down the loan. There is no other way for this to play out. That is why banking crises are so pernicious. They truly are balance-sheet recessions in that there is no other choice except for the collective balance sheet to "recess" or "recede." There must be shrinkage, and this only causes asset prices to fall.

What can we say the central bank is doing while all this is occurring? The central bank is accommodating a deleveraging of the banking system while funding a buildup of debt. As we shall see, both of these activities are fundamentally unhealthy over time, but the central banks have no choice (figure 6.3).

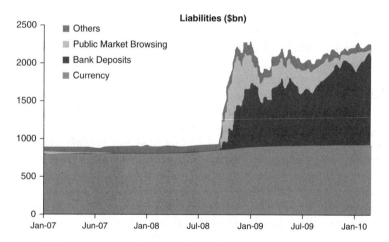

FIGURE 6.3 Federal Reserve Liabilities: Big Change from Mostly Currency to Mostly Risky Assets
Source: Nomura

Once again, it is important to keep in mind that the liabilities of the Fed in this new age of banking are not the creation of money. This is a common mistake of those who say that the central banks are printing money to get out of the problem. It is the furthest thing from the truth. This money is not printed but *recirculated*. It is not new money but old money that finds its way to the central bank and collects 25 basis points.

Why would banks put their money here? They do not have any other use for it. Banks do not want to lend, and people do not want to borrow. The credit engine in the United States, while now functioning better, is still weak and sick. We should think of excess reserves as oil in the oil pan of a car. A car has a system that requires oil to lubricate the engine, but sometimes there is only a need for a certain amount of oil. The remainder of the car's oil, which is in excess of what is required, drains to the bottom and is not used.

These excess reserves sit across from the government debt and mortgage debt assets purchased in quantitative easing by the Fed and are funded mostly by these excess reserves. The obvious question here is what happens to the assets of the central bank when the liability excess reserves (which are assets of the banks in the form of cash) are needed to create loans? This is the $64,000 question. Never in modern history have so many excess reserves been sitting idle in the central bank. If banks suddenly get into the mood to lend, these deposits could be withdrawn by the central bank and then the assets have to shrink.

In the specific case of the Federal Reserve, we will show that the essential role of the U.S. central bank is to stabilize Fannie Mae (FNM) and Freddie Mac (FMAC). The private banks in the United States have terrific LDRs at .62 percent and solid capital bases of about 16× leverage in a remarkably short time. The reason real estate prices are soggy, however, is because Fannie Mae owns half of the mortgage market in America and funds itself through the brain-dead mortgage-backed securities market—*not* through deposits. So, banks are doing well and are looking for new lines of business, and their stock prices are showing it. But the real estate market may crawl along the bottom for a considerable time until Fannie Mae and Freddie Mac are recapitalized or are somehow rehabilitated. As of this writing, 20 percent of U.S. homes are still "under water" (i.e., the amount owed on the mortgage is higher than the value of the home).

There is one risk here. Figure 6.4 shows what happened in 1994 when the U.S. economy finally recovered from the savings and loan crisis of 1989. While banks were licking their wounds from 1990 to 1993, they were very busy buying government bonds rather than lending money to the private sector. See Figure 6.4 to see this buildup. The purple from 1989 to 1993 shows the buildup of government debt to bail out the savings and loans and help out the economy after it entered a recession due to the drop in asset

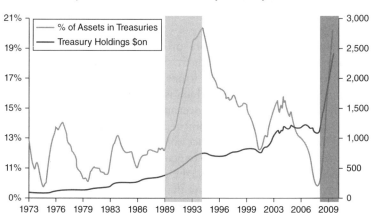

As with S&L crisis, banks will likely buy bonds to
recapitalize with no-risk assets; they could buy US$1.5tn

FIGURE 6.4   Bank Holdings of Government Debt: The Fed Had to Take Debt on
Its Balance Sheet or Rates Would Have Spiked
Source: Nomura

prices. By 1994, the economy exited the slowdown and a boom ensued.
Banks no longer had an appetite for government debt and were inclined to
create risk assets such as car loans, mortgages, construction loans, and loans
for manufacturing; hence the price of bonds dropped as many players sold at
the same time. Consequently, yields rose and caused a crash. Knowing when
the risk appetite for banks is returning is the key to getting bond prices right.
The United States was exiting the slowdown as 2014 drew to a close, but
the Federal Reserve may need to keep rates low, since Europe's banks are in
terrible shape. This may keep yields lower for longer.

When the all-clear sign does in fact appear, what happens to our current
configuration as the preference for risk shifts? Figure 6.4 shows us that as the
banks moved away from holding government debt to lending once again to
the private sector, the holdings of government debt went from 20 percent of
the balance sheet back to 11 percent of the balance of the banks. Guess what
happens to prices of something when suddenly no one wants it? The prices
of government bonds fell hard, and bond yields rose dramatically. This was
the big bond crash of 1994, when yields on the 10-year bond shot up by
several hundred basis points and caused the great bond crash of 1994.

Cut to 2015, and many people are asking what happens to bond yields
if massive government holdings at the Fed (funded by cash provided by the
banks) can no longer be "funded" or paid for by the banks. What if the

banks want to turn this cash into risk assets, such as loans to consumers or businesses? What is the interplay (the tug of war) between this cash that may seek to exit holdings of government bonds and enter a risk trade by way of a loan for a car or for machinery?

This problem is made all the more problematic in 2015 and 2016 because the locus of much of the bonds at stake is in one place. The Fed is a monopolist of government bonds. It has been the sole buyer of these bonds (the opposite of a monopolist, which is the sole seller). It can dictate terms to the seller of bonds (i.e.., the government). If it suddenly goes into the market and is forced to sell government bonds when the banks are in a mood to lend and offload their balance sheet or cash and sovereign risk (while the private sector is in a mood to expend or spend), no one is around to buy these bonds. Both the banks *and* the private sector are engaging in risk-taking behavior. There are concerns that a bond market crash could ensue. Table 6.4 shows that the big three central banks combined hold government debt on their balance sheets that is equivalent to about 25 percent of GDP. This is a big number, and it is a very risky poker game. If one central bank starts to sell its bonds because the economy is healing, this could bring about a crash in the country, which is still building up its government debt load (loose monetary policy). Table 6.4 shows the levels of debt and what we are talking about in dollar equivalent. Central banks have total assets of about $16 trillion. This is about 25 percent of GDP. And the Federal Reserve alone has more than $2 trillion of government debt. It absolutely will move markets if it decides to offload some of these bonds.

There is, of course, a delicate interplay when it comes to understanding where the cash that banks want back and the same cash that the Fed needs to fund government bonds will end up. Some say that excess reserves just won't

TABLE 6.4 Central Banks Comparisons Globally: The Column at Extreme Right Shows Risk Profile (U.S. Best Balance Sheet)

Country	GDP ($BN, IMF '14 EST)	Central Bank Balance Sheet ($BN)	Central Bank Balance Sheet/ GDP	Reserves/ GDP	Currency in Circulation/ GDP	Bonds/ GDP
United States	17,438	4,172	23.9%	15.6%	7.0%	12.5%
China	9,761	4,801	49.2%	32.0%	10.1%	13.5%
Japan	5,228	2,038	39.0%	18.4%	15.6%	31.3%
Europe	13,203	3,034	23.0%	4.2%	9.9%	0.0%
United Kingdom	2,627	661	25.2%	18.8%	3.7%	23.7%

move that quickly—and can't. (Peter Stella is a retired expert on central bank balance sheets from the IMF and claims that this fear of a sudden move away from central bank deposits to risk-taking lending is overblown. Conservative economists say that hyperinflation is right around the corner. Then again, they have been saying this for years.)

The correct answer is that there has never before in modern history been a circumstance where trillions of dollars lying at the Fed, which are funding trillions of dollars of government debt held by the Fed, suddenly are unwound and leave to fund risky assets. The market has many self-correcting mechanisms. For example, if there is a sudden surge in demand for loans for cars or machinery and interest rates suddenly rise (because banks force the Fed to sell bonds and turn the cash into risk assets), then rates may spike and in turn squash newfound risk appetite.

Table 6.5 is illustrative of the size of the issue, in that it is an addition of all the major central banks' balance sheets put together. It is easy to see how many government bonds are currently sitting on the balance sheets of these banks by looking at the asset side. The U.S. Federal Reserve has the largest absolute amount of bonds on its balance sheet with about $2.2 trillion. This is about 15 percent of GDP. In contrast, the Bank of Japan has about $1.6 trillion dollars of Japanese government bonds (JGBs) on its balance sheet, which is a whopping 32 percent of GDP. This may rise to 50 percent of GDP if the full force of Abenomics is brought to bear as planned.

There are some interesting peculiarities here. Look at the liabilities side of this combined balance sheet. Voluntary reserves are about US$4.8 trillion. This is money in the West that is sitting idle by banks and deposited into the central bank for a pittance. This is happening because banks simply do not have the confidence to lend and because there is no appetite to lend.

TABLE 6.5   Combined Central Bank Balance Sheet Globally: Central Banks Own $6 Trillion in Government Debt; ECB Has $1 Trillion in Bank Debt

Central Banks Summary (USD BN)

Total government bonds	5,759	Voluntary reserves	4,728
U.S. Treasuries held by the Fed	*2,181*	Required reserves	3,125
U.S. Treasuries held by PBOC	*1,317*	Money in circulation	4,424
U.K. Bonds held by BOE	*623*	Others	2,204
JGBs held by BOJ	*1,637*		
Bank debt held by ECB	1,015		
Risky asset	1,652		
Gold	450		
Others	5,830	Capital	225
Total assets	**14,706**	**Total liabilities and capital**	**14,706**

Think about it: 10 percent of GDP is just sitting and gathering dust. Western Central banks are desperately trying to get this money back in circulation.*

On the flipside, you have required reserves. Almost all of this is in China. China has been dealing with the opposite problem of a booming real estate sector that will not go down. It is dealing with an asset price surge that has forced the PBOC to *force* banks to hold their cash at the central bank in the form of deposits that receive about 1 percent. China can, if it wants, lower the required reserves, but it still is concerned about asset inflation. So the tug of war continues. China bottles up the excess liquidity of the world in the form of required reserves, and the West has almost the same amount of cash sitting around that it wants to circulate in the economy.

Furthermore, if the Federal Reserve does shrink its balance sheet, there is much concern around large fixed income funds like PIMCO. A sudden rise in yields across the yield curve could do great damage to the capital of the retirement holdings of older people. People who are holding the actual funds could see a loss of capital as the value of these funds drops. This is political dynamite in a rapidly aging population. Politicians will put immense pressure on policymakers to stop the carnage in the bond market. This may cause the Federal Reserve to implement policies to discourage banks from taking risk and, instead, reconsider holding government bonds. This is all terra nova for policymakers globally, and outcomes are uncertain. An unwinding of this vast proportion has simply never been tried before. Anyone who claims to know how this will unwind is as deluded as the person who predicted the outcome of World War I accurately in 1914. It is impossible to know, and there are myriad forces at play that can push things one way or another.

Learning Tools: 06_The_End_Of_Mercantilism.pdf

This presentation on central banks is a good navigational tool to help understand central bank balance sheets as well as other forces, such as hedge funds, private equity funds, and sovereign wealth funds. A classic work on this topic is *Essays on the Great Depression*, edited by Ben Bernanke.

---

*In January 2015, the European Central Bank announced a package with its affiliates that it would buy an additional $1.3 tr in government debt, bank debt, and other risk assets. This brings the total central banks holdings to slightly under $20 trillion. This is approaching 30% of global GDP.

CHAPTER 7

How Bankers and Policy Rescuers Affect Stocks, Foreign Exchange, and Property

Do banks really have that much of an effect on asset prices given the other forms of credit? The answer, of course, is yes. Look at Figure 7.1. We saw this in a previous chapter and it is a vital chart for understanding the investment cycle. Global liquidity is like the phenomenon of high and low tides. There is never more or less water in the world in any one day; it is just that the moon's location affects the water. When the moon is passing over Asia, water levels in Asia are pulled up by the moon's gravitational force. Water levels in the Atlantic Ocean on the other side of the Earth are pushed lower.

Figure 7.1 is a vital chart that shows this effect. Right now in 2015, rates in the West are zero, and there is an extreme low tide of credit. The Western countries are together experiencing a deleveraging of balance sheets, which is necessary to correct the extreme and unsustainable imbalances caused by the global financial crisis. Some countries in the West are moving back to normalcy more quickly than others. In general, however, here is an extreme low tide underpinned by zero rates, which are necessary to help banks and businesses have wider spreads between cost of funds and returns on assets. As we mentioned earlier, equilibrium is achieved by a falling loan/deposit ratio (LDR), which can get to about 0.8, and a falling leverage level, which can get to about 12–14.

At the same time, Asian and other emerging markets are having a high tide because their currencies are tied to the U.S. dollar and their banking systems are healthy. As a result, they are receiving inappropriately low interest rates. Their rates need to correspond to U.S. dollar–based rates or their currencies would rise rapidly in value. With low rates and a liquid banking system with low leverage, they have been on a bonanza; their LDRs are

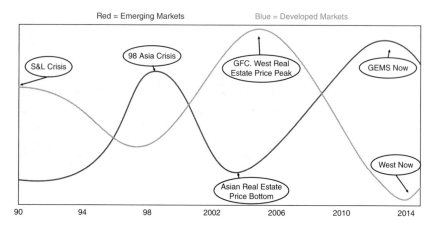

Red = Emerging Markets   Blue = Developed Markets

FIGURE 7.1   Western and Eastern LDR Movements (1990–2014): Uncapped LDRs Create Massive Instability

rising from 0.8 to 1, and their leverage levels are rising from 13–14 times to 17–19 times. Australia, a case in point, has seen a large increase in leverage and a very high LDR of 1.2. As can be seen in Figure 7.2, Australia is a classic example, compared against Spain. As Spain collapsed in both LDR and leverage levels, Australia has risen. In turn, Australian property prices have risen by about 50 percent since 2008, and Spain's property prices have fallen by about 50 percent.

Spain's prices fell off a cliff as the LDR fell back to 1 from 1.7. This meant that Spanish banks were closing out loans and writing off bad debt while Spanish savers had to increase savings and forgo luxury activities, as well as watch property prices dive. In this environment, rates in Europe and the United States had to be cut to accommodate the pain. As this happened, Australian rates also fell, since the Australian dollar is very much tied to the euro and the U.S. dollar. So as rates were cut, Australian banks had a chance to increase leverage and keep the LDR high. Leverage for the banks went from 15 in 2008 to 21 by 2014. Subsequently, housing prices rose substantially.

At this point in the cycle, Australian prices are among the most expensive globally, and Spanish prices are very cheap. An average apartment in Barcelona or Madrid is about half of the price of an apartment in Sydney or Melbourne. Many Chinese entrepreneurs are wandering around Spain now, buying up properties. At the same time, they are lightening up on Australian properties. The differential between Australian and Spanish prices is becoming irresistible, so we may be seeing a moving of the low tides toward

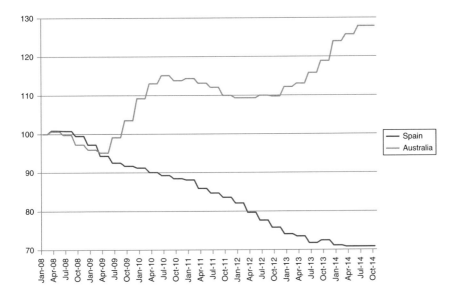

FIGURE 7.2   Spanish and Australian House Prices: High Australian LDR in Funded Boom while Falling LDR in Spain Caused Falling Prices

Australia and the high tides toward Spain. At this point, I am much more of a buyer of Spanish property than Australian property; the same goes for banks as well. As we shall see, property and banks tend to move together, but the banks tend to move 6 months or so in advance of property—on the way down and the way up.

Similarly, China has had a polar opposite experience compared to the United States in the past few years. Figure 7.3 shows the powerful advance in Chinese property while U.S. property prices collapsed. This is exactly what one should expect. While the average prices of U.S. houses fell 30 percent and have only been recovering recently, the average prices of Chinese homes are up 30 percent. In fact, they are up much more than this in cities such as Beijing, Shanghai, Guangzhou, and Shenzhen. This is because China had a liquid and functioning banking system in 2008, which was then given zero rates. We cannot forget that more than 70 percent of China's total trade is with the United States, so the currency is, for all intents and purposes, linked to the U.S. dollar. I have heard very solid bank portfolio managers say that China is the 13th district of the Federal Reserve.

As with Spain and Australia, I would rather own U.S. property than Chinese property now. This is not because China's property sector is about to crash. This kind of thinking is muddled, in my view. The point is that

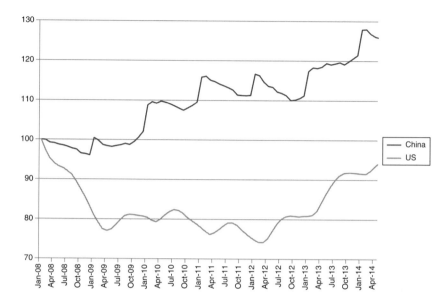

FIGURE 7.3   Chinese and U.S. House Prices: Rising PRC Leverage Created Price Boom; Falling U.S. LDR Caused Fall

I think the currency has peaked. In this sense, a big move in the Chinese yuan renminbi (CNY) for the Chinese—who have been able to amass large amounts of wealth—means that the world is very likely not going to get any less cheap.

My argument is that the government does not want to see the CNY strengthen beyond 5 to the U.S. dollar. So the government will, over the course of the next few years, accelerate capital outflows, and real estate around the world will appear absurdly cheap compared to the stratospheric levels of prices in Beijing and Shanghai. Think about being able to buy 8 or 9 apartments in Barcelona for the price of just one apartment in Shanghai. The same is true for Los Angeles, even for houses near the beach. A nice apartment in Santa Monica with a view of the ocean is still a fraction of the price of an apartment in an upscale neighborhood in Beijing or Shanghai. Plus, there is a sense in which property acts as a store of value for Asians that is not apparent to Western economics. This is historical in nature, but many Chinese people prefer property over investment any time. In addition, mainland Chinese have had a terrible experience with their own stock (it is down 60 percent from the top) market but have managed to make fortunes in property. As a result, they will go with what they know and have had good luck pursuing.

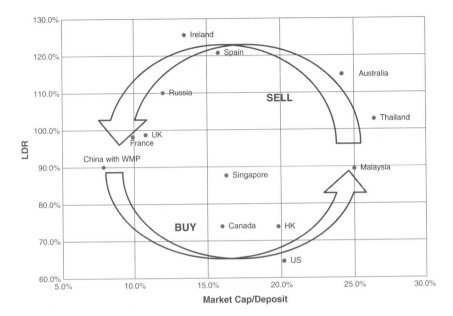

FIGURE 7.4 Schulte Bank Valuation Model: Uncontrolled LDRs Cause Constant Cycles of Instability

Figure 7.4 is a favorite of mine because it shows very nicely how the financial system works. The countries with the high tide discussed above are the ones that are moving from the bottom left to the top right. The countries with a low tide need to have low rates to accommodate a drop in the LDR through painful deleveraging.

This really shows the theme of my book in terms of price action. The X-axis is a pure valuation parameter that cuts out all the noise of intangibles, capital structure, and other cost structures. When we get down to the pure essence of what a bank's value is, we can reduce it to the faith of a depositor who places his cash in that bank that the cash will be available on the next day at 100 cents on the dollar. The ultimate value of a bank lies in its deposit franchise. The value of a bank does not lie in its ability to raise vast amounts of long-term debt from capital markets. Therefore, that is the denominator of the number of the X-axis. The numerator is market cap. This is purely the value that Mr. Market places on the bank today. As we have demonstrated amply in this book, the stock prices of banks are a smarter beast than other stocks, in my opinion. They have an uncanny way of sniffing out problems several quarters before the problems arise. So, market cap/deposits as a way to get to the pure essence of a bank's franchise value and the value that the market (the stock price) places on this is an excellent way to look at banks.

We see a world where the market cap/deposits goes round and round in a cycle. I submit that any economic model must be built around credit indicators like this, or these economic models have absolutely no value whatsoever. (This is the main lesson of the global financial crisis and so many other crises that economists have completely missed.) The market cap/deposits for the banks usually go to a high of about 30 percent (or 30 cents of market cap for every dollar of deposits) at the top of a cycle. This is simply doing an aggregate of market cap for all publicly traded bank stocks and looking at it against all deposits for the banks (these numbers are easily retrievable from any number of websites). It corresponds to a bank passing through a peak of 1 on the LDR. After this, bank stocks will fall, since Mr. Market realizes that the use of wholesale funding is more risky than using deposits to fund loan growth. After this, market cap/deposit will glide down to about 20 percent and hold there. When a full-blown crisis starts, the LDR is usually about 1.2–1.3 for a period of time that could range from 12 to 18 months. This is the peak of asset prices (property and currency values included). Prior to the crisis hitting in a full-blown way, stocks will have another leg down and hover at about 15 percent of deposits.

When the banking crisis hits and credit stops, what is generally intensifying the crisis is the sudden withdrawal of wholesale funding from banks that are scared out of a country because these bankers observe credit downgrades from ratings agencies, isolated defaults, falling property prices, or a weakening of the currency. In general, though, we harken back to the immortal words of John Maynard Keynes. Bankers, he says, are always ruined together. They are "ruined in a conventional and orthodox way along with their fellows, so that no one can really blame them."[*] In other words, bankers almost always go over the cliff together. Thus has it always been.

At the peak of a financial crisis, investors should watch these market cap/deposit numbers like a hawk. These numbers will tend to collapse to 5 percent to 7 percent at the peak of a crisis, when the panic is at its most extreme. At this point, it is probably prudent for investors to start bottom fishing. Politicians at this point are dragged into a rescue because they are presented with a fait accompli by bankers, which goes like this: The banking system is collapsing. All credit will stop soon. Social disorder will take over if you do not step in and do something. Politicians on the right (call them the Austrians) will say that a cleansing is "long overdue" and banks that extended themselves too much need to shut. Politicians on the left (call them

---

[*] J.M. Keynes, *The Consequence to the Banks of the Collapse of Money Values*, 1931.

the Keynesians) will say that fiscal deficits are needed to provide some boost to the middle class as unemployment rises. Thus is the debate we have seen for a century. I submit it is all noise, since the banks will not function again until bad assets are pushed overboard. LDRs need to adjust downwards from 1.3 or so to .85 or so, and tangible leverage needs to adjust downwards from 30× or so to 15×. The laws of gravity of financial systems are such that whether you use a mix of Austrian or Keynesian economics, a recovery will not come about until liquidity has been restored to the banking system. So, why is the banking system left out of the economic modeling of cycles? It beggars the imagination. Furthermore, we saw in the previous chapter that Keynesian deficit spending is nothing other than foam on the tarmac as the damaged economic airplane comes in for a landing. The foam prevents a large and deadly fire as the damaged plane lands. Keynesian economics does nothing to fix the plane in the air. In other words, Keynesian economics may be a necessary evil, but it is a subsidiary and accidental element to a much larger and powerful adjustment of the credit system. It is a palliative, not a cure. It is preventative medicine for a chronic injury that *might* prevent further deterioration.

So, as governments intervene, it tends to be at the level of 5 percent to 7 percent of deposits. This was the case with both the U.S. and U.K. banks in 2008, for instance.

LDRs AND DETERMINING CURRENCY VALUES

To bring home the point, Figure 7.5 shows up another important data point about the effect of excessive LDRs on currencies. LDRs are an important way

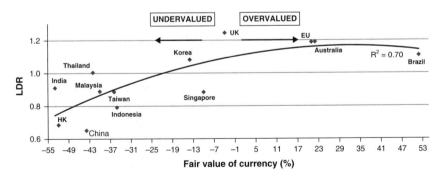

FIGURE 7.5 LDR versus Fair Value of Foreign Exchange: As LDR Rises, a Country's Asset Prices Rise as Leveraged Buyers Splurge
Source: China Construction Bank

to determine the extent to which currencies are overvalued, and Figure 7.5 shows the relationship. Countries with a low LDR are those that have not yet fully deployed their deposits. In other words, the banks have not turned all their deposit liabilities into loans. So, there is scope for creating more credit for citizens of various jurisdictions, and the value of real estate and other assets can be inflated. The fair value of the foreign exchange rate should reflect this.

The most accurate reflection of any foreign exchange rate is justifiably based on some form of purchasing power parity. A basket of goods in one country should, more or less, be the same as a basket of goods in another country, as expressed in that country's currency. This is called purchasing power parity (PPP). That is the principle of Figure 7.5. The X-axis shows the fair value of a country's exchange rate based in PPP. The Y-axis shows the LDR. It should be seen as no surprise that the higher the LDR, the great is the overvaluation of the currency, because after all of a country's domestic savings are used up, additional wholesale borrowing from international banks drives up values for assets to unsustainable levels. This is because the ability to drive up asset values (homes, buildings, cars) by any additional value depends on any extra additional money from the outside world. This money has come in only *after* all of the domestic savings of a country have been deployed into leverage to drive up asset prices. Do you think that international wholesale lending is going to find bargains after locals with far better knowledge and intelligence have picked over the assets? I very much doubt it. This is the problem with wholesale lending. They are, by definition, latecomers to the party. This is part of the problem that wholesale lending bank Standard Chartered faces in 2015. It got caught holding the bag in China commodity warehousing, Indonesian coal companies, and Indian energy deals, among others. They lent into the peak of the commodity boom and are now paying the price with a 50% drop in the stock price in 12 months.

The result of Figure 7.5 is that Brazil and Australia are the most exposed currencies globally. They have both been accidental beneficiaries of China's infrastructure buildout and both have shipped billions of tons of coal, iron ore, and other commodities. China's physical infrastructure is now built out, and Australia and Brazil have borrowed heavily against future commodity production from the ground. This is a problem for both countries, because cities such as São Paulo, Sydney, Rio, and Melbourne are among the most expensive cities in the world. Something has to give, and presumably that something will be the currency. This is because the financial systems of both countries take time to deleverage, adjust prices, and replenish savings. This is not a good place to be for equity investors.

THE BEST INDICATOR FOR VALUE FOR FINANCIALS

Do price-to-earnings ratios (P/Es) tell us anything about bank stocks? If you try to find a correlation of P/Es and other fundamentals for any time in the credit cycle, good luck. It is highly likely that you will find nothing but a random scatterplot of dots on a chart of P/Es relative to just about anything. P/Es simply do not matter when it comes to banks. This is because the stock prices of banks have far more to do with capital structure than with earnings. Bank stocks seem to be more interested not in *how much* money banks make as much as *how* they make money.

Stock prices have a way of sniffing out "unsafe" earnings that are high but unsustainable. In this way, the absolute amount of earnings per share (EPS) is an irrelevancy. And the state proves that out. See Figure 7.6 for a snapshot in time. It shows the P/E of banks globally against the LDRs. P/Es and other measures create the same conclusion: P/Es have correlations close to zero with most criteria in bank stocks.

In Figure 7.6, we see a phenomenon that I have noticed for many years: As the return on equity (ROE) goes up, the P/E goes down. This is, prima facie, somewhat surprising. As the ROE goes up, one should expect a bank stock to fetch a higher multiple. After all, the capacity to create earnings on

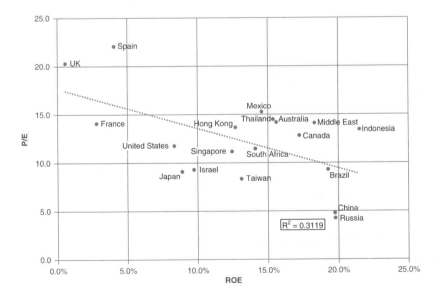

FIGURE 7.6 P/Es and ROE for Banks: P/Es Have Nothing to Do with Bank Valuations and Should Never Be Used

a certain equity base is actually accelerating. The reason the P/E falls and the stock is derated as ROE accelerates is simple.[1] The only way to "goose" earnings for a bank that has exceeded its normal ability to create an ROE of 12 percent to 14 percent is by wholesale borrowing as the LDR exceeds 1.

Again, this is the theme of this book and the proof of the folly of thinking that wholesale funding is a legitimate way to create shareholder value, belied by the way that stocks behave after a bank has achieved an artificial ROE of about 18 percent to 20 percent. Not only are P/Es an unreliable gauge, but when banks move to wholesale borrowing as the LDR exceeds 1, the P/Es bend backwards and decline. This shows that wholesale banking causes a derating of a bank stock and destroys shareholder value. So beware of banks with low P/Es and high ROE. They are cheap for a reason, and often correctly are ferreting out danger.

WHAT ABOUT ROE AS A MEASURE IN ITSELF?

Many people use ROE to look at bank stocks, but this also belies a big problem. Many banks in the world are funded in their capital structure entirely by retained earnings. ROE offers false signals, because as banks engage in wholesale borrowing, the capital structure changes to a more dangerous type of funding. By definition, as the LDR passes 1, banks must borrow through long-term loans, and this becomes part of the capital base. So, the ROE *rises*, and at the same time, the quality of earnings goes down because it is predicated on debt that is international in nature and can leave tomorrow. ROE does not take this into consideration. That is why, even though P/Es have a low correlation, the overall correlation is actually negative. In other words, as the ROE goes up, the P/E tends to go down.

The bottom line? P/Es are largely irrelevant in analyzing banks and will, more likely than not, tell you counterintuitive information. The better the ROE, the lower the P/E. This is because an ROE above 15 percent usually is generated by dangerous and unstable wholesale funding, which Mr. Market rightly concludes is very risky and, therefore, merits a derating.

AS WITH ALL LIVING CORPORATIONS, RETURN ON CAPITAL IS EVERYTHING

This is why the banks like Credit Suisse, Deutsche Bank, and Barclays are problematic these days: They are *not* funded predominantly by deposits but mostly by long-term debt. Deutsche Bank is not really a bank; it is a financial holding company funded by long-term debt. Only one-third of its balance sheet is deposits. Two-thirds of its balance sheet is long-term debt. The same is true for Credit Suisse. If you add the long-term debt to the equity, you arrive at the return on capital (net income divided by total equity plus long-term debt). Of course, deposit liabilities are not included in this calculation. This is an entirely reasonable, accurate, and sensible return on capital calculation, which, as we will see, is the precise way to measure value for a bank. After all, the long-term debt is a real liability of the banks and must be included in the capital structure. Deposit liabilities are what makes a bank a bank. People have trust and confidence that the money they deposit today will be theirs for the taking tomorrow. The bank gets to keep these deposits as long as the bank maintains full faith and credit of the depositors. The bank is not obligated to return it at a certain date. This is obviously true of checking deposits that sit around bearing zero. Long-term debt, on the other hand, must be returned to bondholders when the debt matures. It does *not* belong to the bank but accrues interest while the principal must be returned to investors. This is the difference between deposits and principal. One is capital and one is deposits. The difference is clear for all to see. A bank is like any corporation. Long-term debt and equity are the capital base from which the bank grows its earnings.

This is an important difference. Principal is a true debt liability that has covenants and a host of legal obligations that simple deposits do not. Indeed, most banks have no long-term debt and massive long-term debt is a very new phenomenon in the history of banking. The difference between deposits and principal is vital to understanding why the European banks are stuck in the financial quicksand from which the ECB is trying to extract them. Vast amounts of long-term debt need to be refunded to keep the assets alive. Without relief from the ECB, the market is telling us that the long-term debt funding of these banks is problematic. Finance companies (non-bank financial institutions) do not rely on deposits and usually blow up in a crisis as short-term funding (6 months to three years) is pulled while long-term assets (five years to 30 years mortgages for house and buildings) need to be funded. If this debt is pulled, the assets must be sold and a domino effect occurs. This is why the ratings agencies are forced to play a game of keeping investment ratings on banks that are trading like they are going out of business. If the banks are downgraded to junk status (BBB+ or below), institutions such as insurance or pension funds that hold the debt of the banks (not the deposits) very often must sell the debt as a fiduciary obligation to *their* shareholders. Thus, central banks must enter the fray and prop up the balance sheet of the banks by buying the debt. This is way beyond the protection of shareholders. It is the protection of equity shareholders, bond holders, *and* the viability of the pension and insurance system that fund themselves through vast holdings of bank debt. There is a lot at stake,

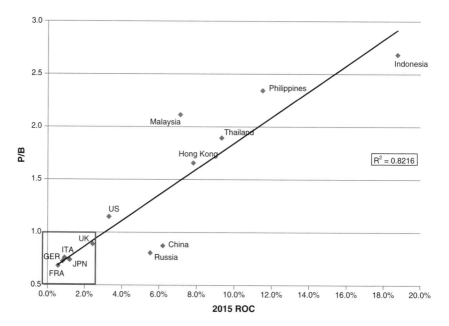

FIGURE 7.7 Return on Capital versus Price/Book for Global Banks: Return on Capital Works! The Banks at the Bottom Left Are the Broken European Banks

which is why so many "Austrian" economists and free-market purists hold their noses and agree to this form of socialist economics.

Furthermore, common sense matches the opinion of the market. As can be seen from Figure 7.7, this is the problem with the world. Five members of the G7 have broken capital structures. This does not include the Swiss banks, which also are in that square and have problematic capital structures. Over the years, these universal investment banks accumulated insufficient equity capital through retained earnings and, at the same time, accumulated long debt (they issued hundreds of billions of dollars of debentures to pension and insurance funds) to fund their balance sheets. This caused a collapse in the return on capital, which precisely explains the appalling valuations being attached to the equity valuations. As an example, Deutsche Bank at the end of 2014 was trading at 0.5× book. This is one of the worst valuations globally, and reflects its terrible returns on capital.

Similarly we can see that the banks in Japan, France, Italy, and the United Kingdom are all creating returns on equity that are very poor, indeed. The average for this group is less than 2 percent. (Notice that the U.S. banks have achieved some degree of liftoff, with accelerating returns on capital at 4 percent, and are being rerated.) But the U.K. and European banks have returns below 2 percent at a time when the cost of capital is still 6 percent or 7 percent. This is not a sustainable equation. The fundamental understanding of markets (and one that I think reflects reality) is that if the return on capital is greater than the cost of capital, stocks rise. If the return on capital is below the cost of capital, stocks fall. This explains perfectly the situation in the European banks now.

Indeed, Figure 7.7 tells us that bank stocks are being driven by return on capital. The greater the return on capital, the higher the price/book the bank receives. This seems axiomatic. Right now, the Indonesian and Filipino banks have among the highest returns on capital globally and also have some of the healthiest LDRs globally. Thai, Malaysian, and Hong Kong banks are right on the line and follow this trend. One of the exceptions is China, where the banks are offering high returns on capital, high dividend yields, and strong bond price performance but have been languishing for two years due to the impression that they have higher non-performing loans than they are admitting. Time will tell if that is really the case.

If we bring this down to the stock level, Figure 7.8 shows a fairly uncanny relationship between returns on capital and valuations of price/book. This makes great sense and is a robust way to examine whether to buy banks. In Figure 7.8, for instance, we might conclude that Metro Bank is somewhat overvalued. And we might conclude that Bank Mandiri is undervalued. Funds that do pair trades could sell banks that are on the left side of the line and buy banks on the right side of the line. This is based on

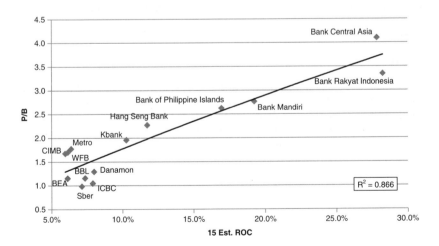

FIGURE 7.8 Return on Capital versus Price/Book: Global Emerging Market Banks Don't Have Bonds, so ROE = ROC

a mean reversion idea that return on capital, over time, is an ideal way to examine valuations on banks.

In conclusion, P/Es are as likely to deceive as they are to assist when it comes to buying or selling banks. They can create a perception of cheapness (especially at the top of a cycle, when ROEs are high), but this could be a honey trap and lead to losses. ROE by itself tells us little unless we incorporate the capital structure of a bank, which may have large amounts of long-term debt. This is why return on capital is ideal. We showed that returns on capital and the price/book have fairly uncanny predictive ability. There are anomalies among and between banking systems, but return on capital in alliance with price/book is very helpful. In periods of extremes on the upside and downside, the best parameters to look at are market capitalization/deposits and LDR. This gives a sense of valuations in the extremes of the bubble, which usually tap out at 30 percent or so and offer selling opportunities. And they offer buying opportunities when the market cap/deposits bottoms out at 5 percent to 7 percent, when there is panicky selling. This is actually a great buying opportunity.

Learning Tools: 07_ROC_For_Banks.pdf

This file contains an analysis of return on capital for financials, which shows the winners and losers in this situation.

Endnote

1. Of course, the correlation on the line of best fit is low, but it is clearly a downward sloping line. This shows that, in particular, the P/E is not an appropriate measure of value for banks. In general and more importantly there is a clear derating of P/Es for stocks that will actually fall as the ROE accelerates. This can create the perception that a bank is "cheap" when in fact the P/E is offering a warning signal.

Interlude

CHAPTER 8

Why Government and Institutions Get Suckered into Debt Binges

*The whole problem with the world is that fools and fanatics are so
certain and wiser people are full of doubts.*
—Bertrand Russell

The development of financial bubbles and subsequent busts I have described in previous chapters now looks surprisingly obvious and predictable. Unfortunately, economists used almost *none* of these rather obvious tools in their prediction of the downturn. There are predictable danger markers and these should be included in all models used to identify and head off dangerous financial bubbles. The market is *not* designed to self-correct; it is designed by bankers to maximize profits at the expense of the commonweal. Greed does not have a built-in moral compass. So, economists and ratings agencies need to incorporate the credit markers noted in previous chapters and do a better job of downgrading banks and/or publicizing hidden dangers so consumers and policymakers have a chance to react. Examples we looked at are:

1. Loan/deposit ratios (LDRs) above 1.15 are dangerous. Let's put it this way: Find a financial crisis that was *not* preceded by a financial system with a loan/deposit ratio of 1.15. You can't.
2. Market cap/deposits of banks above 30 are high and problematic. These high valuations tend to indicate bubbly overvaluation for banks and are more a sign of danger than a sign of health.

3. Bank market cap/total market cap of a country above 25 percent is a warning. In most banking crises, it is important to watch the market cap of banks relative to the market cap of the entire stock market. When the banks get close to 30 percent of market cap of the total market, then there is danger. This is also a sign of extreme valuation. A safe number should be 12 percent to 18 percent of market cap of the entire stock market.

4. Entities such as the International Financial Accounting Standards Board should never have been allowed to actively advocate for the creation of offshore investment vehicles to create hidden leverage. Liabilities should only ever be found squarely on the balance sheet of a financial entity and not hidden away in some obscure vehicle.

5. Ratings agencies should be forced to include market-based mechanisms in their consideration of ratings. Take the example of Petrobras, the national oil company of Brazil. The market currently is showing that the stock is trading at 0.4× book value for several quarters. This is indicating extreme distress in the company, yet S&P as of February 2015 is indicating that the company is investment grade. Equity and fixed income investors are all too often baffled about why ratings agencies are so far behind the curve when market signals are showing loud and clear that there is a problem.

Current account deficits of 3.5 percent to 4.5 percent of gross domestic product (GDP). The flipside of any excessive LDR is always a high current account deficit. The United States in 2007 had a current account deficit of more than 4 percent and a budget deficit of more than 3 percent and no one was warning the investor community. If this were a developing country, the IMF and World Bank would have been screaming about such conditions. There needs to be equal treatment for developing and developed countries—standards that apply to one group need to be applied equally to all. Too often, however, economists dismiss a large current account deficit if it is funded by "high-quality" capital account inflows. They do not realize that these capital account inflows (loans, short-term investments in stocks and bonds, foreign direct investments or FDIs) are almost always pro-cyclical and reinforce frothy domestic activity. When the going is good, capital account inflows rush in. When times turn bad, turning around a large current account deficit will require a devaluation of the currency (just when the LDR and high debt loads peak out) and then the capital account drains as international investors are scared off by recession, devaluation, and falling asset prices. The system is a setup for suckers who are both wholesale lenders and late to the game in equity and fixed income. High current account deficits and high LDRs together are toxic. Look at Spain in 2007. No one was raising the alarm bells when the LDR was above 1.60 and the current account was 6 percent of GDP. This was not a Spanish miracle. It was a Spanish nightmare waiting to happen. The balance of payments system we have in place for the world is *not* self-correcting. It is pro-cyclical in that capital account inflows will tend to rise as the current account deficit rises (in a boom) and fall when the current account turns to surplus (in a bust).

6. Bank stock prices that inexplicably start to fall for a protracted period of time in the midst of an otherwise-rosy credit cycle. Look at the stock price of Citi in 2005. It peaked and began going sideways one year before the crisis was unfolding. The stock prices of banks are fairly smart indicators of things to come. No one was asking questions when the stock price of Lehman Brothers began to go sideways and fall in 2006 despite record profits, yet it was telling us important information. The quality of earnings for banks is far more important than the quantity of earnings.

7. *Leverage below 20.* When the aggregate tangible leverage (leverage minus goodwill) is above 20, problems arise. Again, show me a banking crisis and I will show you a banking system with leverage of 30× or more. The leverage of Lehman was 40× when it collapsed in September 2008. The leverage of Bear Stearns was about the same. Currently, the German banks (Deutsche Bank in particular) and Swiss banks still have quite high levels of leverage, so this merits close examination.

8. Banks need to be chastened about self-involved profit motive. Savvy politicians should know that a credit crisis will drive them from office and prevent banks from getting out of control for their own self-preservation. When banks go down, governments go down soon afterwards.

The markers I have described above are like human temperatures or blood pressure. They are entirely objective and offer guides to health and danger. Why do these booms and busts keep happening if there are independent, verifiable, and repeatable markers? After 25 years of watching people fall into leverage traps over and over again while working for many financial institutions on three continents, I began reading many books on the psychological elements of how humans make financial choices.

WHY ARE WE COMFORTABLE CRAWLING INTO BUBBLES AND STAYING THERE DESPITE DANGERS?

The puzzling question is simple: How and why do individuals and groups get suckered into one financial bubble after another (usually at the top of the market) that ends up popping and subsequently causes vast societal damage, instability, painful unemployment, and often war? More importantly, why do the policymakers in charge of maintaining a civil and stable society enact rules and policies that are inherently unstable and lead to great human misery and political chaos?

The simple, correct, and ridiculous answer is that humans love bubbles. We love making them and we love climbing inside them. While we are in a bubble, we will actually attack anyone who points out that we need to get out of the bubble or dangerous events will befall us. We are all too often the authors of our doom. This sounds preposterous, but it is absolutely true. We love moving into bubbles, bringing in the furniture, and decorating them. We are social animals who need to belong, and bubbles give us the feeling of belonging. They make sense because the group says so. We end up using excessive leverage and buying overpriced assets for the very simple reason that everyone else is doing the same thing, so it can't be a bad idea.

We engage in irrational behavior because we want to belong and fail to ask questions.

Let's take a couple of texts that I think are seminal works that try to understand why people—as a group—take collective decisions that were smart at the beginning but end up being against the collective self-interest. For this is what happens in financial catastrophes. The group at first sees an aim or an objective that is ostensibly smart, but then it pursues some distorted idea of the initial process and the endeavor ends up being a disaster. All kinds of folly befall people when they are in a bubble (military, political, religious, or financial, for they are all the same) and use all sorts of absurd justifications to maintain a course of action that leads to human misery. (Recall the papers produced by the U.S. Federal Reserve in 2007, which said that there was no indication that the real estate market was in danger!)

The two-time Pulitzer Prize winner Barbara Tuchman wrote the seminal work *The March of Folly* to describe how large groups of people (in fact, she was only interested in horrendous decisions made by large groups that turned into multigenerational catastrophes) make unbelievably stupid decisions that, at the time, seemed perfectly rational and, indeed, full of alleged self-interest. Among other historical examples, she cites the folly of World War I, the Vietnam War, and the destruction of the Catholic Church by the Medici Popes.

Another woman who offered illumination on this issue is Margaret Heffernan, who wrote a bestseller called *Willful Blindness*. She uses more modern anecdotal evidence to show how delusional and deranged thinking enters institutions quietly and silently through the floorboards, causing incredible damage to humans during perfectly preventable situations such as financial catastrophes, offshore oil explosions, or death from unheeded cancer-causing substances. It goes on and on. As with Tuchman, Heffernan demonstrates that corporate, financial, religious, or health-related phenomena in which groups engage in deranged thinking have remarkably similar dynamics.

In the context of financial markets, let's weave together some of the thoughts of Tuchman and Heffernan. Why do we make mistakes when it comes to processing perfectly objective financial data that can be easily calculated by one and all in repeated experiments? The easy but absurd answer is that we seek out data to satisfy our desires. Indeed, the research departments of many banks were looking for data in 2007 and 2008 to show that things were fine. Central banks were doing the same. This is a natural human weakness not only in financial fiascos but also in corporate, religious, and health-related issues. We use our five senses to receive sensory data that is in fact subjective and that can satisfy inbuilt biases and beliefs about ourselves. As Martin Heidegger put it in a profoundly simple way, "Desire creates perception."

Why do we seek data to support our desires? We have a genetic fear of being left out!

What is the starting belief about ourselves that is inbuilt, genetic, and all too natural? We are social creatures and we want and need to belong. Therein lies the foundation of financial bubbles. So much research points in the direction of the stark reality that we just do not want to be left out. We would rather be wrong than alone. We need the group to make sense of ourselves, so without the group we are missing something. Heffernan goes into fascinating detail on the genetic foundation of belonging in her book. We are, all too often, at the mercy of our genes without knowing it. It takes a great deal of strength and insight to go against the tide. Warren Buffett said you should buy when others are selling and sell when others are buying. Alas, Heffernan makes the fascinating claim that our genetic makeup tells us to belong and fit in. This is the core of so much human misery. We do things because others are doing them and not because they are smart or wise.

The corollary to this is that if the group says something is good for me, then the group knows better than I do. Both Tuchman and Heffernan make the point that we are designed to obey and fit into the group whose decisions we would rather adhere to than be exiled. So, when a financial bubble comes along, we jump straight into the center of it and we ride it into oblivion for the simple reason that everyone else is doing the same thing. Myriad examples in Heffernan's book show that we are genetic lemmings whether we like it or not. One striking example is an asbestos mine in Montana which Heffernan visited. Even with overwhelming evidence that asbestos is bad for humans—and with many of the town's population dying of lung cancer—the vital need for employment and the power of the group astonishingly caused the people of the town to continue to work in the mine until it was shut down by the government. Heffernan asked many of the townspeople why the owner of the mine offered to give free lung X-rays each year. The people she interviewed thought it was because the mining company was looking after the miners' interests. This is a chilling example where the group can cause people to take action that is in direct opposition to their own interests.

HUMAN FOLLY: BELIEVING IN SOMETHING IS BETTER THAN BELIEVING IN NOTHING, AND INJUSTICE IS BETTER THAN DISORDER

Let's dig down a little further and see what other forms of crowd delusionality are at work in bubbles. Many other absurd forms of thinking can be derived from following the group without any reflection. We saw that the group offers a context for meaning. It offers safety. It offers a belief system of what can be seen as good and bad. So—the group should direct us. Right? Most of the time this is correct. But often this can go off the rails when it comes to excessive greed, religious fervor, racism, or plain cruelty.

The common misperceptions that cause people to be dragged into financial bubbles revolve around a few core beliefs. People are not so much gullible as they are designed to believe that the group knows better than they do. The corollary of this is that the group should direct us. Furthermore, we are designed to avoid conflict. Another corollary is that wrong beliefs are better than no beliefs. If all of my friends believe that house prices will go up forever, then we should go along with this.

In bubbles, there is an air of invulnerability, and the naysayers must be discredited.

Another of these core human beliefs is the following: *Injustice is better than disorder.* Order, therefore, is better than justice. If people think that orderly accumulation of as much credit as possible for as long as possible is a good thing, then so be it. If society says that the accumulation of credit is a social good that is to be pursued for its own sake, then why question this? In bubbles, there arises an air of invulnerability. The project, the bet, the trade, and the investment simply cannot go wrong. So, why not borrow and use leverage to increase the bet? (When I was inside Lehman Brothers in 2007, this is exactly the way it felt.) Those who are on the outside and warn about the consequences of an excessive buildup of debt can be ignored because they do not understand the "group." They just don't get it. Those who protest can be ignored, delegitimized, and pushed away as being fools. "We get it and they don't."

When this group psychosis takes over, issues of prudence and justice are thrown out the window. And as principles are thrown out the window, as Tuchman demonstrates with many examples throughout history, when the group makes mistakes, a delusional psychosis takes over and the group protects itself against mistakes at all costs. No one wants to find the source of the problems or to learn from past mistakes. So, any mistakes are covered up, dismissed as random pitfalls. Or, they are called *black swans*, which can't possibly happen again. The ex post facto justifications in financial bubbles are precisely a sign of the bubble and not an excuse for why thinking went wrong.

While in these financial bubbles, the group psychosis becomes very rigid. In his prescient article in the *New Yorker* on the Chicago School of Economics, John Cassidy makes exactly this point.[1] The Chicago school had gathered so much credibility and confidence over several decades that it became a power unto itself, with no one around to ask questions. No one was asking why a school so famous and revered kept on failing at predicting recessions and downturns. No one asked why the Chicago School did not even use credit in its models. No one was asking questions—and they were living in a bubble. When I wrote about the dangers of a rapid buildup of debt prior to the bursting of the Asian bubble in 1997, people in my firm wanted to have me fired and the financial secretary of Hong Kong called me a "second-rate hack analyst." The group will go a long way to destroy those who point out the bubble. This is true in finance, religion, health care, auto safety, and many other endeavors. The Cassandra or whistleblower needs to be destroyed for the group's delusionality to be maintained. (Cassandra was the daughter of the King of Troy and warned him not to let the Trojan Horse enter the walls of the city or Troy would face total destruction. Cassandra was thrown from the walls of Troy, and Troy was destroyed when the Trojan Horse was allowed into the city. We always kill the messenger.)

We jump into bubbles because we crave conformity. We are designed to adapt to the habits of our peers. (Heffernan makes the point in her book that belonging activates opioids for our brains as a genetic reward for "hanging in there.") The group offers meaning. And the group actually does help, a lot of the time. But excessive fitting in, when taken to extremes, causes people to become blind to risks. The meaning offered by the group means I need to seek out data to confirm my beliefs. No one wants to be the bearer of bad news, and this goes right to the top. The top brass do not want to hear the bad news, so the Cassandras are killed off. The absence of vigilance and excessive risk-taking are, according to Heffernan, a kind of group derangement.

When we are tired, we are even more prone to join the group, because we are too tired to think for ourselves

In the workforce of banking, there has been a terrible ethic of overwork for the sake of overwork. This causes what Heffernan refers to as economized thinking. When we are tired, we economize, and the first thing to go is our social and ethical thinking. Tired minds are gullible and morally blind.

So, believing is easier than doubting. A tired mind is obedient and unquestioning. We focus on order. We ignore consequences. Authority becomes our conscience. We follow the "true believers" and we learn the short-cut language to fit in. Is it any wonder why so many chronically overworked people in banking (and these people often come from great families and previously had well-functioning moral compasses) end up making terrible ethical choices that, over the years, have wrecked the reputations of one bank after another?

In this kind of deluded dynamic of chronic overwork and tiredness, we give up seeking out risks. Heffernan makes the case that this not only happened in banks but also at British Petroleum. We have selective bias. Our imagination fails us as we stop considering worst-case scenarios and we stop having contingency plans. This was in fact the conclusion of a government study that examined why the Federal Reserve failed to see the whole crisis coming. The conclusion of the report was that the Fed failed in that they had no contingency plans. Their collective imagination was nowhere to be found. They did not see it coming because they were in a collective psychosis, such as the ones described by Tuchman and Heffernan. No one has a monopoly on truth. And when we are overworked or tired—whether it is a derivatives trader in New York or an oil rig worker in Louisiana—judgment falters and we make mistakes.

11 RULES TO AVOID GETTING PULLED INTO A BUBBLE

When we attack the messenger or try to discredit any criticism of our own self-constructed bubbles, we are trying as a group to discount important data points that will help us make better decisions. This elimination of the facts that do not correspond to our worldview (or bubble or delusion, call it whatever you like) is referred to as *cognitive dissonance*. How do we avoid cognitive dissonance, and how do we avoid getting sucked into bubbles? Avoiding this pitfall is the key to long-term wealth creation. The reason is simple. Markets are designed to kick us in the teeth. They only ever bottom out and rise after every one has sold (i.e., when there are no more sellers). And they only ever peak and begin to fall after every one has bought the market (i.e., when there are no more buyers, markets cannot go up). Good investors must think counterintuitively and go against the grain. Susan Cain's book *Quiet* is also excellent in this regard, for she asks us to acknowledge the outsiders, the introverts, and the Cassandras who may have better insight than the noisy and overconfident alpha males. This is the same idea that Warren Buffett propounds: Buy when others are selling, and sell when others are buying.

If we combine the wisdom of Tuchman, Heffernan, and Cain, we arrive at some sturdy principles that can offer great wisdom to avoid getting sucked into credit bubbles at precisely the wrong time.

Rule 1: Listen to the Cassandras

Those people who have investment committees for private equity, long-only funds, or hedge funds can also benefit from the combined wisdom of these three women. As difficult as it is, every voice should be heard in the investment committee. The Cassandras should be included at all times. And those who are introverts should always be included, for it is often the introvert who has the best insights. Cain's observant insight is that something like 40 percent of us are introverts, and introverts often consider themselves outsiders and have a unique view on events and the interpretation of these events. Listening to the extroverts all the time is liable to get people into trouble.

Rule 2: Be Aware of the Limits of Your Knowledge

As with the Chicago School, it is wise to keep vigilant about the limits of knowledge. The group should always seek to identify its limits and should always have a devil's advocate to argue the opposite view. The Federal Reserve failed in this regard. The staff did not explicitly encourage opposing views. They did not scout the horizon.

Rule 3: Acknowledge Cognitive Dissonance and Be Disciplined in Debate

This does not mean that there should be an unfocused free for all. Dissonance needs to be structured and practical at all times. Cassandras need to be practical as well. Intellectual bullies should not be tolerated. They destroy the fabric of the group over time. Politeness and a sense of humor should dominate the group investment process at all times.

Rule 4: Create an Atmosphere of Fun and Adventure, Not Fear and Intimidation

During times of great change, people are fearful and confused and are more inclined to allow the group to make decisions for them. A key virtue of the leader is to instill a sense of calm and remove fear as the driving force in decision making. This is because a fearful mind is in lockdown. It does not change, because it does not know how to change. Leadership in an investment committee—or in the battlefield—is all about getting people out of that fearful lockdown and motivating people to take sensible action. In this kind of environment, people need to feel rested and free of fear. A sense of humor is vital in the process of moving people out of fear and into action.

Rule 5: Always Use Examples and Be Concrete

Another vital element of getting people out of fear mode is to use tangible, concrete examples of action that can be taken and that will offer clear options. Putting forward clear examples of how to change and focused means of resolution of conflict is a key element of moving people from fear into a more relaxed mode of change.

Rule 6: Don't Fight a Mob! Have an Executive Committee That Makes Decisions

Openness, Cassandras, controlled conflict, and open disagreement are all important elements of change and healthy progression toward forward movement and smart decisions. There is another element to this as well: It is never wise to fight with a mob. Mobs have a will that can become unruly and destructive. They take on a life of their own and can trample common sense and wisdom. The head of an investment committee needs to have a cadre of trusted leaders who can draw from the resources and occasional wisdom of an unruly mob and come to sound conclusions in a smaller group away from the noise and the haste of conflict, disagreement, and controlled chaos.

Rule 7: Always Go Home at 6:30 P.M. to Prevent Exhaustion

It is becoming all too clear that long hours have a strong tendency to backfire. When we are tired, Heffernan contends, there is a strong tendency for the part of the brain that controls moral judgments and long-term thinking to go on strike. At the same time, the part of the brain that becomes very active is the "flight or fight" limbic system, also known as the "lizard brain." This part of the brain focuses on conflict, short-term survival, and basic needs. Long-term planning and a solid knowledge of consequences go right out the window when we are tired. This is especially true when decision-making drags on late into the night. These kinds of sessions tend to backfire. It is always wise to let people go home early and have a chance to recharge and make decisions in the morning.

Rule 8: Volunteerism Is Vital to Keep a Moral Compass

There is another part of this discussion that is vitally important. Too many people in the financial industry work so much that they do not have any kind of outside interests. In particular, they fall out of society in very basic ways, in that they fail to maintain themselves as a part of a community. This includes giving back and offering some form of volunteerism during which people can both contribute to society and feel better about themselves. Volunteerism seems to refresh the soul and offer an improved sense of self-esteem, which feeds into better judgment, a sense of fulfillment, greater calm, less fear, more self-confidence, and a healthier outlook. All of these should be considered ideal outcomes in that they create more productive employees who are happier and create a work environment that is conducive to sound decisions, better cohesion, less selfish behavior, and an overall improvement in team spirit. No one loses from this ideal.

Rule 9: Watch Out for Telltale Signs of Insularity and Groupthink

A few other danger signs of group insularity that are indicative of an organization heading for trouble are:

- When people speak in coded language, and when the environment encourages anxiety about not fitting in.
- When there is a sliding scale of moral thinking and people begin to take unprecedented risks; this is all too common in the investment process and needs constant vigilance.
- When consensus is a desired outcome and when working for its own sake becomes the norm; people should remain focused at work and go home at a sensible hour.

Rule 10: Get The Data and Resources You Need to Make Good Decisions

When people do not have all the information and all the facts—and when they live in delusion or denial—they are impotent and powerless. They undermine the strength of the group and are bound to fail. This is a group that is blind to alternatives. It is a slave to events.

One of the great reality checks of all time comes from the political analyst and Pulitzer Prize winner Ted White. He wrote the seminal book on the 1960 U.S. Presidential election, in which John Kennedy beat Richard Nixon. His thinking on politics and international affairs, including disastrous decisions made by the U.S. government in Vietnam, led him to three conclusions about what constitutes good strategy:

1. Do I have the right personnel and partners? If not, get them. Remove weak or ineffectual leaders quickly, as they can drag down an organization. Promote good talent quickly.

2. Do I have the proper instruments and resources to succeed? If not, get them. If the resources at my disposal are insufficient to get the job done, then they must be acquired or the team will end up spinning its wheels and "working the levers" rather than working toward an attainable goal.

3. Do I have clarity of objectives? If not, move on. One of the main themes of Tuchman's thinking about folly is that, all too often, institutions inherit thinking and ideas that are simply outdated, wrongheaded, or inappropriate for a new set of circumstances. New regimes should focus on questioning every one of the main assumptions and objectives of a previous regime to make sure that new developments, data, or important trends are incorporated. In this way, the organization can be free of outdated or idiotic assumptions. This is especially true for portfolio managers who take over the portfolios of discredited predecessors. A major overhaul of assumptions is often required.

Rule 11: *Always* Beware the Sunk Cost Theory and Change Course When Necessary

Ted White described in crystal clear language the idea of sunk cost theory. It matters not one single iota how many resources have been poured into a project if the means, the manpower, and the objectives are out of whack. Projects must be constantly reviewed on a quarterly basis, and new leadership, resources, and objectives should be put in place if the old ones do not make sense.

The whole point of promoting vitality in organizations is to encourage robust and dynamic decision making in order to keep the group on its toes and beat out the competition with better ideas, agile implementation, and smart thinking. The avoidance of bubble-think and delusionality precisely means allowing honest dialogue at all times. This means that a crucial way to avoid getting into bubbles is to welcome the whistleblower. The whistleblower is the Cassandra.

CONCLUSION: CASSANDRAS MUST REPLACE DELUSIONS WITH A NEW VISION

Be a Cassandra when necessary, but be politically astute while doing it. Avoiding being suckered into a financial bubble or debt-fueled nonsense often means listening to the introvert. Introverts are often the outsiders. He or she may have had a difficult childhood or may have felt different his or her whole life. Introverts are observers and often have great insight vis-à-vis the happy-go-lucky extrovert who always seems to fit in. Susan Cain's book

Quiet is an excellent description of this phenomenon. She lambastes business school models that train people to be aggressive and listen to the loudest voice in the room. In fact, the introverted quiet person may often have the better insight. They may have a truth worth knowing.

The problem with observant introverts and impolitic Cassandras is that, in their enthusiasm to bring forth painful truths, they trample on people's beliefs in ways that reinforce fear and cause people to get backed into a corner. Like a caged lion, people can lash out against those who are bringing forth the unvarnished truth. This can damage the organization. People who want to warn against stupidity, a bubble, a debt disaster, or plain bad thinking must have some political savvy and diplomacy, because they are bringing forth truth that destroys illusions. People whose illusions are destroyed must have something with which to replace the truth. The definition of an iconoclast is a person who "breaks an image." There must be a new image or a new vision to replace the old one as it is broken apart. Cassandras have a role, but they need to be managed.

Are global banks in a delusional bubble with regard to a revolution in financial technology? Yes! In the next section of the book, we will see how being in a comfortable bubble (in a safe cocoon of status quo thinking) is getting many banks into very serious trouble. Imagine if banks like HSBC, Standard Chartered, or Deutsche Bank took the 11 steps outlined above after some senior changes in management. Imagine how much they might change if they revisited all of their assumptions! Imagine how much new life they could breathe into their organizations.

These banks speak in their own language. They have an insular culture and are disinclined to change. They do not review their core ideals and core values in order to see whether change is necessary. They are so big that many wonder if they have the DNA to change. They are closed off to alternatives. They are not interested in reform from the inside. (Contrast this to firms like Goldman Sachs, which are constantly exercising internal reforms, technology upgrades, and talent improvement.) Many of these large behemoth banks are not paying attention to the Cassandras who are warning about the threat from financial technology. In fact, these banks are dismissing or outright attacking pundits who warn about the threat coming from firms like Lending Club, Alibaba, Paypal, and Kickstarter. This is what happens when people are in bubbles. The behavior of the banks is precisely the behavior of entities in a delusional bubble. They are asking for inevitable decline without taking the 11-step test as shown above. It is bad banking not to know how to fix your financial institution. But the greater danger is delusional or deranged thinking, which includes (1) attacking the Cassandras; (2) using insular and coded language; (3) refusing to question basic assumptions; (4) being unable to implement major strategic reviews; and (5) not jettisoning what does not work in favor of new technologies.

John McFarlane is coming to the helm of Barclays in spring 2015 and is expected to make radical changes. I believe that the reputations of many banks have been tainted, and that the current leadership of many global investment banks needs to go. When new leadership enters the game, it is likely that a more radical agenda will be set and that banks will then adjust. Some banks are already doing this, and the equity market is rewarding them. That is what the next section of this book is all about. Who among the banks is ready to embrace the Cassandras, and who among the upstarts is coming along to drive those who live in comfortable bubbles out of business?

Learning Tools: 08_Leadership_in_a_World_of_Folly.pdf

Investing in a World of Folly: Leadership in the Board Room

Endnote

1. John Cassidy, op cit.

Four

The Revolution in Financial Architecture

CHAPTER 9

Why Is This Revolution Happening Now and Why So Fast?

Innovation is always inconvenient and it seems to come at the worst time. Innovation is spawned by crisis because when times are good, there is no incentive for change, improvement, or revolutionary thinking. When financial crises hit, for instance, there is always profound disruption. There are many reasons for this. First, people are thrown out of work as banks downsize. Some banks simply close and everyone is fired. Credit is hard to come by. Businesses become desperate and need funding. Governments become desperate to stay in power and will do anything to get another vote. Governments need growth to stay in power, and growth requires credit. So, political and economic forces rapidly coalesce to create new opportunities for the lifeblood of an economy: credit. Banks that are saddled with bad debt are offered a lifeline by governments, but many of them simply cannot come back to life quickly enough as the next cycle starts. They are the horse-drawn buggy that dies off when the car is invented. Examples here are erstwhile powerhouses like ING, RBS, ABN Amro, Fortis, Washington Mutual, Bear, Stearns, Lehman Brothers, and many others. They either are gone or are shadows of themselves.

Other, new powers need sponsorship and support from regulators who, after all, work for government. Furthermore, politicians always want to shake hands with the popular guy who has money for campaign funding. If banks are in the doldrums, politicians will find new sources of funding and "street credibility" for upright citizens who have not broken the law. Banks are, quite frankly, in the doghouse. Politicians are staying away. They will do the bidding of the credible new entities in California and not those "banksters" perceived as criminals. (An excellent treatment of this is "All the President's Bankers" by Nomi Prinz.)

DO BANKS HAVE THE DNA TO CHANGE?

In addition to the problems banks have been having, the talented people who know how to create alternative methods for creating credit are often the people who were fired from banks in the downsizing. Others decide to leave because the work environment or the pay is unsatisfactory. Still others look at the cost structure and the bureaucracy of banks and rightly decide that the banks in their current form do not have the DNA to make the leap to a more efficient and responsive machine for new means of credit. So, these people leave in an act of professional self-preservation. In this chapter, we will ask and answer the question of whether banks even have the institutional or bureaucratic will to change. I am not sure they do. Large institutions with hundreds of thousands of people have a hard time changing, especially when they are under legal and regulatory scrutiny and when a good chunk of the talent pool has moved on to greener pastures.

TECHNOLOGY IS ADVANCING WHILE BANKS DEAL WITH THE DA

Our world has been in the grip of astonishing advances in technology. The advance in speed, bandwidth, and new products at the same time now allows all of us to do things in small groups that were barely possible with large organizations eight years ago. In the past 15 years, fixed Internet traffic has increased by an astonishing 1,100 times. Mobile phone data have increased 16,000 times. These numbers are expected to increase by multiples again as we head into the end of the decade. So, this underlying phenomenon has created a riptide underneath the technological waters that is causing the careless or the unprepared to be pulled out to sea and drowned. The waters are wild, indeed.

In addition, financial crises cause central banks to drop interest rates, and capital becomes very cheap for those with access to it. Capital becomes very cheap relative to expensive labor, and where is labor more expensive than in banks? Wages in banks are among the highest, especially in investment banks. So, anyone with a viable product that is a replacement for a product offered by an investment bank will very likely be able to provide this product or service to current customers of the banks at a fraction of the price. Furthermore, these people have access to cheap real estate relative to the very expensive real estate of the banks. Lastly, they also have access to now-cheap and -powerful technology, which makes small groups suddenly highly efficient and competitive. The equation for land, labor, and capital now changes and allows small groups of entrepreneurs to go on the attack in virtually every area of the investment banks.

Let's take a few examples. In the area of ecommerce, companies like Priceline, PayPal, Alibaba, and Tencent have come along and now offer an array of services that are, like termites in a house, eating away at the foundations of traditional banking services, taking away lucrative fees from banks, and offering new services at lower fees with higher margins. Companies like PayPal are FDIC-insured entities commanding a large share of payments.

The revolution of the mobile phone with regard to banking services is also having a profound effect on traditional banking services. It is even calling into question the value of the physical bank branch network. If a new depositor can access his or her banking information on the phone, deposit money, conduct transactions, engage in foreign exchange movements, or even make investment decisions, the physical bank branch becomes an unnecessary (and very expensive) trapping of the days of old.

While this is happening, we see many banks dealing with one fine after another for fraud, conspiracy, insider dealing, money laundering, consumer protection violations, antitrust violations, and many other violations that have resulted in tens of billions of dollars in fines. Ratings agencies are also under heavy pressure. So are accounting firms. Much of the landscape that has created the legal, credit, financial, and accounting infrastructure of modern finance is under a cloud of suspicions, legal investigation, and mild contempt from the general population. This is problematic for the sustenance of this ecosystem. Something must change. I submit a new ecosystem is being created in front of our eyes by a new generation of people who have stepped outside of banks. Let's see how this plays out. There is no doubt in my mind that this is not only irreversible but also will accelerate. We need to heed the comment of Andy Haldane from the Bank of England, who surmised that the financial system is undergoing a revolutionary shakeup the likes of which we have not seen in centuries.

EMERGENCE OF NEW AND BIG PLAYERS LIKE BLACKROCK, ALIBABA, AND BLACKSTONE

Large financial organizations that were marginal business to banks are now able to function as competitors to banks. Examples of this are BlackRock and Blackstone. BlackRock is now engaging in quasi-banking activity, offering financial solutions to companies and financial institutions such as liquidity, funding, bridge finance, and financial products that are solutions for corporate and financial institutions encountering problems with funding both existing and new businesses. Blackstone is also morphing into a quasi-liquidity provider. And Alibaba is also very definitely growing new wings in its financial empire.

This is not just happening in the financial industry. Every industry is being affected. Publishing is being affected in profound ways, drawing into question the foundation of an industry that has not changed much in two centuries. Is it about time? The introduction of the paperback book in 1940 was a development that many thought would destroy the hardbound classic. Amazon's book business is creating a world in which self-publishing is now easier and more feasible than ever. Retail is also undergoing revolutionary changes. Education, especially at the university level, is under great pressure to change. Banking is hardly an exception.

TELECOM COMPANIES NOW SEE REVENUE IN BANKING

This technology is available to one and all, and other ancillary industries want a piece of the pie that has been traditionally reserved for the bank. Telecom companies are becoming quasi-banks. Firms like PCCW, SmarTone, and KT are developing financial applications on their services and receiving fees. IT firms like Google and Facebook are eating into banking services. Facebook may be creating a new way to connect marketing, funding, advertising, and customer loyalty in ways that were undreamed of just a few years ago. Credit card firms like Visa, MasterCard, and American Express are now reaching out and grabbing traditional banking activity by having cards that are connected to banking accounts and forming exclusive arrangements with retailers such as Walmart. Let's face it. Banks are under attack from all areas and are putting up a quite weak fight.

Globalization is the most hackneyed phrase around, but these developments in financial technology described above mean a company like Alibaba, whose business is restricted mostly to China, is a global company because deals can be made in Hollywood to bring new films virtually overnight to Chinese audiences without the traditional physical ownership of studios, physical sets, and so forth. Streaming of entertainment will revolutionize how we think about entertainment. The speed of developments with global competition means that technology firms that are not first movers can go "from hero to zero" very quickly.

LEGAL ISSUES: THE SHERIFF AND THE DA ARE AFTER BANKS FOR AT LEAST 20 ECONOMIC CRIMES

There is another serious problem working against the banks as they try to compete with new technology developed by people who are willing to work for much lower wages, are living in far cheaper real estate, and do not have the district attorney breathing down their neck. As far as the banks are concerned, there are a slew of outstanding legal issues that continue to occupy senior leaders in the bank. In the last few years, we have seen a nonstop array of indictments, convictions, and settlements among many banks in the United States, the United Kingdom, and Europe. These are a source of profound distraction and cause deep fear of further infraction. The result is timidity about anything adventurous or aggressive. This includes going into new product lines but also new jurisdictions. Product diversification or change, as well as geographical change, are problematic. The usual response is, probably sensibly, a strategic retreat for a period of time. But the pace of technological change is very rapid, indeed, and banks that dilly-dally too long can find themselves pushed out of business lines that have been disrupted by upstart entrepreneurs.

Examples of legal issues that currently plague the banks include violations of the Trading with the Enemy Act. These felonies have been committed by banks that illegally trade with countries like Iran or various terrorist states in Africa or the Middle East. Another involves money laundering the illicit cash from the sale of narcotics by drug gangs in Mexico that engage in murder, extortion, kidnapping, and robbery.

Other examples of crimes for which banks have already pleaded guilty or have paid fines to settle with the courts include tax evasion, interest rate manipulation, smuggling, bribery of ratings agencies, mortgage fraud, illegal foreclosure of homes, bribery of government officials, predatory lending, undisclosed conflicts of interest, and accounting fraud.

Ongoing felonious investigations include high-frequency trading fraud, violations for trading with countries that have sanctions, foreign exchange manipulation, and fraud with respect to credit default swaps.

In the area of the high-frequency trading scandal, prosecutors and plaintiffs in class action suits have brought forth charges that include fraud, restraint of trade, antitrust violations, deceptive conduct, acceptance of kickbacks, interstate fraud, electronic insider trading, infliction of harm by fraud, and layering (or spoofing) against most of the major investment banks. So in total, banks are dealing with about 12 types of felonies for which they have pleaded guilty or for which they have paid fines. In addition, there are about 11 more serious crimes against which they are defending themselves.

HAVE BANKS LOST THE GOODWILL OF THE REGULATOR?

Life is speeding up precisely at the time that financial regulators are trying to slow things down. This will lead to poor outcomes for those who are the most heavily regulated. Those who are the most regulated are those who are

The Financial reform landscape remains complex

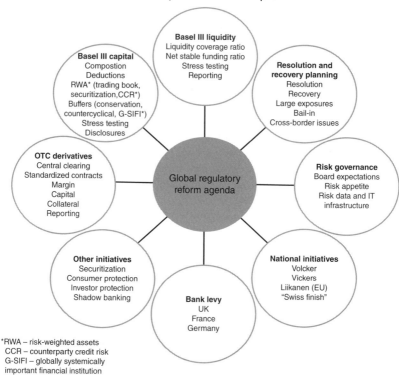

Basel III liquidity
Liquidity coverage ratio
Net stable funding ratio
Stress testing
Reporting

Basel III capital
Compostion
Deductions
RWA* (trading book,
securitization,CCR*)
Buffers (conservation,
countercyclical, G-SIFI*)
Stress testing
Disclosures

**Resolution and
recovery planning**
Resolution
Recovery
Large exposures
Bail-in
Cross-border issues

OTC derivatives
Central clearing
Standardized contracts
Margin
Capital
Collateral
Reporting

Global regulatory
reform agenda

Risk governance
Board expectations
Risk appetite
Risk data and IT
infrastructure

Other initiatives
Securitization
Consumer protection
Investor protection
Shadow banking

Bank levy
UK
France
Germany

National initiatives
Volcker
Vickers
Liikanen (EU)
"Swiss finish"

*RWA – risk-weighted assets
CCR – counterparty credit risk
G-SIFI – globally systemically
important financial institution

FIGURE 9.1   The Regulatory and Legal Nightmare from Hell for Global Banks
Source: Ernst & Young, Financial Regulatory Reform

perceived to have breached the trust of the public. No industry is more vilified now than banking. This vilification has resulted in a host of regulators inside countries who want to prevent banks from engaging in more reckless or criminal activity inside a particular jurisdiction. More importantly, regulators are perhaps more concerned about allowing banks to enter *into* their jurisdictions and so are keen to impose some kind of cap to prevent capital from causing dangerous distortions or destabilizing activity in credit markets. Figure 9.1 shows the web of issues currently infesting banks like a plague of locusts on an apple orchard.

Figure 9.1 shows the issues at hand for banks globally. The following issues are problematic in and of themselves, but as a group they severely handicap banks, effectively causing these banks to compete in a marathon against financial technology firms while wearing a ball and chain around their legs:

1. They have regulatory issues with compliance with Basel III being implemented now.
2. They have issues with derivatives.[1] They need to pay attention to liquidity considerations, which make it hard to lend. This includes the placement of collateral next to these derivatives, which weighs down the balance sheet. Furthermore, many of these derivatives (Level 3 in particular) have problematic valuations and need to be written down to zero.
3. They need to adhere to many local regulatory issues. Many regulators are no longer fond of wholesale lending by banks in financial centers in Hong Kong, Singapore, London, or New York. They are forcing banks to create local entities, which is very expensive.
4. They need to make sure that any technology advances they do make are cleared by regulators in multiple jurisdictions
5. They need to adhere to new rules for consumer and investor protection.
6. In addition, the U.S. banks need to adhere to regulations and new rules (which require constant interpretation) from an assortment of alphabet-soup agencies such as the CFTC, the Comptroller of the Currency, the SEC, FINRA, the Federal Reserve, the FDIC, and the Office of Research at the Department of the Treasury. Oftentimes, these rules are at cross-purposes. These are seven agencies with various kinds of teeth to cause damage to banks as well as to impose fines and/or imprisonment. No wonder banks are simply not in a very creative mood at the moment!

THE TAX MAN

Investors have been focusing on the regulatory issues that are being imposed in a draconian and comprehensive way to prevent any more reckless or illegal behavior. However, another very thorny issue is that the tax man needs more revenues everywhere and there is little patience for banks that have made great sums by being in the business of tax avoidance. The Swiss banks come to mind on this. U.S. banks, in particular, are under great administrative strain as they force their American customers everywhere to comply with onerous administrative guidelines on any kind of transaction of even a few thousand dollars. The Foreign Account Tax Compliance Act makes many international financial institutions nervous about working with individual Americans or American financial institutions. It is no exaggeration that if an American seeks out a private bank in Asia, he will be met with a cold shoulder. Foreign banks who have solid, high-net-worth businesses are shunning Americans because they are afraid of unintended violations of law amid the mountain of paperwork required for every transaction. Foreign banks are terrified after watching Standard Chartered receiving a fine of $300 million for a minor breach of money laundering.

RULES ON SUBSIDIARIES AROUND THE GLOBE

A poorly understood but very important change in regulation has to do with subsidiarization. In early chapters, I explained how excessive loan/deposit ratios (LDRs) have caused countries to become dependent on whimsical wholesale funding. Regulators in several countries have caught on to the danger of large amounts of loose capital coming in one moment and then leaving the next. As a result, regulators are now telling banks that they can only lend inside a country if they set up a subsidiary, capitalize it, and then fund themselves only with whatever deposits they can scrounge up inside the jurisdiction. This means that wholesale banking will die on the vine. I personally think this is a good thing because it will prevent sudden financial meltdowns.

This should not be seen as capital controls. It is the opposite. Regulators are saying, "Please come to our country and do business with us. The only catch is that you can lend only as much as you can create in deposits." This creates great scope for local banks to utilize new financial technologies to compete with global banks in new areas. I am pessimistic that global banks will take on the challenge, because they see subsidiarization as a very expensive nuisance, and competing with entrenched banks for deposits is a tricky business.

LEFTOVER DERIVATIVES FROM THE GLOBAL FINANCIAL CRISIS

There are structural issues on the balance sheets of several banks that inhibit the ability of these banks to increase credit or to alter activity quickly. The major issue for banks like Credit Suisse, UBS, Deutsche Bank, and others is "hard-to-value" derivatives from the old "anything goes" days of 2005 to 2008. These derivatives are real estate–related bonds derivatives, private equities, mortgage-backed securities, and other exotic instruments. Some of these are below their original value and need to be written off; the problem is, no one seems to know just how much they are worth. The totality of these is about US$700 billion, and about US$100 billion are considered hard to value. Regulators have said that since these are problematic, banks have to be prudent and place or "pledge" one dollar of assets against one dollar of derivatives. This is a big problem because there goes another $100 billion of assets that cannot be deployed into loans or economic activity. These assets are glued down onto the balance sheet of the bank and gum up the system with unusable assets that have capital against them. This is a ball and chain around these banks and slows down their innovation and strategic agility.

We can see that the tax man, the sheriff, the DA, the attorney general, class action lawyers, self-serving politicians, and overly zealous regulators are making life for banks very difficult indeed. I have gone through these many roadblocks because so many people ask all the time why the big international banks are just sitting around and watching so many of their divisions being picked off or closed, one after the other. In summary, these banks are dealing with hard-to-change DNA issues, regulators, class action suits, prosecutors, legacy derivative issues from the crisis, Basel III compliance, new rules on global tax reporting, a U.S. Treasury Department crackdown on conduct in the Middle East, and subsidiarization rules. As a result, global banks are behaving like a person who has suddenly walked into a brushfire. They are very busy fighting fires with regulators, prosecutors, lawyers, compliance officers, social responsibility panels, human resources, and other entities both external and internal. How on earth can they focus on their core businesses, never mind adopt the new and often untried technologies that smaller and nimbler banks are adopting in a very aggressive way?

Furthermore, local banks are free of one heavy burden that larger banks have. Global banks like HSBC and Standard Chartered operate in more than 50 countries, and they must make sure that technologies they adopt are suitable for various jurisdictions that may have utterly different views on client confidentiality, disclosure, customer protection, capital commitments, and so forth. So implementation of new initiatives can be problematic and cumbersome.

As an example of how and why some large institutions may lack the DNA to change, one senior IT specialist at a major European bank told me that when he creates one line of code, *it takes two weeks to get approval.* In a world where one initiative needs thousands of lines of code, it is virtually impossible to be adroit and aggressive in a new industry such as financial technology where there are many hungry and aggressive upstarts. Being an upstart is the nature of the beast in financial technology, and new innovations are coming at a fast pace. As an example, while some global banks are still discussing the merits of aggressively implementing new deposit/checking/foreign exchange/stock activity on cell phones, smaller banks like Santander, BBVA, Commonwealth Bank of Australia, and BCA in Indonesia are aggressively moving forth.

The way in which banks are behaving relative to new technologies has all the signs of behavior we see in a sunset industry. These banks have a degree of contempt for some of this new technology. A few of them have a siege mentality when it comes to new technologies. In addition, as banks shrink divisions and create less room for promotion, managers become risk averse and more conservative, making decisions that will please their bosses rather than create new business. Middle managers hesitate and ignore customers. They try to save their skins. New businesses prove too risky, since failure is a sure way to get thrown out. Office politics and short-term-ism rule. Flexibility and aggressive moves to get new business are ruled out as too risky. Businesses go sideways. Profitability suffers. People become more risk averse. A downward cycle is created from which it is hard to recover. (We will also see later that banks like Goldman Sachs have avoided this by aggressively changing and buying new technology in multiple divisions.) This lack of DNA for change makes the banking industry ripe for rapid decline as new technologies come along to challenge financial institutions that have had precious little competition for many decades. We will see what these companies are doing in the next chapter.

Learning Tools: 09_Why_Now_and_Why_So_Fast.pdf

This presentation describes the problems of banks and the ways in which large global investment banks are confronted with a host of legal, regulatory, capital, and Basel III issues that hamper their ability to compete in the new world of financial technology. The presentation shows the impetus for this technological change and the forces causing it to accelerate.

Endnote

1. For a more detailed analysis of the derivative problems, see the PowerPoint presentation on the Level 3 assets problems of the banks (Level 3).

CHAPTER 10

The Revolution in Alternative Investments

We will discuss the dynamism and innovation that the "PayPal Mafia" is bringing to the table in future chapters. First, however, we need to discuss the other large institutions that have been around for some time and that are now spreading their wings and challenging banks in many new areas. They are breathing down the necks of banks as they enter businesses where banks must exit, either due to regulatory pressure or because they simply do not have the balance sheet liquidity to compete. These entities have the flexibility to change and morph. They are also capable of quickly adapting financial technology in their models. We shall see that one firm, Goldman Sachs, is very likely further ahead than any other major bank globally in terms of adapting financial technology for their own use and that of their customers.

Indeed, Antony Jenkins said in the *Financial Times* on December 18, 2014, that "the universal banking model is dead."* In this heretical statement, he indicated that the use of customer deposits from commercial banks is no longer an appropriate way to fund investment banks. Regulators are now stopping this practice and are, in effect, breaking up the commercial and investment bank units into two separate groups. Mr. Jenkins also implied that the speed of technological innovation is the key to the future. Banks with dozens of locations in several continents simply cannot invest in technology in so many places quickly at the same time without making mistakes. Large banks with multiple divisions and with multiple footprints globally are disadvantaged on this score. Furthermore, there is a shortage of capital, which forces banks like Barclays to raise even more capital or shut down divisions. Lastly, many investment banks have lost the confidence of many regulators, and there is ill will in the air, which makes cooperation between

---

*"Barclays Scales Back Global Ambitions," *Financial Times*, December 18, 2014.

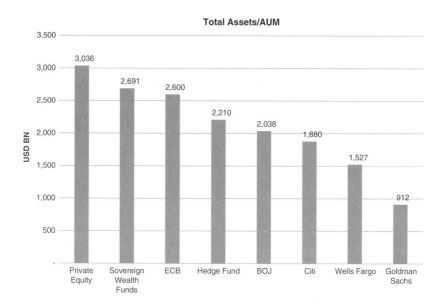

FIGURE 10.1   Can Private Equity and Hedge Funds (Buy Side) Replace the
Sell Side?
Source: Schulte Research Estimates, company websites.

local branches and regulators/central banks problematic. (As a result, we
should anticipate that banks like HSBC will either break up or list entities
inside countries on stock exchanges as separate legal entities. Will HSBC or
Standard Chartered follow the Santander model? I think so.)

Does size matter when it comes to creating alternatives to banks? This
is an important consideration, as size creates momentum and momentum
creates ecosystems. Ecosystems in turn create political support. This political
support creates acceptance and wide-scale use, which produces regulatory
acceptance. We can see from above that private equity is now the largest form
of funding globally and dwarfs the largest banks in the United States, for
instance. Private equity is larger than either the balance sheet of the European
Central Bank (ECB) or Japan (figure 10.1).

Sovereign wealth funds are organs of sovereign governments. These entities are charged with investing the foreign exchange reserves of governments.
These entities have wide mandates and range from public equities, private
equity projects, bonds, and commodities to foreign exchange. They often
engage in projects that are mandates from politicians within the central government. As a result, conflicts of interest often arise as political decisions
are made that may not reflect national interest. Furthermore, these same

politicians may wish to place people inside the funds who are amenable to certain types of investments. As a result, overall performance suffers. Norges has the best reputation among the funds for transparency and performance. On the other hand, China Investment Corporation (CIC) has suffered due to interference and politicization of the fund.

Hedge funds have been growing from strength to strength and now total about US$2.2 trillion. We will see how these funds are funding the boom in Silicon Valley at a time when the banks are mostly excluded from this activity. Hedge funds are spread globally among the United States, London, Hong Kong, and Singapore—and let's not forget that the hedge fund industry in China is only beginning. It will have explosive growth over the coming years and could easily exceed US$1 trillion within five years or so.

PRIVATE EQUITY: MUCH DYNAMIC ACTIVITY TO REPLACE BUSINESSES THAT BANKS EXITED

For private equity firms, their sheer size is a great asset. The top five alone have unleveraged assets of about US$150 billion. Their willingness to engage in new ways to bring life to dying businesses that the banks were forced to abandon is impressive. For instance, the fourth-largest firm, Apollo, is active in trying to resuscitate the mortgage-backed securities business. The reactivation of this business will bring greater liquidity to the residential housing market.

If we look at many of the major buyouts, mergers, or privatizations in the past few years, private equity firms are doing much of the heavy lifting that investment banks were doing in the past. The privatization of Neiman Marcus, for instance, was done by TPG without any help from any major investment banks. The same goes for the buyout of U.S. Foodservice by Sysco. The acquisition of Beats Electronics by Apple was done without any investment bank. Many other financial transactions in the multibillion range are now being done without global investment banks. Furthermore, many technology firms are themselves bypassing investment banks altogether and hiring in-house lawyers and bankers. In this way, there is no need to hire an investment bank at all.

This sends a chill down the spine of investment banks, since even major acquisitions in Silicon Valley are now being done without any participation from banks. For example, Facebook and Cisco have internal investment banking teams and no longer rely on Wall Street banks. According to Dealogic, 70 percent of deals in the area of acquisition did not involve a Wall Street bank. This is up from 25 percent 10 years ago. Apple's purchase of Beats Electronics did not involve banks but in-house private equity specialists. The same goes for the purchase of Oculus by Facebook. California investors are distancing themselves from traditional investment banks rapidly, and this trend seems unstoppable for now.

Furthermore, these financial institutions are offering returns that are multiples higher than the returns offered to shareholders of banks. For instance, the Carlyle Group offered an internal rate of return of 30 percent to its investors. The average for the top five investment banks was a paltry 2 percent return on capital. The return on equity for KKR was 27 percent in 2013. The average return on equity for the global universal investment banks was about 9 percent. The more time that passes, the greater will be the capital bases for private equity, and the more traditional investment banks will struggle to fund what is *currently* on their balance sheets. Private equity funds are very definitely morphing into entities that can offer a broad array of services, and corporations are increasingly relying on in-house advisors, bankers, and lawyers to complete mergers and acquisitions. What's left for the banks?

Another company creating innovation and dynamism in the world of finance is Blackstone. It has US$66 billion in assets and has a portfolio of 72 companies. It has 20 percent of its business in Europe and 10 percent of its business in Asia; the rest is in North America. It has a diverse portfolio that ranges from SeaWorld to Crocs to hydropower. In this space we will also find TPG and Grosvenor. (Grosvenor is very closely allied with powerful political figures in Chicago.) These organizations are very definitely morphing and challenging global investment banks in many areas of traditional funding. In turn, these private equity funds offer capital to high-yield bond funds, mortgage-related entities, and diversified financial companies, which are also threatening incumbent banks. These entities have created an ecosystem of private money that has become an alternative funding source. We will see in a moment that it is these types of companies that are funding the revolution in financial technology—*not* the banks.

HEDGE FUNDS ARE BACKING TECHNOLOGY AND HAVE ABANDONED BANKS

Hedge funds are also morphing and offering new forms of capital to businesses. They are diversifying away from public markets and taking on business lines similar to private equity firms, mortgage-backed entities, and supporters of financial technology in California. To give an idea of how much the hedge funds are moving away from traditional financials and toward technology, I looked at the top 20 tech companies and the top 20 banks in 2007 and tracked their performance. In 2007, the top 20 banks

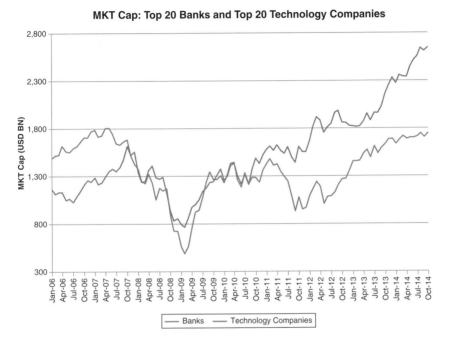

FIGURE 10.2 Global Investors Are Shunning Banks for Fascinating New Technology

globally had a market capitalization of about US$1.8 trillion, while the top 20 companies had a market capitalization of US$1.1 trillion. Cut to the end of 2014, and the market capitalization of the banks is US$1.7 trillion. This represents a drop of 6 percent. At the same time, the market cap of the tech firms moved to US$2.5 trillion, an increase of 127 percent. In other words, the banks are still below their values of 2007, while the capitalization of the tech firms has more than doubled. Figure 10.2 shows the evolution of technology (and a good part of this is financial technology) relative to the banks.

When I explored the top holdings of the largest hedge funds globally, I discovered that most of the top holdings were in fact technology. Furthermore, the top 20 hedge funds globally held almost no banks at all. They owned Amazon, eBay, and American Express. That's about it. But there were no banks to be seen in virtually any of the major holdings of any of these hedge funds. Shouldn't that tell us something? These are some of the smartest people in the world of finance.

The holdings of these funds include many stocks in the life sciences. Hedge fund managers seem convinced that the greatest share of rerating and revenue growth will *not* come from banks, but from (a) an evolution in the human genome; (b) developments in the marriage of biology, chemistry, and transistors to create solutions to diseases by way of human implants; (c) new developments in pill-form drugs for cancer, disease, and mental disorders; (d) developments in military hardware that reduce human casualties; (e) technology that can allow the consumer to bypass the mall, the bank, and the credit card company and shop cheaply from home; and (f) entertainment and educational systems in the home that are exciting, fun to use, and instructive. Banks are simply not on the horizon.

As an example, the top two individual stock holdings of Bridgewater as of late 2014 were Microsoft and Verizon. The top holdings of AQR, the second-largest hedge fund globally, are Google, J&J, Microsoft, and Apple. And the list goes on. There are just no banks. One company that is heavily owned by Och Ziff is China Cinda, an asset management company that is designed to clean up the bad debt of the banks. A few of these large hedge funds own insurance company Metlife and American Express. And that is the extent of the ownership of financials. Is this the sign that it is time to switch? I sincerely doubt it.

As we shall see, there is a real need to clean out the financial system and engage in a fairly radical restructuring of the balance sheet. It is unwise to be an equity shareholder of an industry that is undergoing heavy consolidation. I believe that this is exactly what will happen. Banks like Deutsche Bank, HSBC, Société Générale, BNP, and Barclays are simply too big to survive. Consider: Dinosaurs very likely got so big because the oxygen levels in the atmosphere allowed them to grow larger. At some point, oxygen levels fell by a few percentage points—meteors, volcanos, whatever—and could not support the size. I submit that is exactly what is happening today. The ecosystem can no longer support the absolute size of these entities, and they must break up into smaller and more flexible and dynamic organizations. Furthermore, firms like BlackRock are building horizontal organizational structures that create separate, smaller units with an entrepreneurial spirit. So far, they have succeeded in creating world-class centers of excellence with groups of about 60–100 people. BlackRock is one of the "large" firms that is creating the new enterprise by creating many smaller centers of excellence.

Figure 10.3 shows how large these beasts have become. John McFarlane will enter Barclays in 2015 and will likely break up the banks. Similarly, the FSA is being more aggressive in forcing banks to separate their commercial lending groups from their investment banks. If so, this will cost billions and will force a few banks to close down their investment banks, for the simple reason that the investment bank will no longer have a funding source. Equity shareholders of these banks should be aware: This is not a good time to own these banks. They need to avoid simply collapsing under their own weight

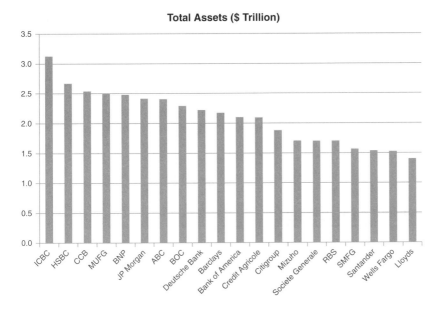

FIGURE 10.3 HSBC, J.P. Morgan, Deutsche Bank, Barclays, BNP, and Citi Need to Shrink

as they find new businesses, close branches, reduce headcount, deal with prosecutors, and write off bad assets. See Figure 10.3 for the largest banks in the world. HSBC, Deutsche Bank, Barclays, and BNP will be under large pressure to reduce assets going forward, and the Royal Bank of Scotland (RBS) is probably in this category as well.

There is one important exception in the investment banking sphere. Goldman Sachs is further ahead than any other bank globally in their ability to maneuver, morph, and adapt to new circumstances. Goldman Sachs is heavily involved in buying private equity stakes in financial technology firms and associated technologies in California. They can now boast a portfolio of financial technology in excess of US$10 billion. They dipped their toes in the financial technology waters years ago and now are reaping the rewards as they integrate these technologies into their client platforms. They have invested in Big Data firm Applied Predictive Technologies. They bought Perzo and used it to develop Babel, an encrypted messaging service that now competes with Bloomberg. They bought a US$450 million stake in Facebook in 2011. They have stakes in Alibaba, PSI, Square, Acquia, Zoom-Systems, and several others. This offers them an ease of comfort to analyze future financial technology, and puts them in the lead among global investment banks.

In the meantime, other global investment banks like HSBC, Standard Chartered, Deutsche Bank, Credit Suisse, and a few others have been unfocused, timid, or careless about the future of financial technology. Goldman Sachs has momentum on this score and is creating its own financial technological ecosystem. Other banks that do not do this quickly will very definitely lose out. Many investors with whom I have spoken wonder if these global investment banks can ever catch up after these years of bumbling about with regulators, lawyers, and prosecutors. My conclusion from talking to a number of my clients globally is that these banks are simply too far behind to catch up and will need to break up and hopefully recreate themselves in some productive way without collapsing under their own weight.

SOVEREIGN WEALTH FUNDS

Sovereign wealth funds are strange creatures. They are part political, part selfish national interest, part capitalist. There is often nepotism, as senior people are placed in positions of power that are related to the leaders of countries or are placed there for political purposes. So, the management procedures and investment processes are often chaotic or nonexistent.

Sovereign wealth funds are using their own money (without any leverage from banks and without any external advice from banks) and their own in-house lawyers to conduct their own investments. The largest globally is Abu Dhabi Investment Authority, at US$775 billion. CIC is up there at US$575 billion, and Singapore's sovereign wealth fund is also a behemoth at US$320 billion. CIC is an example of when sovereign wealth funds are used to clean up messes or to engage in investments for national purposes. When Bank of America and Goldman Sachs were in trouble many years ago, they were forced to sell assets. Bank of America sold its multibillion-dollar stake in China Construction Bank, and Goldman Sachs sold its multibillion-dollar stake in Industrial and Commercial Bank of China (ICBC). CIC (and its sister company, Huijin) was called to the rescue to buy part of these shares in the market (or through block trades) in order to prevent the stocks from precipitously falling.

One of the vitally important dynamics to remember is that many of the decisions of the sovereign wealth funds are political in nature. They will always deny it, but the evidence often points to clear political (or crafty geopolitical) motives. Some of these are secret arrangements between governments that are made for various reasons. A fund like Huijin—the internal local currency sovereign wealth fund of China—engages in pricekeeping operations and is often a forced buyer of stocks to support the prices. As a result, performance of many of these funds suffers. Table 10.1 shows the performance of many of these funds.

TABLE 10.1 Sovereign Wealth Funds by Size and Returns

SWF	Year Founded	Total Assets ($BN)	Annualized Return 1 Year	3 Year	5 Year	10 Year	20 Year	30 Year	Since Inception
ADIA	1976	773	NA	NA	NA	NA	7.6%	8.2%	NA
CIC	2007	575	10.6%	5.7%	5.3%	NA	NA	NA	5.0%
GIC	1981	320	NA	NA	2.6%	8.8%	6.5%	NA	NA
TEMASEK	1974	173	9.0%	5.0%	3.0%	13.0%	14.0%	15.0%	16.0%
KIC	2005	57	11.8%	5.4%	3.7%	NA	NA	NA	4.3%

There was another very important development involving sovereign wealth funds during the global financial crisis that has caused further reputational damage to global investment banks in their dealings with sovereign wealth funds. At this time of extreme distress in the financial system, banks were desperate to raise new capital, and public markets could not digest the large amounts of money that were needed. So, the banks went to sovereign wealth funds to find new capital. Morgan Stanley went to CIC to raise money and was successful. When Morgan Stanley faced another problem and needed more capital, the original investment from CIC was underwater and CIC thought it would be given first priority for a discounted second offering. After all, CIC had saved Morgan Stanley's bacon. Instead, many insiders say that Morgan Stanley went behind the back of CIC and gave the deal to Mitsubishi UFJ Finanical Group (MUFG) in Japan. It was a better deal for Morgan Stanley, and MUFG finally made money on the deal years later. But this was seen as a rebuff for CIC and a public embarrassment. China has a long memory.

Another deal that went south was an investment by the private and secretive China Development Bank (CBD) with Barclays. This deal went sour quickly and caused a great deal of embarrassment for China and CDB, which is considered a vital jewel in the crown of China's financial system. Similarly, investments in Citi, Merrill Lynch, and UBS all went badly south for the two sovereign wealth funds in Singapore. And Temasek's investment in Standard Chartered is seriously underwater. These sovereign wealth fund people talk to each other, and there is a lot of bad blood from the deals that were made in the midst of a crisis and transacted quickly. However, there are too many people in too many of these institutions who feel hoodwinked at worst or misled at best. It will take many years for any of these wealth funds to help out global investment banks after they were systematically burned by so many of them in such a short period of time. We are not talking small amounts: The combined losses by these two sovereign wealth funds through bad investments in these banks can be measured in the tens of billions.

The primary trend we see today among most of these funds is that more of their assets are being externally managed by hedge funds, private equity funds, mutual funds, ETFs, industry-specific funds, or large-scale projects that are government-to-government investments in infrastructure, power, or transport. In this way, sovereign wealth funds can reach out internationally and fund projects with special concessions and rates of return with long-term capital in ways that banks no longer can. Also, these funds are massive passive investors in some of the largest companies in the world.

Another interesting creature is the Abu Dhabi Investment Council (ADIC). It has about US$90 billion in assets and acts as a strictly private equity entity in its investment mandate. This organization does a lot of interesting investments in aircraft leasing, infrastructure funding, alternative energy, and technology. As with other sovereign wealth funds, ADIC has certain internal obligations and must perform national service to the government of Abu Dhabi. So, some of its strategic investments include Abu Dhabi Aviation, Abu Dhabi Commercial Bank, and Abu Dhabi National Insurance. It does no business in public equity markets or in public bond markets. In this way, it has a mysterious presence, as all of its activity is off the radar screen of public pricing.

Lastly, the new competitors to the business of banking are central banks. The Federal Reserve has been doing a tremendous amount of heavy lifting as it tries to avoid a deflationary depression. So, it is buying assets from private banks and quasifinancial organizations in order to prevent downward pressure on asset prices. We covered this in earlier chapters. Suffice it to say that the private sector purchases of risk assets (as well as government bonds) is bringing about a dynamic where central banks now have assets that are a multiple of private banks. Let's not forget that other than currency in circulation, the Federal Reserve owned virtually no other assets prior to 2008. Cut to 2014 and we see that the assets of the Federal Reserve are now almost equal to the combined assets of Citi, Wells Fargo, and Goldman Sachs combined. The balance sheet of the Bank of Japan is now approaching 50 percent of GDP of the country. And it announced in late 2014 its intention to purchase billions of dollars in equities as well. This is an attempt to reflate the economy and remove the danger of deflation on financials assets.

In conclusion, we will see in the next chapter that technology firms emanating from Silicon Valley, New York, London, Scandinavia, and Japan are, like termites, eating away at the foundation of many of the businesses of the banks. This is a phenomenon that has been occurring for the past four years from a standing start. Other firms we described above have been in place for a decade or two and have veteran bankers who split off and started their own firms. These industries, like private equity, hedge funds, mutual funds like BlackRock, boutique banks, and sovereign wealth funds, not only are shunning global investment banks as investments but also are carving out new businesses. In some cases, they are creating entire new lines of business that are a direct threat to the banks. Lastly, firms themselves are taking matters into their own hands and are shunning the tainted reputations of banks, as well as the high fees, and are bringing the business in-house. This combination of activity is a threat to the traditional banking business of global universal banks like Credit Suisse, Deutsche Bank, Barclays, BNP, and Morgan Stanley.

Learning Tools: 10_Non-Bank_Finance.pdf

The presentation attached describes the evolution in private equity, hedge funds, and sovereign wealth funds and the ways in which they are growing and challenging incumbent banks and non-bank finance.

CHAPTER 11

The Revolution in Big Data and SME Lending in the Emerging World

After they created PayPal, owners Peter Thiel and Elon Musk realized that they had created a vast technological infrastructure that had a host of potential applications in addition to the tasks required to create a secure payment system. So they decided to spin out some of this technology and make new applications. Thiel and others have gone on to create many new companies engaged in payment systems, data collection, big data analytics, complex systems for trading various assets, quasi-bank lending systems, cybersecurity, credit card activity, and crowdfunding for projects (figure 11.1).

The fortunes made from earlier companies like PayPal, Square, and others have created a new center of economic gravity. They have created a new hope that a small guy can get rich with a good idea involving ways to gather and allocate money. They have created a new environment for funders with a lot of money who have seen fortunes made from crowdfunding and peer-to-peer funding because banks are in no shape to lend. Ideas are meeting people at a time when great talent either is leaving banks in disillusionment or is being pushed overboard to cut costs. (I believe we will see much greater consolidation in banks in 2015 and 2016, so let's assume many more entrepreneurs will be flooding the streets with good ideas.) Money is meeting optimism and talent in institutions that obey the law at a time when interest rates are zero and people are competing against banks that have been torpedoed by angry regulators, prosecutors, and shareholders. Simply put, a smart man or woman sitting in an investment bank in a career track that is going nowhere has great incentive to go out and make it on his or her own in ways that were undreamt of before. Of course, not all will make it big. But some will. There will be blowups and flakey scammers. But I strongly believe this trend toward what we can call "big data citizen funding" is irreversible.

Elon Musk
- Net worth: $8 billion
- Co-founder and CEO of Tesla, a manufacturer of electric cars
- Founder and CEO of SpaceX, a space transport services company

Peter Thiel
- Net worth: $2 billion
- Co-founder and partner of venture capital firm Founders Fund
- Co-founder and chairman of Palantir Technologies, an analytical software company

Max Levchin
- Net worth: $300 million
- Founder of Slide, a social gaming company bought by Google for $182 million (2010)
- Chairman of Kaggle, a company that provides data analysis services

Ken Howery
- Net worth: $2 billion
- Co-founder and partner of venture capital firm Founders Fund

Luke Nosek
- Net worth: $1.5 billion
- Co-founder and partner of venture capital firm Founders Fund
- Co-founder of Halcyon Molecular

FIGURE 11.1 Billionaires Are Creating Their Own Financial Ecosystem
Source: Schulte Research websites

We have a perfect storm of energy, momentum, and money swirling around creative centers in London, San Francisco, and other cities, while banks are bogged down by compliance, shrinking margins, prosecutions, massive fines, poor morale, and high costs. The buzz in the world of technology has created a need for speed and bandwidth. It seems that the only thing holding back greater innovation in the phone or the computer is technology. So, firms who know there is profit in speed have brought about astounding advances in speed and bandwidth as witnessed by Table 11.1. Think about how much we can do on the phone that was impossible only three years ago. From 2014 to 2018, companies like Cisco estimate that

TABLE 11.1 Astounding Speed of Technological Advance

Parameter	2000	2014	2018 Forecast	2000–2018 Improvement (× times)	2014–2018 Improvement (× times)
Global Fixed Internet IP Traffic Petabytes/month	75	42,000	86,500	1,100	2
Global Mobile Data Traffic Petabytes/month	<1	2,500	15,000	16,000	6
Processor—No. of Transistors (months)	21	5,000	80,000	4,000	16

Source: Cisco

the traffic flow through the cell phone system will increase by 6×—not 60 percent! This means it will be six times more than what it was in 2013. As an example, it will be conceivable to run an entire home entertainment system on a phone by 2017.

The highway is being built at speeds undreamed of just a few years ago, offering a vast scope of possibility for new types of companies and new types of data management to emerge that can allow local commercial banks to widely distribute financial products and collect money safely and securely. It will allow marketing companies to create entirely new campaigns through social networks. It allows retail to create personalized products and bypass the physical store. It allows manufacturing to lower costs, create rapid ubiquity anytime and anywhere in the world, and have perfect fidelity in the ever-cheaper products it sells globally. Education companies can create digital education tools that can reach hundreds of millions of people with no schools. Financial services can foster innovations that connect anyone in society to any financial transaction anytime and anywhere. And these firms can do this with superior returns.

The need for speed is now wedded to an entrepreneurial class with lots of equity funding to create solutions to unmet needs at far lower prices with far lower costs. This is, in essence, the dilemma of the bank. These companies are reducing complexity by consolidating many functions into one go-to conduit. They are increasing productivity by eliminating mail and turning the bank branch into a museum piece—similar to the phone booth of old. These companies are increasing the speed and manipulation of data with instant reporting, something most banks have not yet figured out. They are creating clever programs to alert users of financial services about bogus fees being charged by the bank. They are reducing transaction costs and creating greater profitability per transaction, something the high-cost banks cannot fight. These new technology companies are saving time, reducing paper trails, and eliminating both real and bogus fees, which the banks have considered the privilege of an elite few. In essence, financial technology has now found a back door to the fortress that was "the bank" and is exploiting it in every area. Meanwhile, the banks are unaware of the intrusion and are acting as if all is well when the status quo is changing by the day.

Let's break this all down and look at the various divisions to see how these banks will be affected by the above phenomenon. Global universal banks like Deutsche Bank, Citi, J.P. Morgan, Barclays, BNP, Société Générale, Credit Suisse, and Morgan Stanley have eight divisions:

1. Investment advisory/wealth management
2. Derivatives
3. Credit cards
4. Commercial lending

5. Stock and bond trading
6. Alternative investments
7. Investment banking
8. Payments and clearing

These will remain mainstays of these banks. No one is saying differently. The point here is that *every one of these* businesses is under threat from financial technology firms around the world. This chapter is about the banks' vulnerabilities and the way in which new technologies have already eaten into bank profitability. As far as I can see, these trends are likely to take on new momentum and accelerate. The opinion of Andy Haldane, the executive director of financial stability at the Bank of England, put a fine point on what I am about to describe: "Banking may be on the cusp of an industrial revolution the upshot of which could be the most radical reconfiguration of banking in centuries."[1]

In the area of wealth management, there are many new technologies coming down the pike that are ingenious. Companies like Wealthfront are entering the fray and offering ways of replicating indices. This software can be automated and offers solutions for tax savings and portfolio management. Furthermore, companies like AlphaClone have ingenious software that can get all available public information on up-to-date portfolios for funds that are known as either good stock pickers or good dividend players or smart fixed income players. In this way, anyone can "clone" portfolios of some of the best investors globally in no time. These and many other tools are now available that put powerful tools into the hands of amateur investors. (For lecture purposes, see *From High Finance to iFinance: Do Not Fear the Digital Revolution*.)

Brad Hintz is a famous bank analyst who writes on this topic. He recently left the highly respected broker/dealer Sanford Bernstein Research and offered some parting thoughts: "Banks, under pressure, have pulled back on commodities and FI trading, leaving a gap in the market to be filled by new actors, such as hedge funds and other lightly regulated entities. Regulation has boosted revenues at clearing houses, which are mainly owned by exchanges."[2] This is the understatement of the century. Many lightly regulated entities are moving into all of these areas at a very fast pace.

WHAT HAPPENS WHEN SALES AND RESEARCH CAN'T BE PAID FOR ACCESS OR IPO RESEARCH?

Another nail in the coffin on the world of equity trading comes from regulators. A combination of new regulations and new technologies may render these divisions redundant. Regulators are deciding in unison that fund managers who use the equity services may no longer pay for "corporate access." This includes the setting up of meetings during grueling trips to several countries. What if an analyst and the sales team can no longer be paid by investment banking? What if an analyst and the sales team can no longer be paid for their relationships with corporations? If funds are banned from paying for these activities, then the raison d'être for the research/sales/trading platform for equities ceases to exist. Most long-only funds and hedge funds now trade through electronic platforms, anyway.

AFTER THE REGULATORS, NEW TECHNOLOGY IS LEADING TO END TIMES FOR HIGH-TOUCH BANKING

Regulators and technology are taking away the equity trading platforms of investment banks. They are taking away the commodity trading platforms. And slowly but surely, they are taking away the fixed income platforms, as fixed income trading also becomes mechanized. Take away the advisory function, because corporate access and much of the front-facing business of trading stocks, bonds, and commodities evaporates. This is problematic for labor, in that many business schools, for instance, still prepare people for roles such as research and sales, and these roles are disappearing in favor of entrepreneurial roles connected to information technology. Some of these business schools, as they say, did not "get the memo." A few examples among a multitude of that which can more cheaply and more efficiently replicate the functions of advisor, salesman, and analyst are Estimize, eToro, EquaMetrics, and SecondMarket. Table 11.2 shows how these companies threaten the sales/trading/research function.

As we saw in the previous chapter, many large corporations are also taking their mergers and acquisitions (M&As), legal, and advisory businesses in-house. I showed multiple examples of how firms like Facebook and Microsoft are creating their own mini-investment banks inside their companies and abandoning the use of investment banks for M&A as well as advisory roles. This also presents problems for the investment banking side of the business. Is this development due to mistrust? Is it due to the poor reputation banks have for inappropriate conduct in multiple areas? Or does it have to do with the rapid nature of the change in nascent industries? If so, does this mean that people on the ground who are owners of businesses and are intimately familiar with obtuse technologies in Silicon Valley tend to have better judgment than bankers in New York or even in San Francisco? It is probably a combination of all of these.

TABLE 11.2 Excellent Tools for Research in Equities and Fixed Income

Company Name	Largest Investor	What They Do	Who Can They Threaten?	Comment
Estimize	Contour Venture Longworth Venture	Algorithm to reduce bias, get better data sets.	Equity research division of banks	Raised US$1.5 million Claims more accurate than Wall Street 69.5% of time
eToro	Spark Capital	Dynamic algorithm trading platform. Allows users to replicate the financial trading activity of others.	Legacy/existing stock, commodity, and FX markets	Threatens exchanges
EquaMetrics	N/A	Powerful algorithm for trading (Rizm).	Replace intelligence of: Fund managers Asset managers Investment advisors	Raised US$5 million
SecondMarket	Social+Capital Partnership	Connects private/public investors with unique investments. Allows companies and funds to raise capital.	Existing stock markets	Raised US$35 million so far and is also backed by Li-Ka Shing and Temasek
Trefis	Semyon Dukach, Stephen Marcus	Can replicate all valuation methods. Allows users to break down company earnings and derive stock prices.	Equity research division of banks Valuation experts	Could be standard tool for all PMS

I have pointed out that there are significant problems with the advisory, broker/dealer, and investment side of the business. I predict that some of these divisions, especially equity sales/trading/research, will be downsized, sold, or closed soon. (Standard Chartered Bank closed its entire equity sales and research group in Asia in January 2015.) This trend will likely start in New York and spread to London, Hong Kong, and Singapore. Other hubs like Frankfurt, Geneva, Zurich, Tokyo, and Shanghai will likely follow. Indeed, China may entirely leapfrog the multiyear and painful decline of the high-touch broker and create purely electronic trading platforms without large and expensive sales or research teams. My experience of working inside a Chinese bank is that senior management looks at research and asks, "What's the point?"

There is not only a revolution in new financial technology upstarts who are creating grassroots solutions to research, funding, and banking. Many people in the heavyweight firms that dominate commodities, foreign exchange, banking, and fixed income are leaving to create exchange platforms that are more efficient, have better technology, and are much cheaper than existing players. This means that commissions for trading in commodities, foreign exchange, equities, bonds, and derivatives are falling fast. This puts a further squeeze on banks and causes further cuts in spending. Banks are forced to go further down the experience chain to hire cheaper people who are going up against ever larger and more sophisticated hedge funds, for instance. Over time, many hedge funds despair about the quality of people in many broker-dealers and stop dealing with them. They no longer feel like they are losing out to access to information when they switch off activity with a certain Wall Street bank and elect to move onto a cheap exchange to transact trades. Cost-cutting begets lower quality, which begets customer resentment, which begets less business. It is a downward spiral from which it is difficult to recover.

CROWDFUNDING IS THREATENING TRADITIONAL LENDING

Now, let's take a look at the more traditional banking side of the business and the new technologies that are coming along and putting a dent into the traditional banking activity. Crowdfunding originally was a response to the effects of the global financial crisis. Banks were saddled with losses, fines, prosecutions, reduced capital, and general fear of the market, and loans dried up. So, ingenious people came along who tried to create new forms of credit. Crowdfunding is just one of these responses.

Crowdfunding has morphed into several variations on a theme. One of these is a system whereby consumers pre-purchase the initiator's services or products; this variant is widely used by artists, musicians, and film producers. (Watch what Alibaba does with Lionsgate Films on this. The companies have agreed on prefunded films, which Alibaba will stream inside China. This is a new form of film funding that is truly exciting and could alter the economics of filmmaking.)

Another is widespread equity funding of companies by individuals. This is true capitalism, as it is a diversified group of people using nothing but cash to fund a good idea. There is no bank debt. There is no banker. It is a crowd of people who are willing to fund a good idea. (This is at the heart of Kickstarter and is true diversification.) Let's remember that stock markets are now just a big exchange-traded fund (ETF) where money that goes into equities is spread equally over all stocks in the Dow 30 or the S&P 500. There is no differentiation, so ETFs are a kind of socialism. Stocks receive a larger capitalization by a distribution of wealth by a remote and arbitrary decision-making machine. Big-cap stocks get larger, and small-cap stocks get smaller.

Table 11.3 shows a few of the leading contenders that have had a big influence in the world of crowdfunding.

From 2011 to 2013, the amount of funds raised by crowdfunding had grown from US$1.5 billion to US$5.2 billion, and the number of crowdfunding platforms had more than tripled. North America and Europe currently dominate, but Asia is, I believe, catching on quickly. These crowdfunded projects tend to be short in duration. They are launched quickly and usually completed in about 10 weeks. Some commercial bankers may want to say that this is only a drop in the bucket, or that this is an untested fad that is bound to blow up. This view may be naïve. A multibillion-dollar ecosystem is building up around these companies and dozens more that comprise a new form of funding, which also includes marketing, advertising, and buzz for new products. This is nothing short of the creation of a better, smarter, faster financial ecosystem that includes marketing, advertising, technology, entrepreneurship, and far lower costs compared to many banks that are lost in the universal banking model of the 1990s.

This new ecosystem being created involves funding, entertainment, marketing, advertising and social networking. It integrates crowdfunding with Facebook and other crowd venues (such as Kickstarter and the ones named above) to create a way to fund new ideas for products that are tied into the advertising for the product, ideal demographics for the product, and a self-feeding buzz that can catapult a well-funded product using nothing but word of mouth and the ever-present Like button.

TABLE 11.3 A New Breed Finding New Credit Methods and Reducing Nonperforming Loans

Company Name	Largest Investor	What They Do	Who Can They Threaten?	Comment
Bilbus	Seedcamp	Financing, e-invoicing, and cash flow forecasting. Strengthening working capital.	White collar: accounting professionals, commercial bankers	Will annihilate the back office
FeeFighters	Hyde Park Angels (acquired by Group in April 2013)	Helps compare payment providers to find the cheapest merchant account provider, or credit card processor.	Square and other existing payment disruptors Beating banks but now these disruptor firms are cannibalizing each other	Deflationary
Funding Circle	Union Square Ventures	Peer-to-peer platform connecting investors with established businesses who want to borrow in the U.K.	Bank margins and the physical need for a banker	Deflationary
iwoca	Talis Capital	Flexible funding structure for ecommerce sellers relying on credit score transaction data and business's selling accounts.	Bankers and physical banks	Deflationary
Kabbage	Thomvest Ventures David Bonderman	Online provider for working capital to small business. Lends money by gathering data sources from eBay, Amazon, UPS, PayPal to determine loan amount.	Bankers and physical banks.	Smart; celebrity funding list
Fund2.Me	N/A	Allows entrepreneurs to list their ideas, and connect with investors for funding purposes.	Bankers and physical banks	May attract small business from China to seek funding in HK through online investor

A fascinating documentary on this is a *PBS Frontline* show called "Generation Like." These established companies and upstarts, which are helping to create demand for new products, are morphing into a new ecosystem that involves value-added advertising, marketing, and social buzz. Unlike the banks, none of these companies are facing multiple criminal charges. They are using social media like Facebook to create sales for new ideas that would never be funded by bank credit. Furthermore, some brands are created literally overnight and receive funding overnight because millions of people on Facebook click *Like*. In turn, these new companies create a generation of devoted customers who can bypass traditional financial services because they are technologically savvy and can use alternative means to spend, invest, and save their money. It is a new ecosystem, which the banks think is a passing phase, if not an irritating and flaky nuisance. They are flat-out wrong.

THE JEWEL IN THE CROWN FOR FINANCIAL TECHNOLOGY: SME LENDING

Another area that I think is the jewel in the crown of all these new industries is the small- and medium-sized enterprise (SME) market. It is a cliché to say that most businesses are small businesses, but it's true. Of 27 million businesses in the United States, 21 million have less than five people. This means that almost 80 percent of the firms in the United States are small businesses. Now, add to this the statistic that banks reject 80 percent of small business applications. And let's add in the fact that loans to small businesses during the global financial crisis have fallen by 30 percent. We have a starved market where potentially millions of customers have no access to credit to start businesses.[3]

Companies that have come forth to fill this enormous gap include Kickstarter, Kiva, Indiegogo, and Lending Club. Table 11.4 shows their businesses, profiles, deal structures, and other data. Many people now call these people "citizen lenders." Lending Club is a variation on this theme, as it collects a pool of capital and is more like a private equity firm in that it offers an internal rate of return to those who fund the entity. Kickstarter, Indiegogo, and Kiva do not have any sort of interest rate charged on funds. It is pure equity in return for a prearranged product, reward, or service.

Should banks be worried? Many of the bankers in the United States and United Kingdom with whom I have discussed this issue have a somewhat cavalier attitude. I wonder if this cavalier attitude is merited. Francisco Gonzales is chairman of BBVA in Spain. His take on all of this is simple. He inferred that banks that are not prepared for such new competitors face certain death. I have gone further in my own research to international portfolio managers

TABLE 11.4 Crowdfunding Is True Diversification and Citizen Funding

	Kickstarter	GoFundMe	Indiegogo	Fundable
Year Founded	2009	2010	2008	2012
Total Fund Pledged (US$)	1 billion+	390 million	200 million	180 million
Industry Focus	Creative projects	Personal use or charity	Personal use, charity, or start-up business	Small business or start-up
Type of Crowd-funding	Reward-based	Donation-based	Reward-based	Reward-based Equity-based
Fee Charge	5% of raised fund if funding goal achieved	5% of raised fund	4–9% of raised fund depends on the scheme you choose	A flat monthly fee of US$179
Successful Funding Cases	Pebble, a customizable watch for iPhone and Android, raised $10 million in funding.	A victim of the Boston Marathon bombing raised over $800,000 to pay for medical costs.	Ubuntu Edge, a smartphone and desktop computer in one device, raised $12mn in funding.	Plum raised $760,000 to develop software to control household lights from smartphones.

and have said that investors should only buy banks that have IT specialists under 40 years of age on their boards of directors. Without a cadre of "young lions," banks lack the aggression, curiosity, and innovation to move ahead. I fear, however, that such initiatives may be watered down or eliminated due to hypervigilant compliance that is suspicious of any new activity. The "police state" atmosphere may prevent many global banks from being able to respond to this siren call from the likes of BBVA.

Banks that do not have a history of criminal activity—and are therefore not all hung up with district attorneys and attorneys general—do have leeway to act. They have the good faith of the regulator and are, therefore, offered more rope. Banks like Commonwealth Bank of Australia (CBA) do not have an adversarial role with their own regulators. Therefore, they can hire people like Rob Jesudason as a CEO of Asia and implement revolutionary technology systems without a stupefying maze of do's and don't's. The old saying for banks goes as follows: "The lower the behavior, the higher the regulation." So far, Australian banks have not been ensnared into the web of illegality that currently dominates the scene in the West.

The companies in Table 11.4 have made terrific inroads into the world of crowdfunding. The amounts are low—only a few billion. But these companies are a few years old. Furthermore, there are many more behind these four companies. Another that is growing quickly is Funding Circle, which now has a lending portfolio of almost US$500 million. It was only founded 16 quarters ago, and its current nonperforming loan rate is 2.2 percent, on a par with the U.K. banks that have been offering loans for decades. Why is this happening? Dan Hyde in *This Is Money* said that in a survey, almost 80 percent of borrowers preferred to go through peer-to-peer (p2p) funding over banks if they are seeking a loan.* This information is important and banks should pay attention to this powerful global trend that is, I believe, only just starting and that is irreversible.

There is another important reason why this is happening. An important theme of this book is the way in which banks have earned the enmity of the common man, while other companies have come along over the past decade and earned respect. The effect of branding is extremely important. Financial technology companies have not only preserved their brand value but have also dramatically improved their branding, while the branding of the banks has fallen sharply. For example, one survey from Accenture asked: "What company would you pick if it were a bank?" Fifty percent of people polled would prefer companies like Square. PayPal and Apple were also preferred. One out of four people would prefer a branchless digital bank. More than 70 percent of people polled saw a bank as nothing but a transactional institution and had no personal ties to it. For now, anyway, the regulatory, legal, branding, and reputational winds are very definitely blowing toward financial technology and away from traditional banking. Many banks have tossed their reputations overboard in the past few years. At the Annual General Meeting of shareholders of Deutsche Bank, one disgruntled shareholder took the microphone and asked the assembled board of directors, "Is there any scandal in which Deutsche Bank is *not* involved?" That says it all.

When there is this kind of a shift in public perception, can you guess who a Congressman or Senator wants to court for campaign money? Access to Congress and steady behavior creates influence. According to the *Silicon Valley Business Journal*, in the latest election cycle, Silicon Valley's biggest political contributors gave more than US$50 million in campaign donations, making this group one of the largest contributors in the country.

---

*Dan Hyde, "This Is Money" column, *Daily Mail* (June 2014).

Interestingly, the split was roughly 55 percent Democrat and 45 percent Republican. Of the 13,000 individual citizens who gave the most, almost one-third of this group came from Silicon Valley. As campaign contributions shift away from banking toward financial technology, regulations will change. One example of this was the Jobs Act. Aimed at promoting private equity rather than bank debt as a means in setting up entrepreneurial activity, the Jobs Act passed in the House by a vote of 390 to 23. This bill legalized equity-based crowdfunding and was less than 50 pages. Now, contrast this against the Dodd-Frank bill, which is a regulatory ball and chain on the banks as a result of their bad behavior and is 14,000 pages. Guess who will win out?

This trend is important because in Nomi Prins' book, *All the Presidents' Bankers*, she has gone through the presidential papers of several 20th century administrations and, starting with President Rooosevelt, she notes that Wall Street was the first stop for campaign contributions. In his 1980 campaign, President Carter turned to Wall Street for a significant portion of his funding. (Up-and-coming Boy Wonder, Robert Rubin, helped Carter raise money.) Of course, Ronald Reagan received a lot of his funding from Wall Street and eventually picked Donald Regan as his Secretary of the Treasury. Regan was CEO of Merrill Lynch.

This is no more. Raising money from bankers in a high-profile way does not work in this day and age. Hence, we see more campaign contributions coming from a new generation of California-based financial technology entrepreneurs who are socially liberal but have a hybrid form of libertarian economic thinking. They advocate a liberal agenda in social affairs but want the government to stay out of everything else. This is, in a strange way, the polar opposite of traditional conservative Republican thinking.

BIG DATA, CROWDFUNDING, AND THE SME: THE MAGIC FORMULA

In the past two years or so, a new chapter is being written. If there is a new capacity to sift through vast amounts of information—billions of bits of information on consumer habits in seconds—if there is a new source of gathering capital through crowdfunding, why not combine these to create new ways of lending that banks cannot do because they lack the flexibility, regulatory goodwill, innovation, and ingenuity? In other words, if a company like Intuit or Indinero comes along and offers software to help companies manage their receivables or payables, won't this information, which is shared with crowdfunders or smaller, more flexible banks (and highly accurate), allow these institutions to gain confidence to lend to various companies since they will have a better picture of the liquidity conditions of a company? What if these companies went further and offered software to help these companies manage tax, payroll, and overall working capital considerations?

If these companies can gather pools of capital and also manage the real-time software that is a constant examination of cash management, then they can become a genuine partner of this company and feel comfortable investing with them. They can have true and accurate information on taxes, payroll, and working capital. Furthermore, these lending pools can bypass ratings agencies that have tarnished their reputations by spurious rating activity, which helped the issuer more than the buyer of debt. This is precisely what is underway in a big way globally. The epicenter of this is in the United States, but it is spreading quickly to other parts of the world. I believe this phenomenon hit Asia only in the latter half of 2014. The one bank in Asia that is rapidly implementing this idea is CBA. CBA does not sell this software; it gives the software to companies for free. In this way, both the company and the bank act as partners and can have transparent information each day at 9 A.M. about the liquidity conditions of the company.

Other banks that are rapidly implementing these types of systems are BCA in Indonesia, UOB in Singapore, and CBA in Australia. Santander in Spain has an extensive financial technology platform, which puts it ahead of HSBC and Standard Chartered. BBVA gets it and is running ahead of regional giants. U.S. Bank also has a good reputation for grabbing onto this technology. By and large, however, the larger global universal banks have been sleepy. It boggles the imagination why these banks do not adapt this technology more quickly. The answer is clear for all to see. The larger universal global banks have so tarnished their reputations that instituting any global initiative is virtually impossible because these initiatives must be passed through dozens of regulators who are not that inclined to be cooperative because of history of mistrust. They simply do not believe the banks who say, "We are sorry and we will never break the law again." The infractions of too many banks are as long as your arm and have infected hitherto-sacred institutions such as the London Interbank Offered Rate (LIBOR) daily fixing, which is what the world's system used to be based on. Global FX markets have been tarnished by illegal behavior. Banks have received heavy fines for manipulating the Japan interbank market. The bad behavior has infected many equity and bond exchanges. This behavior has infected foreign exchange markets in every major financial center. It has infected credit default swap markets. It has affected commodity markets. Local regulators are not in the mood for illegal activity or irresponsible lending practices that can cause an economy to implode overnight. In this way, slow-and-steady activity by clean and law-abiding equity-funded crowdfunders, SME software entrepreneurs, peer-to-peer lenders, or trusted regional banks may win out. It is unlikely the global universal larger banks will have their regulatory probation lifted any time soon or will have become small enough to flexibly and adroitly go on the offensive. Absence of trust and excessive size hinders them severely.

These smaller, entrepreneurial organizations now have the goodwill of regulators, the capacity, the technology and wherewithal to break into the SME market. And they can do it because monolithic banks are in legal and regulatory quicksand. Think about it. The largest unmet need in the world is the SME. This is a company with between US$500,000 and $8 million in revenues and anywhere from 3 to 30 employees. There are millions of these companies, especially in the emerging world. And they are utterly blocked from bank credit for an assortment of reasons.

One of the reasons why growth is not higher in the emerging world is that there is a plutocracy of wealthy, landed gentry who have access to credit (it is only ever a small number of families—between 8 and 20—who control economics in the emerging world) and tens of thousands of small companies that are deprived of credit. These companies are forced to get credit from often unregulated financial entities or outright loan sharks. They pay extortionate rates of interest, in the neighborhood of 30 percent to 40 percent. What if they bought software (or were given software) by a crowdfunder who could monitor and verify the weekly or monthly operations of this entity by watching its liquidity conditions, payroll, tax payments, and working capital requirements? A crowdfunder (or a smart bank) could quickly command market share and clean up for one simple reason: These entities, which could have comfort by analyzing (on a daily or weekly basis) the cash balances of a company, could lend to these companies and charge interest rates of 15 percent or 18 percent with a high degree of certainty. The company doing the borrowing at 18 percent would see these rates as a tremendous relief compared to extortionate levels of borrowing rates of 40 percent, which the company was paying in the past from very unpleasant loan sharks and the like. Everyone wins. Word will spread and others will join the bandwagon. Some of these small companies will become big companies and a virtuous circle will ensue. Ecosystems will form and banks either will be forced to change or will create the seeds of their own demise by refusing to grasp technological change.

EXAMPLES: BRINGING TOGETHER THE DATA TO CREATE NEW OPPORTUNITIES AND RELIABLE CREDIT RATINGS

If these companies can grow to critical mass and avoid bad lending problems, there is a good chance they can disrupt the funding structure of millions of SMEs globally. They can offer 30–180 day credit products with a good degree of confidence because they understand the business of their client better than most. They can gather capital and act as a private equity funder using traditional bank products and a far cheaper rate than banks. They can enter the equipment leasing business. They can enter real estate funding under similar funding structures. They can easily steal away trade finance, since banks have a heavy burden from Basel II with regard to funding trade finance.

It is not inconceivable to see these companies entering into wealth products for the families of these companies. It would be easy to envision these financial technology companies offering tailored financing. It would also be easy to see how these firms could use financial supply chain optimization, because they would eventually grow large enough to potentially have data on both buyer and seller.

So far, a company like Funding Circle can offer credit far faster than a bank and can offer a slightly better rate. And in this cycle, the nonperforming loan rate of Funding Circle is currently *lower* than the average for U.S. banks. As and when they grow larger, these financial technology crowdfunders can gain economies of scale and really eat into traditional bank businesses. The finance function can be automated. Cash flow can be made more transparent for all to see. And the early feedback is that these new types of software allow a company to understand their firm better than ever before, never mind the lending entity. These companies are not out to create false fees or bogus charges and engage in criminality. Companies like Intuit want to make money from creating good software.

Companies like Kabbage can go further and enter into the world of the individual. It can turn the analysis of data into a microevent and offer money to people based on elaborate analysis of their e-commerce activity. Kabbage can offer cash in one day. Companies like UPS have entered into agreements to allow Kabbage to examine shipping histories. Kabbage is growing at more than 250 percent per annum, and if it achieves some kind of critical mass, there is no telling what it can do with smart analysis of big data. The savings to the customer could be enormous.

The bottom line is that companies like Intuit create new financial systems that integrate invoices, payments, and accounting records with all sorts of devices like phones, computers, and tablets. They can create customized features for various industry environments. They offer flexible, fair, and cheap software packages. There is no downloading. There are no contracts. A customer can cancel at any time. Why is this, as yet, still confined to the United States? Why is it not spreading into emerging markets? You watch. This revolution is slowly spreading across the Pacific Ocean. Companies like Moody's Analytics are stealthily using their U.S. technology bases to sell these types of bespoke software to companies, but this trend is very young.

TABLE 11.5 Payment Systems Are Bleeding into Social Networks

Company Name	Largest Investor	What They Do	Who Can It Threaten?	Comment
Alipay	N/A	Can provide 500 million customers with all bank services without a physical bank. Allows individuals and businesses to execute online payments.	Providers of individual payment systems (cards-only, online transfers) PayPal	No legacy technology Breaking the rules Keep an eye on Yuebao (collectively received RMB 6.6 billion in deposits from Alipay users)
Adyen	N/A	Improving the efficiency of online and credit card payments as well as offering face-to-face payments.	Providers of individual payment systems (cards-only, online transfers)	NA
BitCoin	N/A	Digital currency that allows P2P transactions. An alternative foreign exchange.	Central banks, real foreign exchange Macroeconomists	Gimmicky?
Dwolla	Union Square Ventures, Village Ventures,	Foreign exchange movement at low or no cost.	Providers of payment systems, payment terminals	5 years old
Square	Starbucks, Citi Ventures	Allows users to swipe credit card through the use of smartphones. All in one payment, inventory management, ordering, item sharing.	Providers of payment systems, solutions, and terminals	Marquee list of participants Have raised more than US$300 million Antifraud system that shows where the transaction was made
Tenpay	N/A	Bolting credit card API to the phone and bypassing cards.	Providers of payment systems (cards-only, online transfers)	No legacy history; breaking all the rules

PAYMENT SYSTEMS

The last area where there is a more recognizable story is in payment systems. The traditional retail sector (books, magazines, household items, luxury items, cosmetics, etc.) is in a tailspin because virtually anything anyone wants to buy anywhere in the world is available online for a lower price. Needless to say, this is all deflationary due to the hyperefficiency with which companies like Amazon interact with these payment systems. The world of payments moves away from physical/retail activity with high rents to a private cyberworld of private purchases of ever cheaper items. All of this can be done more efficiently, more quickly, and with instant global pricing comparisons and payments, which will always search for the ever better discount. Table 11.5 shows what existing payment systems are able to do.

Second-generation payments have already begun and are moving the system in different directions. This is similar to the way in which funding is tying itself to social networks. These payment systems are also tying themselves to social networks. Not only are these companies, such as Klarna, Venmo, and Stripe, easier and cheaper to use than existing payments systems, they are now flexible enough to be attached to social network entities like Facebook, where people can combine their social activity with their financial activity with the click of a button. The differences among and between checking accounts, savings account credit cards, and charge cards

TABLE 11.6 Fascinating New Experiments in Payments with New Credit Checking

---

Venmo is a payment app that enables you to send money instantly for free with social networking functions. Payments can be made with friends. Money can be held in Venmo account, or "cashed out" to a checking account.

It is fun, simple, and fast. The goal: accepted like Visa and used like Facebook.

Klarna was founded in 2005. It is a Swedish-based e-commerce company that provides payment services for online storefronts. They assume stores' claims for payments and handle customer payments, thus eliminating the risk for seller and buyer.

Most payment systems, like PayPal, require users to have money in their account or a credit card on file before they can buy. But Klarna underwrites the financial risk for retailers until people pay for the goods, either right after checking out or when the product arrives in the mail.

Stripe was founded in 2009 and is an application programming interface that can be embedded on websites to accept payments (no merchant account).

Stripe charges 2.9% + $0.3 per charge, the same rate set by PayPal with no fees for setup, monthly use, minimum charges, validation, or card storage.

Stripe has US$130 million in funding, and is valued at $1.75 billion. Ex-PayPal investors.

---

blur, and companies can even offer a "bridge loan" in funding of purchases. See Table 11.6 for more details about how these companies operate. These companies have high margins and, despite being around for a few years, have strong profit-generating power. Many banks are nowhere to be found in this area.

Learning Tools: 11_Financial_Technology.pdf

The financial technology presentation looks at all of these new technologies in greater detail and lays out the competition, its tools, methods, and who is threatened by them.

Endnotes

1. Quoted in London Business School Issue, Volume 3 (2014).
2. This is taken from a public note of Brad Hintz as quoted in the *Correlate Asia Daily Report*, November 5, 2014 (Hong Kong).
3. The source for these data is Biz2credit.com.

CHAPTER 12

Banking and Analytics — The PayPal Gang, Palantir versus Alibaba, and Hundsun

In his fascinating book, *Who Owns the Future?*, Jaron Lanier tells us that the cloud server will soak up everything in its path. It will know where the lowest price is for anything on the planet. It will become a truly global leviathan that will attract the best advertisers. It will learn all about our likes and dislikes. It is learning our price-points and preferences—our credit rating and our sneakiness. It will quantify everything about us. It will learn our skills and try to replace us. Free exchange of information brings insecurity. The server will become cheap to run, and people will remain expensive. We are willingly giving out knowledge to the server for free. We need to get with this server and remain dynamic and imaginative, or else the world has a cruel message: Salaries can seem like unjustifiable luxuries. Those who sit by idly as the cloud server accumulates more and more to itself will lose out: banking, law firms, universities, music, journalists, architecture, and so on.[1]

So, the new race is the one to dominate the cloud. The cloud is a cosmic rental storage facility for billions of bits of information for thousands of companies. It is an information system that is abstracted from the buyer and is beneficial because it is a variable expense to the buyer of the service.

There are three parts of the cloud: infrastructure, platform, and software. Figure 12.1 shows the layout of the industry as it stood in 2014. The *software* is all about client relationships, desktops management, communications, and e-mail services. The *platform* is database management, web servers, and development tools. This will be a key element of the whole new industry of credit data management where enterprising financial technology firms will discover efficient ways to distribute capital armed with easily digestible but fantastic amounts of consumer information. The *infrastructure* is virtual machines, networks, and large servers. In this chapter, I will

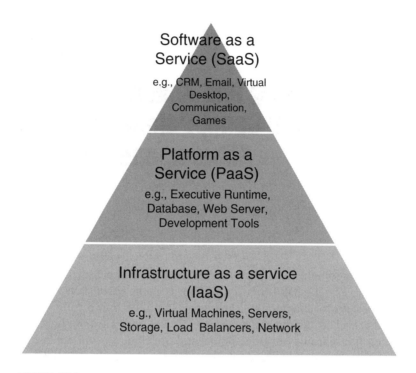

FIGURE 12.1 The Three Types of Cloud Service

discuss ways in which large hedge funds, financial institutions, government entities, and security companies use the infrastructure to digest billions of bits of information for pattern-matching, correlations, causality, and sorting of behavior, price-points, preferences, and so forth. This is the realm of the CIA, DIA, NSA, Citadel, Palantir, and high-frequency trading.

This industry is very new—only four or five years old. In one survey from Gertner and Forbes, companies were asked if the use of the cloud was a strategic part of their customer-facing businesses. In 2010, only one in three said yes. In 2013, two out of three said yes. From the second quarter of 2013 to the second quarter of 2014, quarterly revenues for the cloud increased from US$1.2 billion to almost US$2 billion. Seven years ago, there was virtually no revenue from this business. As can be seen in Table 12.1, the biggest player in this is Amazon, with a 50 percent market share. Microsoft has made the biggest inroads in the past year. Its business was up 160 percent in the first half of 2014. IBM and Google are growing quickly as well. Think about it. In 2009, there was only US$470 million in revenues from these companies. In 2013, there was US$6.2 billion in revenue. Even if current

TABLE 12.1   Annual Revenues in US$ for the Cloud: This Is a Brand New Business

Estimated Cloud Service Revenue	2009	2010	2011	2012	2013
Amazon (AWS)	448	674	1,291	2,035	3,200
Microsoft (Azure)		80	250	1,000	2,000
Google (Cloud Platform)				314	900
Alibaba (AliCloud)	23	69	83	105	125
Total	471	823	1,624	3,454	6,225

rates of growth fall by half, this will be a US$10 billion business within a few years. Trailing these giants is Alibaba's Aliyun (Alibaba's cloud business). It did not even exist in 2009 but saw revenues of US$125 million in 2013. Alibaba is head-to-head with Huawei in this business inside China.

The growth rates for this cloud traffic are astonishing. As expressed in exabytes (10 to the power of 18 bytes or one billion gigabytes), the traffic from 2012 to 2014 doubled. It is expected to double again by 2016. This represents a 40 percent compound growth rate for the period of 2012 to 2016. For the period from 2012 to 2017, Asia is expected to have the fastest growth. This is largely in China. Of this the consumer and business will grow at about the same rate. Asia Pacific is expected to grow from 505 exabytes to 1,900 exabytes by 2017—a fourfold increase. By 2017, it is interesting to note that Asia Pacific is expected to equal North America in exabyte traffic. On this score, let's compare the trends in the United States to the trends in China.

THE PAYPAL GANG SUMMIT: BIG DATA, RESEARCH, CREDIT RATINGS, AND CYBERSECURITY

In the United States, the PayPal gang is busy ramping up the system to a new and stratospheric level of super-powerful data processing of everything that moves. They are working for the government, hedge funds, large banks, and consumer companies. A leading-edge player here—and probably the best example of the future—is Palantir. Founded by Peter Thiel several years ago, Palantir has had explosive growth in the past three years. The initial funding for Palantir came from the CIA. The CIA's venture capital firm is called In-Q-Tel, and it was one of the angel investors. Palantir provides software that can search, cross-reference, and interpret large amounts of data from many sources. Palantir's software has been used to detect fraud and insider trading by law enforcement agencies and banks. Its clients include U.S. government agencies such as the CIA and FBI, Bank of America, J.P. Morgan

Chase, and News Corp. In 2013, it had estimated revenues of US$450 million. The current value of Palantir is estimated to be US$9 billion. (Let's also keep in mind that Amazon has a US$600 million contract with the CIA, presumably for international sales, since it is illegal for the CIA to operate domestically.)

Having started as an entity that was funded by the government, Palantir now has 60 percent of its revenues from the private sector. It was surmised that the financial impropriety at HSBC with drug cartels in Mexico was discovered by way of the CIA. It would not be a stretch to think that Palantir might have had a role to play in this investigation.

Palantir's reach is extensive, to say the least. The company now has a right and a left hand. The right hand is Palantir Gotham. This entity analyzes structured and unstructured data (for example, data found in e-mails, news reports, books, and websites) into a single information model providing relationships that can be understood by nontechnical staff. It enables users to Palantir to search multiple large datasets simultaneously to identify relationships. Gotham's clients include U.S. government agencies the CIA and FBI, who use the software to seek patterns in large amounts of data to track terrorists, drug trafficking, and cybercrime.

The left hand is Palantir Metropolis. This entity is the financial services arm and provides powerful quantitative financial analysis software. This software distributes bank data in a centralized fashion to technical and nontechnical users. Customers include banks and hedge funds. As an example, Steve Cohen at Point72 Asset Management (formerly known as SAC capital) hired Palantir to assist in its compliance and surveillance. It has an "Unauthorized Trading" algorithm that assigns riskiness scores to traders by examining correlations between key risk indicators in the context of overall trading activity. Citi uses Palantir Capital Market software to merge proprietary and vendor data into one platform for equity analysis.

Palantir is a cutting-edge company that is taking financial software and big data to new heights. It helps banks manage internal risk. It helps law enforcement monitor the potential illegal activity of financial institutions with regard to violations of money laundering and antiterrorism. It gathers data for hedge funds to help to discover previously undiscovered correlations among social, economic, and commercial phenomena.

It is almost amusing that top executives at Palantir admit that they have trouble articulating what exactly the company does. They say that it "extracts insight from information." They respond to human-driven queries. They can summarize large datasets, and they visualize datasets by articulating what is going on inside the data. Palantir lauds itself for being able to do the work quickly.

One example of a company that used large data to discover how consumers behave is the following. One company was asked to analyze all of the purchases at Walmart (tens of millions) and find the one common purchase of those that had the best credit rating. Interestingly, the company discovered that people who buy door-stops had the best credit rating. What was the most common purchase of those with the worst credit rating? The deadbeats most often bought mouth restraints for dogs. Is this a matter of mixing up correlation with causation? Maybe, but the experts in big data say without batting an eyelid that when you have millions of data points offering you some fairly sound and compelling correlations, it is folly to ignore these conclusions. In their book called *Big Data*, Kictor Mayer-Schonberger and Kenneth Cukier make the point that correlations can be found faster than causation and correlation is backed up by millions of data points. He makes the point that we still need controlled experiments with carefully handled data. For everyday needs, however, knowing *what*—not *why*—is good enough. In addition, big data correlations can be a harbinger of promising areas in which to explore causal relationships.*

The above is an excellent example of the kind of work that Palantir might do. Also mentioned in Jaron Lanier's book *Who Owns the Future?* are examples of entities that search the globe thousands of times per second for the lowest price for a certain book. A company like Amazon will use this price (whether it is in Belgium, Biloxi, Beijing, or Bangalore) as a new benchmark and beat the previous price. This is known as a *bot*. This bot is an algorithmic program that searches for the lowest prices everywhere and at all times. This world of the bot is one where great fortunes are made by driving prices down rather than up. It drives out the middleman and forces out the marginal producer. The curse of humans is that they love getting good deals. (Amazon is an example of a bot gone haywire. It is constantly driving down prices so fast that it seems that this bot is devouring the shareholders of Amazon. The company can't manage to make money after all these years!)

These bots will always only ever get the best deal possible (priceline.com lives by this) but this means that the bot will drive the price of one industrial or social good after the other to something close to free. This is designed to push all prices to the marginal cost of production. So, we must stay close to this powerful server, as it is the arbiter of prices. This is a super-deflationary phenomenon. It learns all it can about our behavior and then it offers all of the services we create at a price that is the closest to free that can be possibly be achieved. If we do not stay near the server and constantly improve

---

*Victor Mayer-Schonberger and Kenneth Cukier, *Big Data: A Revolution that Will Transform the Way We Live, Work and Think* (John Murray, 2013).

innovation and imagination, we are out of a job. Hence the vital importance of companies such as Palantir, Google, Alibaba, and Amazon. Imagine what will happen as these companies hone their skills better in the world of lending. They will eat inefficient and high-cost banks alive!

Credit card companies, new financial technology, and innovative software by companies like Moody's Analytics are also joining this game. They will crunch millions of data points to find good creditors who are down on their luck and need a short-term loan, for instance. They will eventually squeeze out inefficient and high-cost banking entities. One interesting example of a type of high-quality credit is a woman who is almost finished with her nursing degree and needs a loan. She fits a certain kind of criteria of an excellent credit and will be given a loan in less than a day. Companies have created algorithms to track down women like this and offer them loans. The level of detail about who is most apt to pay back a loan from myriad details of our private lives is astounding. Slight changes in our habits are picked up by some of the most sensitive bots out there. These bots can detect divorce, pregnancy, bankruptcy, new additions in the family, changes in health, changes in mood, and other intensely personal details with startling accuracy.

In addition, Palantir has access to all open information platforms of the U.S. government: health, safety, traffic, budgetary items. It is safe to say that Palantir's systems are firmly embedded into the defense, counterterror, intelligence, and law enforcement establishments. It is emphatic that it abides by all civil liberties protections mandated by the federal government. It is safe to say that Palantir's network is something of a foundation for how data collection, integration, and analysis can help financial institutions in the future.

Another competitor is Kaggle. Kaggle has had PayPal veteran Max Levchin as its chairman since 2011. It is a platform that creates competitions for predictive modeling and analytics. Data miners compete to produce the best models for data posted by companies and researchers. Kaggle charges clients a fixed fee and offers monetary rewards to data miners who seek to answer the human queries of Kaggle's customers. In the past few years, Kaggle has paid out more than US$5 million in "rewards" to data scientists who have helped its customers crack a thorny issue or discover important patterns in certain behaviors. Clients include GE, Microsoft, NASA, and Tencent.

Companies like Palantir and Kaggle are important for all financial institutions because they can breathe life into the imaginations of IT teams at banks about how to data mine consumer behavior (e.g., professional development, changing tastes, patterns of purchasing door-stops, etc.) and find better ways to safely and prudently lend money to those who are most likely to repay the money and also to avoid the deadbeats. It's a very simple procedure. And so much of this is automatic. Furthermore, software is getting cheaper by the day, and there is more information available on the Internet on patterns of individual and corporate financial behavior. Banks who do not aggressively embrace this trend are dead in the long run.

I am not saying we are entering into a new Panglossian world of an end to credit problems, thieves, and con artists. We live in a world of alligators and boa constrictors in all walks of life. I am saying that this world in which we have extremely powerful tools to examine and parse data points to more efficiently allocate credit is very likely a better world than the one dominated by banks that time and again have shown their ineptitude when it comes to allocating capital and managing risk.

I am saying that the hardest nut to crack in the world of credit has been the small and medium enterprises that have traditionally been locked out of the credit world. Is there a reason for this? Are small and medium enterprises composed of perpetual liars and thieves? Of course not. Most work very hard to run family businesses and are honest people. But banks have traditionally not had the economies of scale to make money on this sector when they can make better money on big-ticket, high-margin, low-touch loans to large corporations and governments.

In a world of immense data that can be easily managed among and between the banks and the company, there are many ways to open up credit to hundreds of thousands of SMEs. If an SME is a true partner to a bank and offers its data on working capital, inventories, tax, and payroll, the bank can offer not only more credit but also better pricing for this credit. This is a revolution right in front of our eyes. And it is real. Just ask people who bank with Commonwealth bank of Australia. This bank is making this a reality now. And companies tell CBA that the software offered by CBA helps them to know their company better.

One last comment. There is a predilection for some strange reason to pooh-pooh the idea of financial technology as a scam or a passing phase—some adolescent idea that will fade away. I think this is a misplaced notion. I sense that there is powerful momentum and a kind of irreversibility about this. I strongly believe this will only grow larger. And regulators, users, governments, and banks need to get their heads around this sooner rather than later. To ignore this trend as a passing phase is foolish and costly.

ALIBABA'S CLOUD BUSINESS: THE FUTURE OF BANKING

We go to the other side of the world and see that, in China, Alibaba is doing precisely this. It is aggressively morphing from a company that is a combination of PayPal, eBay, and Amazon into a company more like Palantir and Google. Alibaba is achieving this through a number of smart moves that may create one of the most interesting hybrid companies the world has ever seen. Alibaba not only looks like Amazon but also has shades of Palantir and resembles the entertainment element of Disney. So, Alibaba is morphing into a four-headed creature in e-commerce, entertainment, banking, and information analysis.

The bread-and-butter of Alibaba is the equivalent of Amazon and eBay. Alipay is a separate entity but is similar to PayPal. It is likely to list inside China and have an H share listing in Hong Kong in 2015. Like PayPal and eBay, it is probably wise to have a separate listing. This will allow it to have a higher valuation, and they are in fact different businesses and belong apart.

Alibaba is gluing other interesting entities onto this framework that revolve around consumer behavior: driving, dating, learning, fun, languages, lifestyle, and buying goods that can be mailed by Alibaba to the home. Figure 12.2 shows how Alibaba is becoming a lifestyle company. This diagram shows how Alibaba is *already* like Google, Dropbox, eHarmony, Amazon, Twitter, Spotify, Orbitz, Uber, and ING Direct.

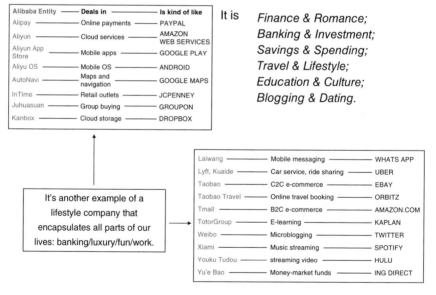

Summary of Main Businesses – Alibaba is a Universal Internet/Banking Services company and a Lifestyle company

Alibaba Entity	Deals in	Is kind of like
Alipay	Online payments	PAYPAL
Aliyun	Cloud services	AMAZON WEB SERVICES
Aliyun App Store	Mobile apps	GOOGLE PLAY
Aliyu OS	Mobile OS	ANDROID
AutoNavi	Maps and navigation	GOOGLE MAPS
InTime	Retail outlets	JCPENNEY
Juhuasuan	Group buying	GROUPON
Kanbox	Cloud storage	DROPBOX

It is *Finance & Romance; Banking & Investment; Savings & Spending; Travel & Lifestyle; Education & Culture; Blogging & Dating.*

It's another example of a lifestyle company that encapsulates all parts of our lives: banking/luxury/fun/work.

Laiwang	Mobile messaging	WHATS APP
Lyft, Kuaide	Car service, ride sharing	UBER
Taobao	C2C e-commerce	EBAY
Taobao Travel	Online travel booking	ORBITZ
Tmall	B2C e-commerce	AMAZON.COM
TotorGroup	E-learning	KAPLAN
Weibo	Microblogging	TWITTER
Xiami	Music streaming	SPOTIFY
Youku Tudou	streaming video	HULU
Yu'e Bao	Money-market funds	ING DIRECT

FIGURE 12.2   Alibaba Knows Everything about 500–600 Million Chinese
Source: Adapted from Quartz

ALICLOUD AND HUNDSUN: THE MOTHER LODE OF ALL FINANCIAL DATA

There is something else going on with Alibaba, and the other part of this entity that is less understood is more like Google and Palantir and less like eBay and Amazon. Alibaba has built its own cloud server from scratch and called it Aliyun. This is very important, because Alibaba decided to build all of its infrastructure internally with no outside entities. This is referred to as a "No IOE" policy. In other words, the technology that Alibaba used to build the infrastructure is not from Intel. It is not from Oracle. And it is not from EMC. It is, indeed, indigenous technology built internally.

There is an element of paranoia here—justifiable paranoia, that is. The Snowden leaks of NSA material showed that everything is open to the U.S. government.[2] The NSA reads just about anything and has cracked any code there is. Governments from China to Germany are now aware of this. So, countries like China that are overcoming a century of humiliating occupation (at one point in the early 1900s, China was occupied by 12 different countries) are flexing their nationalist muscles and saying they do not want any cyberimperialism. This is understandable and expected. China has a very capable spying service, which is very likely on a par with the NSA. It wants to preserve its secrets from the prying eyes of the U.S. government. So, it has concluded that it will build its own technological architecture. Furthermore, we shall see that the phenomenal technological firepower achieved by the likes of Palantir has scared China into creating its own equivalent.

Since its establishment only a few years ago, AliCloud (Aliyun) has more than one million customers and it has generated almost $100 million in the three quarters to December 2013. Cloud computing and Internet infrastructure are a powerful combination. See Figure 12.3. With Taobao and Tmall, Alibaba has access to the spending habits and price-points of hundreds of millions of Chinese people. With Alipay, Alibaba has access to the credit histories of hundreds of millions of people in literally thousands of cities across the country. With the dating service called Momo, Alibaba has access to preferences and demographic information of 140 million adults in nearly every city in the country. And with Weibo and Tango, Alibaba has access to a social network that makes Facebook pale in comparison.

Inside China, the cloud market is growing at more than 40 percent per annum and now accounts for only 3 percent of the global cloud market. In this space, Alibaba has a commanding share. Tencent, Shanda, and Baidu are all competing in this market. But the real competition here comes from Huawei. Huawei is the gargantuan technology company founded by a PLA

AliCloud (Aliyun)–Highlights

- AliCloud offers cloud computing services, including:

  (a) Elastic computing, (b) Database services & storage, (c) Large scale computing services.

- Users include (1) Sellers on Alibaba's marketplaces; (2) Start-up companies; (3) Internal use.

- IT infrastructures are developed internally ("NO IOE" policy: no IBM, no Oracle, no EMC).

- Important to ensure server stability when facing high web traffic.

- Around 1 million customers are using AliCloud computing service as of Dec 31, 2013.

- Cloud computing & Internet infrastructure contributed $90 million in revenue from Mar—Dec 2013.

- Big data analysis is the future. The integration of Hundsun would be unbeatable.

The Big Data Goldmine

- Consumption behavior data:	Taobao and Tmall
- Payment behavior data:	Alipay
- Finance and investment data:	Yu'E Bao and Hundsun Technologies
- Location data:	AutoNavi, Momo
- Social network data:	Weibo, Tango, Momo

FIGURE 12.3   Alibaba Sees under the Skirt of *All* Chinese Financial Institutions

Army colonel. Think of IBM, GE, and Apple all in one company! Huawei is the real competition for Alibaba in this space. Time will tell just where this competition goes. So far, the software infrastructure is 70 percent of the market. Infrastructure is about 20 percent of the market. In the software sector, Alibaba is the dominant player. In effect, then, Alibaba commands the field in the first inning of this buildout. Estimates show that this business will be close to US$1 billion by 2018.

AliCloud's customers are remarkably diverse. Customers include companies in pharmaceuticals, utilities, government security, tourism, weather trends, near-field communication mobile support, gas distribution, telecom, and IT solutions. It is basically the entire economy located inside the AliCloud. And this is only three years old. Imagine what will come next! (See Figure 12.4.)

What's next is Sesame! Sesame is Alibaba's new credit rating service for consumers. In the United States, 85 percent of people have some form of credit rating through a Social Security card, credit cards, phone data, sensor data, or browsing data. In China it is only about 25 percent. This is *only* 350 million. Alibaba's ambition is to have reliable credit ratings on all Chinese over the age of 14 fairly soon, so even youngsters can have cellphone accounts or credit cards for school or other purposes. The numbers being thrown around so far are in the neighborhood of 900 million people who could conceivably have reliable credit ratings and be able to get credit. So, a company like Alibaba (whose market share in phone e-commerce is more than 80% and whose market share in peer-to-peer e-commerce is 90%) can

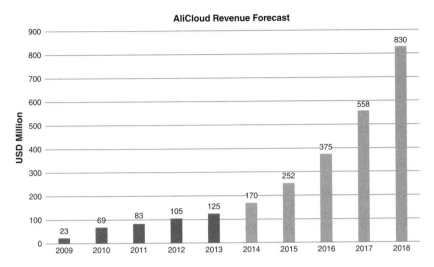

FIGURE 12.4 Beware the AliCloud—It Will Grow Like a Weed
Source: Schulte Research, Alibaba

realistically hope to achieve these ambitions. Imagine a world where a company like Alibaba or Tencent could have reliable credit data on 15 percent of the earth's population. This is precisely why Alibaba needs AliCloud. In this way, we should conclude that Alibaba will become the world's largest ratings agency within three years.

HUNDSUN: A VAST ARRAY OF INFORMATION ON FINANCIAL SERVICES

Now we arrive at the mother of all information lodes. In a brilliant move, Jack Ma bought a controlling interest in a company called Hundsun. Hundsun was developed by 12 software engineers in the 1990s. The 12 sold their 22 percent interest to Jack Ma's personal company Zhejiang Rongxin for US$522 million. Because this investment involves sensitive technological infrastructure for the banking sector, banking laws prohibit foreign ownership; this is why Hundsun lies in the private company rather than inside the listed entity. The remaining 78 percent of the company is listed on the Shanghai Stock Exchange and its ticker is 600570. The Ministry of Commerce sanctioned the deal in late 2014, so the relationship has been cemented.

Hundsun is a unique company. Imagine a company that is like IBM and Cisco and that has built the infrastructure for PIMCO, Fidelity, J.P. Morgan, Prudential, and Bank of America Merrill Lynch. Presumably a good portion of this information will end up being stored in Alibaba's AliCloud. If we combine the industries for which Hundsun has built the backbone, it runs the full gambit of financial services. These include securities, banking, asset management, insurance, treasury management, and exchange solutions. And it also includes the infrastructure for the new derivatives markets in China, including futures and options markets that were just opened in early 2015.

Hundsun also has a great deal to do with internal security for China. For instance, like Palantir, it also is involved with anti–money laundering, internal compliance platforms for banks, and internal controls for trading. But it also serves functions akin to exchanges like NASDAQ. Hundsun has built the backbone for the futures and options exchanges to be launched in 2015. It also operates systems that manage fund sales, margin accounts, and security exchange platforms. As a result of the integration of these tools in the Alibaba arsenal, Table 12.2 shows the raw data that can be analyzed inside the AliCloud to discover where people shop, how they drive, what they buy, how much they want to spend, where they travel, how they insure themselves, when they will buy a house, how they want to entertain themselves, and what they want to learn about and read.

There really is no one company like it in the world. This company can conduct human queries on just about anything. How many insurance policies are there? How many miles did Chinese people drive last year, and where? What kinds of movies do people want to see? Where do people want to go on vacation? What kind of analysis do investors in equities and fixed income like to use? How do Chinese construct portfolios for their future? Who needs to get rid of certain inventories? Who is a good credit and needs working capital for 90 days? In what way will Chinese use the futures and options markets? This is a unique and massive amount of data on the largest population in the world, and it is generally closed. But this is just getting started! Perhaps most important of all: What if companies like Alibaba, Palantir, and Tencent are able to more accurately predict GDP trends better than any government entity?

TABLE 12.2   Alibaba Information Powerhouse Is *the* Entire Consumer Spectrum

The Alibaba Powerhouse Combines:	
E-commerce:	Home, clothes, health, books, beauty, weddings, school
Travel:	Plane, hotel, car, boat, train information
Banking Data:	Liquidity, portfolios, insurance, working capital, inventories
Alipay:	Habits, trends, lifestyle, demography, warning signs
Big Data:	Personal, corporate transactions, credit ratings
Financials:	Futures, options margins accounts,
Entertainment:	Crowdfunding of shows, films, music, streaming

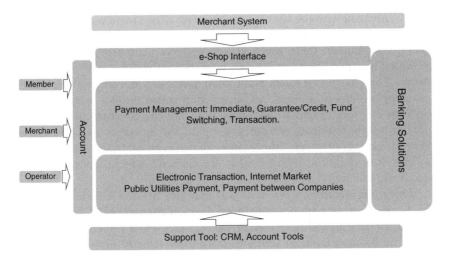

FIGURE 12.5 Hundsun Built the Backbone Connecting Banks with Consumers

Think about this further. Look at Figure 12.5. It shows the power of the information that is part of the Hundsun infrastructure built over the past several years, which conceivably (and in all likelihood is part of Alibaba's cloud) will now be able to be mined by Alibaba entities. If one sees corporate transactions going on live, it is possible to get a good real-time sense of where GDP is going. It is possible to get an up-close-and-personal sense of consumption trends, entertainment likes and dislikes, and fund flows within the economy. It will be possible for government entities to track corrupt officials and their cash movements. It will be able to seek out money laundering. It will be able to have a reliable sense of funds flows among and between various asset classes. The opportunities for data analysis (for better and for worse) are infinite.

FINAL ANALYSIS: THERE IS NO SUCH THING AS PRIVATE INFORMATION FOR ANYONE

What we are seeing in front of us with Alibaba on the one hand and Palantir/Amazon/Google on the other is the largest and second largest economies in the world competing for data hegemony. Both of these entities are indisputably joined at the hip to the government of their respective countries. When I was traveling around the world presenting my clients with a bullish analysis of Alibaba in the fall of 2014, I was asked a perplexing question. Some investors asked whether it bothered me that Alibaba was so closely entwined with the Chinese government. When I laid out the intimate connection among and between Google, Amazon, Palantir, and the U.S. federal government, there was a sheepish silence. This is because there is an inbred bias that China is the only country that watches and controls its people. There is a sense inside the United States that government intrusion into people's lives in minimal and lies within constitutional protections. If the Snowden files taught us anything, it is that the government can issue hundreds of thousands of warrants on e-mail and messages under the guise that a crime *might* happen. Almost none of these are contested. Some would say this is a violation of the Fourth Amendment, which concerns illegal search and seizure.

One thing is certain. There is no way that Jack Ma and Alibaba would be able to do what they are doing without the tacit consent of the government and the military. In addition, it is certain that Jack Ma is present in meetings when the People's Bank of China discusses any issue of financial technology with the banks. Similarly, Amazon, Google, Microsoft, and Palantir are absolutely joined at the hip with the political and military structure in Washington, D.C. I mentioned the US$600 million contract that Amazon has with the CIA. In addition, Palantir received money for its start with funding from the CIA's private equity arm.

Another sticky wicket for both of these entities (Alibaba and Silicon Valley quasi-banking activity) is the inevitability of regulation. History shows us that regulation almost always arises out of abuse. Fires in shabby textile mills that killed young girls in Manhattan in the early 20th century brought about modern fire codes. A bursting dam in Pennsylvania in the late 18th century brought about safety codes for infrastructure. The Depression in 1929 brought about the Securities Act of 1934. The calamity that was the great recession of 2007 brought forth the 13,000-page Dodd-Frank Act. The admittedly nascent financial technology industry has not crossed the line or committed any large-scale fraud of serious crime—*yet*. It is inevitable that this will happen. So far, however, these people are the new "respectable" crowd to be seen with and to receive political contributions.

The number-one problem I see for this industry is not a shortage of ideas, money, or smart entrepreneurs. It comes from conservative regulators who lack the imagination to see that a great trend has begun that is virtually unstoppable. Those who let it take its course will prosper and develop rapid sophistication and wide acceptance. China and the United States are examples of this. Those who prevent this from happening will cause their financial systems to remain backward and inefficient, full of bloated, unprofitable, and inefficient banks. Joseph Tsai, vice chairman of Alibaba, said that the financial services industry in China was "very antiquated" and that e-commerce could help to reform and develop the current system.

With Alibaba, Tsai asserted that the economy could "shift from one focused on the state to one focused on the consumer."[3] On the other hand, he admitted that there had already been setbacks. One example he mentioned was the suspension of the ongoing rollout of the online money market fund Yu'e Bao. Another was the central bank's decision to block plans for a virtual credit card. Why? This would hurt the state credit card monopoly Union Pay. One has the feeling, though, that reform is high on the agenda in China and that Union Pay will need to give way or get more efficient. China is not messing around here. It is trying to create a technological infrastructure that is as good or better than that of the United States.

The elephant in the living room here is the censoring of information. Gmail is blocked all over the country. Bloomberg only partially works. Sites are regularly shut down. There are hundreds of words and phrases that are immediately shut down when they appear on the Internet. An army (literally) of people regularly monitors millions of messages and deletes those it deems inappropriate to the political elite. This has to change. How can Shanghai possibly become a financial center if Bloomberg, Gmail, and other vital messaging systems do not fully function? A free flow of information is vital. China is a long way from this. Something will have to give. The Chinese government has great insight by letting companies like Alibaba and Tencent do what they are doing. But there is a new political cold blast blowing through China that is a reaction to the runaway corruption of the 2009–2012 years. Ideological purity and a vicious anticorruption campaign are sweeping through the country (which in my opinion is long overdue and necessary). China needs to balance progress in technology with both political stability and ongoing credibility of the Communist Party.

As it is now, the development of the technological infrastructure in China is on a par with most of the OECD and it has done this in a very short period of time. Interestingly, Alibaba has done in seven years what six or seven companies in the United States have taken 15 years to achieve. Alibaba is eBay and it is Google and it is Amazon, and Uber, and eHarmony, and ING Direct. I think we should all watch next what Alibaba does in the distribution of pharmaceuticals within China. More importantly, I think the industry that Alibaba will dominate is the streaming of films. Alibaba has hooked up with both Sony and Lionsgate to distribute content in China. This may spell the end of cable within a few years as more movies are watched through Internet streaming and as new technologies enhance the experience of watching movies using a phone that can display the image on a wall as a projector or in a 360-degree experience.

The possibilities are endless and the competition is intense. But companies like Alibaba, Palantir, Google, Apple, and Amazon are first movers and have phenomenal cash piles to dominate any subsector they choose to enter. One chart to show the way in which industries can be overturned by rich and entrenched first movers is the way in which Apple is stretching its wings in many different areas. Figure 12.6 shows what can happen if Apple decides to get into the credit card business with Apple Pay. It can disintermediate many companies and become a middleman among cards companies, merchants, banks, and the consumer.

Facebook will increasingly be used as a source of financial technology to raise money, transfer funds, settle accounts, pay bills, and other activity. Alibaba will become more like Disney and less like eBay. Facebook may become more like a multicultural virtual financial center where finance, buzz, brilliant marketing, and the "experience" can create "virtual"

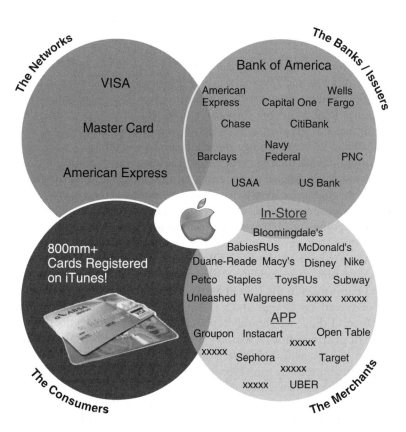

FIGURE 12.6 Apple Was Alone 7 Years Ago and Now Connects All with Its 700 Million Users
Source: Adapted from Goldman Sachs

industries overnight. Airbnb will challenge hotels in every country in the world. Uber will change how we all get taxis in countries all over the world. Intuit, Kabbage, and Indinero are companies that will change how small and medium companies raise money. Prosper, Kickstarter, and Zopa will alter how people fund projects. Palantir will change the way we understand the mining of data. Banks will struggle to keep up with this phenomenon, but I am not hopeful. The cloud server is the center of this. We need to take heed of the advice of Jaron Lanier: "People who want to do well, as information technology advances, will need to double down on their technical education and learn to be entrepreneurial and adaptable. For information and money are mutable cousins."[4]

This book is intended to offer a roadmap to provide for those in the financial industry (individuals, brokers, information providers, and banks) a way to understand where this revolution in information and financial technology is going. The cloud server—and the billions of bits of information on it, which includes detailed financial behavior of billions of people—is where we are all being drawn toward. The closer we get to it and the better we understand it, the better our chances of not being left behind in a world of economic feudalism and ultimate poverty. One of the more conservative financial institutions in the world is the Bank of England. Andy Haldane is the executive director of financial stability. He recently said: "Banking may be on the cusp of an industrial revolution, the upshot of which could be the most radical reconfiguration of banking in centuries."[5] To say that we may be on the cusp is a profound understatement. The revolution has started. As usual, those most affected by the revolution—the banks themselves—do not seem to see it coming. Hannah Arendt said that revolutionaries are those who see power lying in the street and pick it up. Thousands of entrepreneurs are picking up capital, information analytics, raw material for corporate and individual credit scores, as well as good management off the streets and are now creating a new banking industry. It is always a bottom-up operation, and only ever starts at the periphery. It is a bare-knuckles fight between the future and the past. Between the traditional bankers of the past and the financial technology innovators of the future, I know whom I will bet on!

Learning Tools: 12_Alibaba_and_the_Paypal_Gang.pdf

This presentation looks at the ways in which the PayPal gang have diversified into data analytics, cybersecurity, and cloud services. It also looks at Alibaba and its future with Hundsun and AliCloud.

Endnotes

1. Lanier, op cit.
2. The best book on this is not Glenn Greenwald's. In my opinion, the better book is *The Snowden Files* by Luke Harding (2014, Random House). In February 2013 alone, the NSA downloaded two billion messages inside the United States alone. Imagine what it downloaded around the world.
3. "Alibaba Targets China's Financial Reform and Healthcare Sectors as Ripe for Reform," *Financial Times*, November 12, 2014.
4. Lanier, Chapter 5.
5. This quote appeared in www.wired.co.uk website. It appeared on September 29, 2013.

The purpose of this appendix is to show the extent to which bank credit still dominates most countries globally, even though many have advanced capital debt markets. In most countries the average bank debt/gross domestic product (GDP) stands at 121 percent, and the government debt/GDP stands at 116 percent. India's banking system still remains one of the most primitive in the world with a small bank credit/GDP ratio of less than 60 percent. The bank credit/GDP for the UK, on the other hand, is the highest in the world. This explains why the Bank of England has been keeping interest rates low in order to allow these banks to sell assets and reduce leverage. (See Figure A.1.)

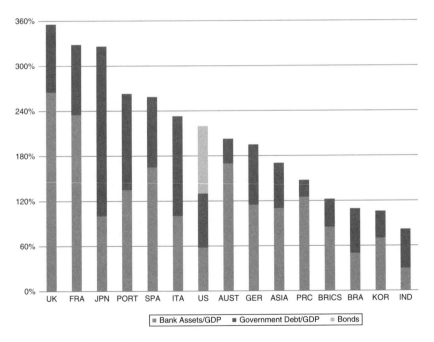

FIGURE A.1 There Is No Doubt about It: Bank Credit Matters
Source: IMF, World Bank, CIA Factbook

Much of the world has bank loans that are about 80 percent to 90 percent of GDP. It is true that capital markets in the form of equity, corporate debt, and government debt make up a lot of the pie, but it is accurate to say that bank debt dominates globally. Even in the United States where capital markets are very advanced, bank debt still counts for about 55 percent of GDP. This is clearly significant.

Bibliography

Ahir, H., & Loungani, P. (2014, April 14). "There will be growth in the spring: How well do economists predict turning points?" *VOX*.

Aubrey, T. (2013). *Profiting from Monetary Policy*. St. Martin's Press.

Biz2Credit. (n.d.). Retrieved from Biz2credit.com.

Blinder, Alan. (2013). *After the Music Stopped*. Penguin Press.

Bruce, J. (Director). (2013). *Money for Nothing: Inside the Federal Reserve* [Motion Picture].

Carpenter, S., & Demiralp, S. (2010). *Money, Reserves and the Transmission of Monetary Policy: Does the Money Multiplier Exist?* IMF Working Paper.

Cassidy, J. (2010, January 11). After the blowup. *The New Yorker*, pp. 28–33.

Cain, S. (2012). *Quiet: The Power of Introverts in a World That Can't Stop Talking*. Crown Publishers.

Clover, C. (2014, November 11). "Alibaba looks to transform 'antiquated' state-dominated sectors." *Financial Times*.

Das, S. (2014, October 29). "'Coffin corner' threat to financial stability." *Financial Times*.

Easterly, W. (2002). *The Elusive Quest for Growth: Economists' Adventures and Misadventures in the Tropics*. Cambridge: MIT Press.

Feldkamp, F., & Whalen, C. (2013). *Financial Stability: Fraud, Confidence and the Wealth of Nations*. Hoboken: John Wiley & Sons.

Friedman, M. (1962). *Capitalism and Freedom, 40th Anniversary Edition*. University of Chicago Press.

Grunwald, M. (2013). *A New New Deal*. Simon & Schuster.

Haldane, A. (2013, August 29). *Andy Haldane: "Banking may be on the cusp of an industrial revolution."* Retrieved from WIRED.CO.UK: http://www.wired.co.uk/magazine/archive/2013/09/ideas-bank/a-financial-forecast-from-the-bank-of-england.

Harding, L. (2014). *The Snowden Files*. New York: Random House.

Harris, Shane. (2014) *@War: The Rise of the Military-Internet Complex*. Houghton Mifflin Harcourt.

Heffernan, M. (2011). *Willful Blindness: Why We Ignore the Obvious at Our Peril*. Walker & Company.

Huerta de Soto, J. (1998) *Money, Bank Credit and Economic Cycles*, 3rd edition. Ludwig von Mises Institute.

Keynes, J.M. (1935). *The General Theory of Employment, Interest and Money*. Cambridge University Press.

Keynes, J.M. (1920). *The Economic Consequences of the Peace*. Harcourt Press.

Lanier, J. (2014). *Who Owns the Future?* New York: Simon & Schuster.

LeBor, A. (2013). *Tower of Basel: The Shadowy History of the Secret Bank that Runs the World*. Perseus Books.

Madrick, J. (2014, September 25). "Why the Experts Missed the Recession." *The New York Review of Books*.

Mayer-Schonberger, V., & Cukier, K. (2013). *Big Data*. John Murray.

Maltzer, A. (2003). *A History of the Federal Reserve*. Volume 1: 1913–1951. University of Chicago Press.

Prins, Nomi. (2014). *All the Presidents' Bankers: The Hidden Alliances That Drive American Power*. Nation Books.

Raguran, R., & Zingales, L. (2004). *Saving Capitalism from the Capitalists*. Princeton University Press.

Rogoff, K., & Reinhart, C. (2009). *This Time Is Different*. Princeton, NJ: Princeton University Press.

Rothbard, M. (2008) *The Mystery of Banking*, 2nd edition. Ludwig von Mises Institute.

Schumpeter, J. (2012) *Capitalism, Socialism and Democracy*, 2nd edition. Stark Publishing.

Shambaugh, D. (2008). *China's Communist Party*. Berkeley: University of California Press.

Skidelsky, R. (2010) *Keynes: The Return of the Master*. Penguin Books.

Stell, Benn. (2013). *The Battle of Bretton Woods*. Princeton University Press.

Stiglitz, J. (2013, January). Stable Growth in an Era of Crises: Learning from Economic Theory and History. *Ekonomi-tek*, 2(1), 1–39.

Tuchman, B. (1985). *The March of Folly*. New York: Random House.

Index

Page numbers with suffix t refers to tables and those with f refers to figures